BELIEVING
in an
INVISIBLE
GOD

A Memoir of Faith and Doubt

CHRISTINE PILGRIM

Believing in an Invisible God
A Memoir of Faith and Doubt
Christine Pilgrim

To contact the author:
christinepbelieves@yahoo.com

Edited by:

Mary Ethel
Mary Ethel Eckard
Frisco, Texas

Library of Congress Control Number: 2025920860
ISBN (Print): 978-1-966561-30-9
ISBN (Hardcover): 978-1-966561-34-7
ISBN (eBook): 978-1-966561-31-6

DEDICATION

To the God who finally answered,
and to Miles, Maddie, Rainy, Autumn, Jaxson, and Ava—
you are the proof that every prayer was worth it.
This story is for you.

ACKNOWLEDGMENTS

To the God who never stopped speaking—even when I swore You were silent. These pages are proof of Your patience with me.

To Miles—my pajama-pants hero. Thank you for carrying what I couldn't and making me laugh when I wanted to quit.

To Maddie, Rainy, Autumn, Jaxson, and Ava—you are the fruit of so many prayers. Watching your faith grow has been my greatest joy.

To Judy— thank you for loving us fiercely and showing what it looks like to cling to God with both hands.

To Denise and Shannon—thank you for your sharp eyes and fact-checking superpowers. You made sure this wasn't just my dramatic version of events.

To Mary Ethel Eckard—thank you for believing this book mattered and helping me share it with others who wrestle with doubt.

And to you, the reader—thank you for stepping into my story. My prayer is that in these pages, you hear not just my words—but His voice.

CONTENTS

INTRODUCTION

Let's be real—I didn't just doubt God.
I practically turned it into a side hustle.

I was the President of the "I'll Believe It When I See It" Club.
Founder and lifetime member.

Faith? Lovely for other people.
Me? I wanted proof.
Evidence—something undeniable.

Sure, I grew up believing in God—Sunday school, bedtime prayers, plus my mom's whispered warning that "Jesus is watching" anytime I lunged for my sister's lip gloss.

But faith?
It always felt like trying to nail Jell-O to a wall.

My relationship with God wasn't a grand spiritual romance.
It was a confusing situationship—mixed signals, long stretches of silence, and plenty of doubts.

Some days I was all in, hands raised like a prodigal daughter on a caffeine high.
Other days, I was halfway out the door, mentally swiping left on faith.
And on my worst days, I flat-out ignored God.

I liked certainty.
Stuff you could peer-review.
Preferably with a pie chart.

Faith felt risky.
Like skydiving... with a parachute you're *pretty sure* came from eBay.

And yet... while I doubted, something in me still hoped.
Even as I rolled my eyes at other people's "God stories," a tiny part of me
wanted one too.

Not a fortune-cookie verse. Not a vague prophecy. Not just "a feeling."
I wanted God to speak.
Direct line. No middleman.

And here's the thing—
for the longest time, nothing happened.
No lightning bolt. No secret code in the clouds.
No Morgan Freeman voice booming from the heavens.

Then one ordinary day, something shifted—quiet, easy to miss.
A thought that wasn't mine. A peace that didn't make sense.

If you're skeptical, I get it.
So was I.
But this didn't feel like me talking to myself—it felt like someone
answering.

And once you've had that happen—even once—you can't un-hear it.
That whisper was the beginning of the undoing—and the remaking—of
everything.

That whisper changed me.
But it didn't fix me.

There were doubts.
Ugly cries.
Days when faith felt like running through molasses in flip-flops.

But God never stopped chasing me.
Even when I challenged Him to prove Himself.
Even when I mistook His silence for absence.
Even when I gave Him my best spiritual side-eye.

He kept showing up—patient, gentle, no guilt trips.
Just steady presence... waiting for me to stop spiraling long enough to
hear Him.

And once you hear Him, it changes you.
Suddenly you're the one talking about God like He's real.
Like He actually shows up in parking lots, coffee shops, and on random
Tuesdays when you're ugly-crying on the kitchen floor.

You sound like the person you used to roll your eyes at.
Hi. It's me. I'm that person now.

Because God doesn't just speak to the polished, perfect, monogrammed-
prayer-journal crowd.
He speaks to the messy ones.
The snack-loving, skeptical, spiritually complicated souls.

People like me.
People like you.

I think I finally get why Paul kept insisting, "I'm not lying, I swear!"
(Yes, that's basically in the New Testament.)
Because when God actually talks to you—when something supernatural
drops into your very real, very ordinary life—you can't help but blurt, "I
know this sounds crazy, but I promise I'm not making it up."

So here's my promise: this story is real. Messy, imperfect, hilarious at times—but true.

After all the doubting, here's what I know now:
God is real.
He's personal.
And yes—He still speaks.

Not only to the "Super Spiritual" with matching Bible highlighters.
But to regular, wandering people like us.

If you've ever prayed and wondered if your words just bounced off the ceiling...
If you've ever whispered, *"God, if You're real, You're going to have to show me..."*
If you've secretly hoped there's more to faith than hype and hashtags—

Then buckle up—this is your invitation.

You might laugh, cry, roll your eyes—but by the end, don't be surprised if you whisper, "Okay, God ... I'm listening."

CHAPTER 1

The Sheep Who Wandered… Again

And the Shepherd Who Refused to Quit

I didn't storm off from God.
No slammed doors.
No dramatic "We're done here" speeches.

I just… wandered. Quietly. Slowly.
Like a sheep who forgot it was part of a flock and thought, *Eh, I'll just go over here for a while.*

Ask ten people about their relationship with God and you'll get ten different answers:
  - "I've loved Jesus since I was in diapers.
  - "God? We're on a break."
  - "Circle back after coffee, carbs, and five years of therapy."

And then there was me—a professional drifter with spiritual whiplash.
Technically, I was raised Christian.
Think: Jesus loves you—but clean your room first.

Sunday School? Check.
Vacation Bible School? Double check—with crafts that left glitter in my hair for years and snacks that were somehow *always* animal crackers.

Flannel-graph stories of brave boys with slingshots. A Sunday School teacher in a floral skirt who smiled like she'd just come from tea with Jesus Himself.

I believed it all.

I sang "Jesus Loves Me" louder than necessary—full Broadway understudy energy—secretly hoping the lead got laryngitis so I could have my moment.

I was all in.

Or at least... I thought I was.

Somewhere between flannel graphs and adult reality, something shifted.
No lightning bolts.
No rebellious tattoo phase.

Just a slow leak. Like a tire you don't notice until you're riding on the rim, wondering when everything got so heavy.

It started with questions.

The kind you don't ask in Bible study because they ruin the vibe:
- *What if we only believe in God because we're scared not to?*
- *What if He's real... but indifferent?*
- *What if this is all just made up?*

I never asked them out loud.

I was a nice, Midwestern girl with a strong sense of politeness and a vague
fear God might smite me with lightning.
Or worse—another endless Midwest winter.

So I smiled.
Nodded.
Sang the songs.
Recited the prayers.

And quietly stuffed my doubts into the corners of my soul like laundry
shoved under the bed five minutes before company comes over.

I wasn't rebelling—I was just tired, confused, maybe a little hurt.

Some days spiritual.
Some days skeptical.
Some days just trying not to yell at slow drivers.

Then came *another* one of my wandering seasons.
I knew I needed something.
I just didn't know what.

That's when my sister Denise heard about a Christian women's conference
in Wisconsin.

I didn't want to go.
Too far.
Too much effort.
Too many enthusiastic hand-raisers.

I made excuses.
But Denise? She's relentless—in the best way.

A holy bulldozer in a cardigan—equal parts grit and grace.

The kind of sister who leaves three voicemail messages until you finally call her back.

"If you don't want to drive," she said, "I'll buy you a plane ticket."

That ticket changed everything.

Looking back, I didn't see it coming.
God was about to flip my world upside down on that trip.
Even now, the memory still ties my stomach in knots—like a rollercoaster I didn't sign up for.

Denise would've done anything to get me there—and I couldn't figure out why.
It felt like Someone had circled my name on His calendar... and refused to erase it.

I didn't know it yet, but God had set me up.
A divine ambush with a boarding pass.

And here's the wild, tender, completely unfair part:
I had been running away from Him.
And He came after me.
Every time.

Not with thunder or anger.
Not with guilt trips.
Not with a divine "I'm disappointed in you" text.

He just... came.

Like a parent spotting their toddler drifting toward traffic—He sprinted, scooped me up, dusted me off and whispered, *I've been here the whole time.*

Even when I rolled my eyes at "divine intervention" and called it coincidence.
Even when I almost took a job that would've wrecked my life.

I didn't know it then, but I'd already been saved from more than I could count.

Even in the nights I cried into my pillow convinced I was alone—except somehow, I wasn't.

That wasn't luck.
That was Love—capital L.
Divine. Undeserved. Persistent.

Jesus once told a story about a shepherd who left ninety-nine sheep to find the one that wandered off.
That day, I realized—He meant me.

And if you've ever felt like maybe He means you too?
Spoiler: He does.

Because if you're the one who wandered—He's already on His way.

Not to shame you.
Not to lecture you.
But to carry you home.

That's what real love does.
It doesn't quit.
Doesn't roll its eyes.
Doesn't keep score.

It leaves the ninety-nine.
It shows up for the one.
It shows up for you.

> *"What do you think? If a man owns a hundred sheep, and one of them wanders away, will he not leave the ninety-nine on the hills and go to look for the one that wandered off? And if he finds it, I tell you the truth, he is happier about that one sheep than about the ninety-nine that did not wander off."*
>
> — **Matthew 18:12–13**
>
> ❧ **God's love is personal.**
> He pursues the one. No one is too lost or forgotten.

END OF CHAPTER REFLECTION

1. Ever feel like you've wandered a little too far for God to bother tracking you down? (Spoiler: you haven't.)

2. Looking back, do you see moments that felt like coincidence—but maybe, just maybe, were God pulling some strings?

3. What would actually shift if you believed God isn't sighing at your wandering but sprinting toward you like you're worth the chase?

CHAPTER 2

Dear God, Are You Even There?

One Woman's Loud Whisper for Proof

I couldn't fake it anymore. I was done smiling through sermons, done nodding like I believed while secretly thinking, *Am I just talking to the ceiling again?*

I had to know.
Not guess.
Not assume.
Not play church-girl pretend just because everyone else seemed convinced.

I needed truth.
The kind that could hold my questions without cracking under the weight of my ache.

So, in a moment that was equal parts childlike curiosity, grown-up exhaustion, and maybe just a sprinkle of sass...
I challenged God.

Yep—I threw down the gauntlet with the Creator of the Universe.

Did I ask for thunder? A burning bush? Nope.

(Although, let's be honest—that would've been amazing.)

I just whispered:
"If You're real... show me. Prove it. Or I'm out."

Yes, I basically gave God an ultimatum. Bold move for a girl who still apologizes to Siri when she mishears me.

I didn't need theory.
I didn't need a Sunday habit.
I needed a God who was personal.

One who could handle my mess, my sarcasm, my doubts.
One who wouldn't make me memorize Leviticus before pulling me close.

Looking back now, I laugh at my audacity.
Me—one woman out of billions—shaking my fist at heaven like, *"Hey, God! I need a sign or I'm out!"*

But here's what undoes me:
God didn't flinch.
He didn't roll His eyes.
He didn't ignore me like a flaky boyfriend.

He met me.
Right in my mess.

Because what I really wanted wasn't proof.
It was peace.

But at the time, I couldn't tell the difference.

And peace doesn't usually arrive overnight.
It takes its time.
But when it comes—you know.

For me, the longing I had carried longer than anything else was this: I wanted to be a mom.

Forget fame—I wanted lullabies.

Forget six-pack abs—give me six-pound babies with fuzzy heads and sleepy eyes.

(Although abs and babies together would've been nice too, if we're making a list.)

But life had other plans.

None of them came wrapped in pastel blankets.

The years slipped by faster than I could calendar them.

Each birthday felt like a loud reminder that time was running out.

Month after month.

Hope would rise—cue dramatic movie music—

Then faceplant into disappointment.

I begged God through tears:

"If You're real... if You love me... why give me this longing only to leave it unmet?"

I didn't want clichés.

Didn't want a throw pillow reminding me that "Everything happens for a reason."

I wanted answers.

But silence is what I got—and it hurt.

Here's what I know now: God doesn't waste pain. He transforms it.

He doesn't dangle dreams to tease us.

He reshapes them.

Not to punish.

Not to withhold.

But to give us something far better than we were begging for.

My story didn't play out the way I wanted.
It stretched further than I thought I could walk.
But in the end, it was deeper and richer than the picture-perfect life I'd been sketching in my head.

I came to see God not as a clipboard-carrying boss with spreadsheets, but as a tender, wildly creative Father with zero interest in them.
One who sat with me in the silence.
One who let me fall apart in His presence and never once said, *"You should be stronger than this."*

We're told we're made in His image, right?
So maybe longing, heartbreak, and deep love aren't signs we're broken.
Maybe they're proof we're human—and deeply loved.

Even in my doubting, God stayed close.
Even in my questioning, He answered—just not the way I expected.

No thunder.
No flashing lights.

But oh... the timing.

A stranger saying exactly what my soul had been whispering.
A door opening when I'd already stopped knocking.
A prayer answered before I dared to voice it—like Someone had been listening all along.

And sometimes?
A voice.
Not vague.
Not maybe.
But clear.

So clear it yanked me from sleep—heart pounding—in the middle of that women's conference I hadn't even wanted to attend.

That night, He gave me exactly what I'd asked for: words from Him to me. Personal. Direct. Undeniable.

Words that wrapped around my heart and have been echoing in my spirit ever since—reshaping everything.

And that's why I'm sharing my story.
Not because I'm special.
But because God is.

He didn't speak to me because I earned it.
He spoke because I asked.
Because I got honest.
Because I was willing to wrestle.

Stick with me and you'll see real-life, can't-make-this-up proof that God is absolutely real.
Wild, no-way-that-was-coincidence moments. *Believe me, I tried to call it luck. Skeptic-me had all the excuses ready.*

I get it—you might think, *"She's exaggerating. Nobody's life works out like that."*

But listen, I am not about to meet God one day and explain why I lied in a book with His name all over it.

When I meet Him face-to-face, I want Him to say,
"Thanks for telling the truth—even the messy, crazy, awkward parts. Thanks for helping other doubters find their way home to Me."

Every word you're reading is real.
It happened.

It changed everything.

If you've ever stood in your kitchen, stared at the ceiling, and whispered,
"God... are You even there?"
You're in the right place.

Because He is there.
Closer than you think.
Waiting—not for perfection—but for honesty.
Waiting for you.

And that night at the conference?
It was only the first crack in the dam.

What followed were moments so specific, so personal, I still shake my head when I think about them. Moments I couldn't make up if I tried.

Some will make you laugh.
Some might make you cry.
And a few might just make you whisper, *"Okay... maybe He's real."*

END OF CHAPTER REFLECTION

1. Ever been desperate enough to throw down a challenge at God? *And did you secretly duck for lightning ... or at least unplug the toaster just in case?*

2. What's the one longing in your heart that refuses to die—and have you ever actually told God the truth about it? No filters. No churchy answers. Just raw honesty —like I did, ugly crying into a pillow, whispering, *"This isn't fair, God."*

3. Can you remember a time when life lined up so perfectly you thought, *"Okay... that couldn't have been random"*?

CHAPTER 3

The GPS Said 'GOD'— But I Kept Recalculating

Confessions of a Spiritually Disoriented Sheep

Ever yell at your GPS like it personally betrayed you?
That was me—with God.

Except I wasn't just ignoring directions.
I was pretending I didn't even have a destination.

I'd sit in silence—no music, no distractions.
Just me, my thoughts, and a big, aching question:

Do I really believe any of this?

Not just the polite "Sure, I believe in God" kind of answer. I mean midnight-hour belief—the kind that holds up when life hurts and prayers feel like they're bouncing off the ceiling.

And let's just say it out loud: believing is hard.
We're not "supposed" to admit that, right?
But come on—it is.

Life gets dark.
Pain kicks in the door uninvited.
God feels quiet.

And belief?
It doesn't always feel like a sweet Sunday school answer wrapped in flannelgraph Jesus smiles.
It feels more like a wrestling match—one where you're clearly losing, flat on your back.

And yet Scripture lays it out so simply: if you believe, you will be saved:

> *"That if you confess with your mouth, 'Jesus is Lord,' and believe in your heart that God raised him from the dead, you will be saved."*
> — **Romans 10:9**

Just believe.

On paper, it sounds so freeing—but to me, it felt impossible.

Believe what, exactly?
That Someone I can't see, hear, or text back is running the universe while my life feels like it's unraveling?

That's like asking me to trust a parachute I've never tested—while already falling.

> *"We live by faith, not by sight."*
> — **2 Corinthians 5:7**
>
> **♪ Easier said than done.**
> I like maps, proof, and receipts—God seems to prefer mystery.

That verse tripped me up for years.

Because I wanted sight.

Proof.

Something I could circle with a red pen and say, *"There. I see it. Now I believe."*

But apparently, faith was supposed to be this invisible thing.

And we are supposed to believe in this invisible God.

Honestly, God felt more like Wi-Fi.

Everyone else claimed they had full bars, and I was in the corner waving my phone in the air like, *"Hello? Any signal up there?"*

They acted like they had unlimited data on the God plan. But me? Zero bars.

People would say, *"God told me..."* or *"I really felt the Lord say..."*

And I'd just blink at them.

Where were they signing up for these divine conference calls?

Was there a VIP hotline?

A God-only group chat?

Because I was getting nothing.

Silence.

Static.

And a soul-deep hunger for something real.

I didn't want religion.

Didn't want rituals.

I wanted truth.

The kind that could hold my whole weight without snapping in two.

And I wanted to know if that truth had a name.

Was it Jesus?
Or was this all just wishful thinking dressed up as faith?

So I did what I do best: I wrestled.
I questioned.
I ran circles around my faith until I was dizzy with doubt.

And God? Oh, sweet, patient God.
He didn't flinch.
He let me ask.
He let me shout.
He let me cry into the void.

And then... slowly... He began to answer.

Not with fireworks or angelic fanfare.
Not with a glowing finger writing on the wall.
But with quiet, personal, can't-make-this-up moments.

Whispers that said, *"I see you. I hear you. And I'm here."*

Yes, here's that sheep story again—apparently it's my brand: perpetual wandering sheep here.

"Suppose one of you has a hundred sheep and loses one of them. Doesn't he leave the ninety-nine in the open country and go after the lost sheep until he finds it?"

— **Luke 15:4**

🐑 **God's love isn't generic.**
It's laser-focused. If you've ever felt lost or overlooked, know this: He sees you—and He's coming for you.

That lost sheep?

Yeah. Hi. It's me.

Out there wandering, spiritually disoriented, trying to make sense of life with a flashlight of logic and a backpack full of questions.

One minute believing passionately.
The next Googling, *"Is God even real?"*

You'd think at some point God would say, *"Okay, she's a lot. Let's circle back after she's had a nap and some carbs."*

But nope.
He kept chasing me down.

And He didn't play hard-to-get.
No cryptic clues.
No cosmic scavenger hunt.

He just showed up—again and again.

Paths cleared. Strangers spoke words I needed.
Puzzle pieces clicked together I didn't even know I was holding.

At first, I brushed it off.
"Just luck."
"Weird coincidence."
"Okay, maybe the universe is being nice today."

But there were too many puzzle pieces fitting together.
Too many fingerprints that didn't belong to anyone else.

Even skeptic-me had to admit—either God was real, or the universe suddenly got really into curating my life.

And I couldn't ignore it anymore.

Here's what I know now:
God is real.
God is near.
And His love is stubbornly, relentlessly personal.

If you're unsure right now—if you're thinking, *"Yeah, but not me. I'm too skeptical, too scarred, too far gone"*—let me stop you.

You're exactly the one He's coming after.
Not because you nailed Belief 101. Not because you measure up.
But because He refuses to stop chasing.

> *"You will seek Me and find Me when you seek Me with all your heart."*
> — **Jeremiah 29:13**
>
> ❧ **God isn't hiding.**
> He's waiting. Not for perfection—but for pursuit. Even the smallest flicker of faith is enough to send heaven's searchlight straight toward you.

Faith doesn't need to be big.
Jesus said all it takes is a mustard seed.
That's tiny.
Like, you'll-lose-it-in-your-carpet tiny.

And that's still enough to move mountains.

So don't stress about having it all figured out.
Don't panic about believing "hard enough."

Just keep seeking.
Keep asking.
Keep walking.

Because the Shepherd still leaves the ninety-nine for the one.
And maybe... this time... that one is you.

And if it is?
Get ready to be carried.
Because the Shepherd is already on His way.

END OF CHAPTER REFLECTION

1. When was the last time you really stopped and asked, "Do I actually believe this?" Be honest—what came up? *No points off if your first thought was, "I believe I need a nap."*

2. Ever feel like your faith GPS just keeps saying "recalculating" while everyone else seems to know exactly where they're going?

3. What's one tiny, mustard-seed prayer you could toss God's way this week—even if it's just, *"Uh... hey, are You there?"*

CHAPTER 4

No Barn. No Boots.
Just Big Dreams.

Why God Was Raising a Mom, Not a Farmer

Picture this:

A Michigan dairy farm.
Winters so cold they could freeze your nose hairs.
Summers thick with heat, hay, and the unmistakable perfume of cow poop.

Dreamy, right?
That's where my story begins.
Not in a nursery.
Not in a church pew.
In a house that smelled like cows... and dreams that didn't fit the zip code.

From the time I could talk, I knew two things:
I loved Jesus.
And I was going to be a mom.

Not *maybe* someday.

Not *if the stars aligned.*
Set in stone. No backup plan.

While other kids dreamed of fame and fortune, I was naming dolls and planning imaginary baby showers.
Forget glam. Give me Goldfish crackers and a minivan.
Forget red carpets. I wanted spit-up on my shoulder and a six-pound bundle that smelled like heaven.

We didn't have much money.
We had cows.
Lots of them.

And barns. And 4 a.m. wake-up calls. Boots caked in mud. I hated it.

My mom had two speeds: baking like Betty Crocker... and avoiding cleanup like the plague.

She baked cookies, cinnamon rolls and pies that made neighbors swoon. But cleaning up the mess and scrubbing pans? Not her thing.

So I hatched a plan. At eight years old, I made my first big deal.

I marched up to my dad and declared:
"I'll keep this house cleaner than a hospital operating room if you never make me step foot in that barn again."

My dad loved a clean house—he just didn't love that ours usually looked like a bake sale gone wrong.
So he was more than happy to shake on it.
Even farmers know a bargain when they see one.

With the dirt from barns, mud-caked boots, and Mom's bake-offs gone sideways, there was always more mess than one kid could handle.

I worked just as hard as my siblings—just with soap suds instead of tractors and cows.
And let me tell you, Pine-Sol doesn't moo back.

I kept up my end of the deal. That house was clean.

To this day, if the doorbell rings, I don't panic.
No tossing laundry behind the couch.
Martha Stewart would be proud.

I was the second of four kids.
Close enough to be noticed.
Far enough to feel like a backup singer in someone else's show.

Denise came first—three years older, the barn girl.
Strong and slim, Dad's right hand.

Then me.
Then Jim, a year and a half later.
Then Bob, a year after that.

Denise, Jim, and Bob were Dad's barn crew—tractors, hay, cows, manure, the whole deal.
I was the inside crew—scrubbing, dishes, vacuuming, dusting, sweeping.

Me? I preferred soap suds to manure.
Baby dolls to Holsteins. Less mooing, more cooing.

I could shine a floor to perfection...
but I never managed to buff away that backup-singer feeling.

Dad had a nickname for me: "the lazy one."
Sweet, right? Like a Hallmark card dipped in sarcasm.

According to him, if you weren't hauling hay or milking cows, you were lazy. Period.

Denise, Jim, and Bob had barns, tractors and Holsteins.
I had my little red playhouse—an old chicken coop, thank you very much.

They smelled like manure. I smelled like Lemon Pledge.
And honestly? I liked my deal better.

I learned to clean the house fast and efficient—because the quicker I scrubbed, the sooner I could get back to what really mattered: rocking my baby dolls.

That chicken coop was where I kept them all lined up, each with their own names.
I fed them. Changed imaginary diapers. Rocked them to sleep.

It wasn't pretend.
It was practice.

But while I dreamed and scrubbed floors, insecurity crept in.
I wasn't Denise.
I wasn't strong. Or slim. Or Dad's favorite.
I was chubby. Sensitive. Always trying too hard.

School didn't help.
Especially during the annual nightmare called *the weigh-in*.

In front of the entire class.

I'll never forget the number.
The glances.
The snickers.

Humiliation, tallied in front of everyone like it was part of the curriculum.

That's when numbers started to matter—
The scale.
The report cards.
The calories.

And then there were Dad's words:

"You're the laziest kid I have."

"No boy's ever going to want a fat girlfriend."

Maybe he thought it was tough love. Farmer-style motivation.

But his words didn't light a fire.
They lit a fuse.
And I carried that ticking with me everywhere.

And shame? Unlike manure, it doesn't rinse off with a garden hose.
It seeps in.
Sticks.
Lingers.

I was basically running a one-girl maid service, and somehow that still didn't qualify as "work."

He couldn't see the spotless house.
He couldn't see my heart.
He only saw that I wasn't in the barn.
And that meant I wasn't enough.

Here's what he also didn't see: God was already working on me.
Even in the mess. Even in the heartbreak.
Even in that little red playhouse where I rocked my baby dolls like they were real.

Mom saw it, though.

Tender. Faithful. The quiet calm in our chaotic, cow-scented world.

She was the spiritual glue holding us together.
Lighting candles of faith in a house full of noise.

If faith was a fire, Mom struck the match—most likely while baking cinnamon rolls that could make an atheist reconsider.
Honestly, I think her frosting had more altar calls than some sermons.

She talked to God like He was a neighbor stopping by for coffee.
I didn't know it then, but Mom was quietly living out this verse. To her, it wasn't a verse to memorize—it was a way of breathing.

> *"Be joyful always; pray continually; give thanks in all circumstances, for this is God's will for you in Christ Jesus."*
> **— 1 Thessalonians 5:16-18**
>
> **Faith isn't a Sunday performance.**
> It's a daily rhythm—joy, prayer, gratitude—woven into ordinary moments like cookies in the oven and whispered prayers in the kitchen.

She didn't say much—probably because she couldn't get a word in edgewise with my dad around.

That man could narrate a three-part documentary on fixing fences and still have enough air to critique your potato-peeling skills.

But Mom didn't just talk about God.
She showed us. With cookies. With prayers.
With gentle reminders:
"Kids, you never know when God might call you home. Better be packed and ready to go!"

We'd sit there munching sugar cookies, silently wondering if "packed" meant clean underwear or having our hearts right with Jesus.
(It was the Jesus thing. But clean underwear never hurts.)

Dad believed too.
But his gospel came with a tractor.
If the crops were planted and the table was full, that meant he loved you.

Still, his words cut. And they stuck.
Long past the moment they were spoken.

But let the record show—I still stayed out of that barn.

Then there was Jim. My brother. My shield. My defender.
When Dad's words pierced like darts, Jim stepped in like a bodyguard for my soul.

"Knock it off, Dad. Leave her alone."

He saw me.
In a house where I often felt invisible, Jim made me feel seen.
Made me believe maybe I wasn't broken.
Maybe I wasn't lazy.
Maybe I was lovable.

And maybe—just maybe—God wasn't raising a barn girl.
He was shaping a mom.
A mom with big dreams, with a purpose God was already preparing.

But dreams don't just sit quietly in your heart. They grow. They push. And sometimes, God lets you taste them before you've fully arrived.

END OF CHAPTER REFLECTION

1. When you were little, what did you dream of becoming? And if you're honest—does that dream still whisper inside you, even now?

2. What's the first label someone slapped on you—the one that stuck longer than it should have? Lazy, too much, not enough... maybe even "barn-avoider"? How has it whispered in your story, even if you wish it hadn't?

3. Who first gave you a glimpse of God? And what did their version of Him make you believe—about Him, about yourself, about life?

CHAPTER 5

Already a Mother

How God Let Me Live My Dream Before It Was Mine

While other kids sold lemonade or put on backyard concerts, I was hosting baby showers.
Catherine Elizabeth—my favorite doll—was the guest of honor.
There were invitations and tiny plastic cups of water.
By that point, my dolls had been to more baby showers than most first-time moms.
But this wasn't pretend anymore.
This was a preview.

When grown-ups asked, "What do you want to be when you grow up?" it wasn't a cutesy answer.
It was my heartbeat.
Loud. Certain. Unshakable.

Motherhood wasn't part of my plan.
It *was* the plan.

In middle school, I started babysitting for a family with three wild little boys.
They lived miles away. Didn't matter.

I'd hop on my bike—brakes squeaking like they were auditioning for a horror movie, Walkman blasting, no helmet in sight—like I was on a mission.
Not for the money.
For the chaos.
For the chance to be needed.

Then—it happened.
They had a baby girl.

In their infinite wisdom, they asked me—a teenage girl with shaky confidence and even shakier bangs—to be her godmother.

I was floored.
Honored.
Mildly panicked—because suddenly this wasn't just play anymore.

But oh, I was ready.
Ready to love her with everything I had.

I rocked her.
I fed her.
I sang lullabies like I'd been practicing my whole life.

I inhaled that powdery baby smell—70% heaven, 30% mystery formula, 100% addictive.

I changed diapers that would've sent grown men running for gas masks.
And I did it all with this quiet joy in my chest.

Because in those moments, I wasn't babysitting.
I was mothering.

And here's the miracle: God let me taste it.
He let me live pieces of the dream long before it was fully mine.

He whispered, "*This counts. You're already doing it.*"

Looking back, I see it clearly now.
God was nodding.
Not in pity—but in pride.
Yes, I gave you this dream.
Yes, I built that nurturing spirit into your bones.
You're already a mother—even if the road looks different than you pictured.

And I never stopped.
I mothered wherever I could.

I even spent my own money to take other people's kids to Disney World—
because nothing says "I love you" like $40 mouse ears you'll never wear
again.

We didn't grow up with vacations.
But giving kids something I never had? That felt like holy ground.

Love gives—even when it costs you.

> "*The King will reply, 'I tell you the truth, whatever you did for one of*
> *the least of these brothers of mine, you did for me.*"
> — **Matthew 25:40**
>
> ❧ **Motherhood isn't measured by timelines.**
> It's measured in love that shows up early—in the waiting, in
> the babysitting, in every sticky, sacred preview God hands you.

Those memories—sticky fingers, spilled juice, giggles echoing from the
backseat—
they still sit with me.

Not just proof of the dream, but whispers of God's kindness—reminders that He lets us taste joy even in the waiting.

Back then, I thought the previews meant the feature film was right around the corner. I believed it then. I believe it now:
Someday, I'll be a mom.
God gave me this dream on purpose.
And He doesn't hand out dreams He doesn't intend to fulfill.

But here's what no one tells you when you're young and full of faith:

What happens when the dream doesn't show up on your timeline?
What do you do when the years pass and the nursery stays empty?

The waiting changes you.
It sharpens and strips—until you're left with a single choice: do you really trust the One who gave you the dream in the first place?

END OF CHAPTER REFLECTION

1. What was the dream you carried as a kid—the one that stuck, even when life tried to talk you out of it?

2. Can you look back and spot moments where God gave you a sneak peek of that dream—just enough to remind you He hadn't forgotten?

3. When your story hasn't gone the way you pictured, how has God used the waiting to grow something deeper in you (besides patience in long grocery store lines)?

CHAPTER 6

God Still Speaks in All Kinds of Ways

And His Gifts Aren't Just for Bible People in Sandals

I used to think spiritual gifts were only for the holy elite.
You know—the Bible people in sandals who strolled deserts, heard booming voices, and probably had halos that glowed in the dark.

Me?
I was just a small-town girl with big bangs, big questions, and a not-so-big clue how any of this worked.

Still, I prayed like it was my side hustle.
Talked to God about everything—from world peace to why my bangs refused to curl like the girl in the Aqua Net commercial.

But for all my chatter, He never talked back.
No booming voice.
No holy echo.
Not even a divine sticky note on my mirror saying, *"Hey Christine, love you — God."*

Then one day, something happened.
Not a vision.
Not a voice from the clouds.
Something stranger—and somehow more personal.

I was on the Sunday school bus.
Lace-trimmed socks swinging.
The smell of crayons and vinyl seats filling the air.

Praying my usual kid-sized prayers.
Nothing fancy.
Just me, God, and my slightly crooked pigtails.

And then—it hit.
This feeling washed over me.

Not butterflies.
Not goosebumps.
Something I can only describe as... cool warmth.

I know—that makes no sense.
It's like saying crunchy pudding. But it was real.

It was like a quiet, holy chill that somehow felt warm at the same time.
It started in my chest and rushed all the way down to my toes—like God
wrapped me in a quiet, tingling hug that said, *"Hey kid, I'm here."*

At the time, I didn't think, *Ah yes, this is the indwelling presence of the Holy
Spirit.*
Nope.

My deepest thought was probably, *Does everyone feel this? And are we getting
donuts after church?*

But now, looking back, I know exactly what it was.

It was Him.
God showing up.
Not loud. Not flashy.
Just... there.

And that wasn't the only time.

Fast-forward a few years.
Heartbreak.
Confusion.
My Blanket Burrito of Despair era—fleece-wrapped, cereal in hand, convinced my life was imploding in slow motion.

I'd whisper, *"God, please. Just remind me You're still with me."*

And sure enough, that same quiet, cool warmth would come.
Not every time—but always right when I needed it.

Like a divine love note delivered straight to my frazzled soul.

Now, if you're thinking, *Christine, maybe it was just emotions... or low blood sugar... or a really sunny window,* I get it.
I've thought that too.

But it wasn't just a feeling.
It was the peace that came with it.

Like God exhaled into the chaos and whispered, *"I'm not going anywhere."*

Later, I realized He had already promised it:

> *"Never will I leave you. Never will I forsake you."*
>
> — **Hebrews 13:5**
>
> ❧ **He doesn't just show up for prophets and apostles.**
> He shows up for bus-riding, blanket-burrito souls too.

For years, I thought that was my only "spiritual gift."
Holy hugs.

(Thanks, Lord. Appreciate the holy-hug subscription service.)

But then it got wild.

Because one day, I didn't just feel Him.
I heard Him.

Not like, *"Thus saith the Lord"* booming from my toaster.
Not creepy ghost whispers either.

Real.
Personal.
Unmistakable.

Words that cut through my fear and hit my heart so hard, I knew it wasn't me making it up.

And here's the truth—
I realized God had actually been speaking to me all along.

I just didn't know how to recognize His voice.
I didn't know what to listen for.

It wasn't until I finally made it so important that I asked Him point blank:
"Please speak to me. I want to hear Your voice."

That's when everything shifted.
That's when I finally recognized the sound of Him.

And here's the best part—
you can do the same thing.

I'm not special.
I just made it a priority.
I just let God know what I needed.

And when it first happened?
Let's just say subtle was nowhere on the agenda.

No warm fuzzies this time.
More like, *"SURPRISE! I brought clarity, conviction, and you're going to need to sit down for this one."*

From that moment on, everything changed.

And before you think I'm exaggerating, let me say this: there's zero benefit in making up stories about the God I love. Believe me, I was the first doubter in the room—so if anyone tried to explain it away, it was me.

When I stand before Him one day, I want to hear,
"Well done. You told the truth. You didn't water it down. You helped the doubters, the wanderers, the skeptics see Me more clearly—because you were honest."

That's my goal.
Not applause.
Not approval.
Just His voice saying, *"You helped bring them home."*

The same God who whispered to prophets and walked with apostles?
Yeah. He still speaks.

To regular people.
To skeptics.
To snack-loving, slightly sarcastic souls like me.

And maybe... to you too.

Because once you've heard Him for yourself—even once—you'll never un-hear it.
And you'll never be the same.

And yes—I'll tell you exactly how it happened later in my story. Trust me—you won't see it coming. And that's what makes it unforgettable.

END OF CHAPTER REFLECTION

1. Have you ever felt something you couldn't explain—peace, warmth, a quiet knowing—and thought, *Was that God?* What did you do with it?

2. Ever wonder if that moment with God was real—or if you just needed a snack and a nap?

3. Can you name a moment when you desperately needed God—and He showed up in a way you didn't expect?

CHAPTER 7

You Can't Earn Grace

And Neither Can I—But We Keep Trying Anyway

After all my wandering from God—after the heartbreak, the silence, the theological dumpster fire—I started tiptoeing back.

Not with fireworks or fanfare.
More like a guilty kid slipping into the back pew, smelling faintly of doubt and last night's Doritos, praying no one noticed.

I went back to church.
Not because I felt holy.
Not because I felt healed.
Because I had run out of other ideas and honestly needed a lifeline.

I was bone-tired, lost, and terrified I'd already blown my one shot at God's love.

So I prayed again.
Not in those beautiful, Pinterest-worthy prayers the Bible study ladies recited.
Mine sounded more like awkward voicemails:
"Uh... hi God. It's me. Not sure if You still... take calls?"

And just like that, I was in.

Back in church. Signing up for everything.
Bible studies? Yes.
Volunteering? Absolutely.
Christian radio? Sure.
Even creative substitutions for swearing—because apparently, "Cheese and crackers!" counts as sanctified.

If there was a spiritual checklist, I was training for sainthood.

And at first—it worked.
I felt connected.
Encouraged.
Hopeful.

I even dragged my siblings into it. Denise and Jim jumped right in, and suddenly our phone calls sounded like late-night 1-800-JESUS infomercials.
We were quoting Scripture like movie lines we'd memorized.
We were ridiculous.
And I loved it.

Jim was dating Shannon back then. I got them both on the Jesus train.
Meanwhile, my faith life looked like a Pinterest board—color-coded, organized, and way too much.

But underneath all that glittery devotion was a quiet, gnawing fear:
What if I'd messed up too much?
What if my losses were punishment?
What if God was holding out on me because I had let Him down?

So I got busy.
Good behavior became my bargaining chip.
Performance became my way of begging God to notice —like I was hacking a cosmic rewards program.

But that was never the point.

God wanted a relationship.
Not just me hustling and reporting in, hoping I'd earned a gold star.

He wanted a conversation.
Me talking to Him.
And Him talking back.

All my striving had drowned out the very thing He wanted most: connection.

I thought if I could just keep all Ten Commandments—all the time—then maybe I'd finally qualify for blessing.
But let's be real: I couldn't.
One slip, one failure, and I was back to feeling like I'd failed the whole test.

It was exhausting.

And then one day, I actually slowed down long enough to read what Jesus said about the commandments.
Ten rules I could never keep perfectly?
He boiled them down to two: Love God. Love your neighbor.

Jesus said it like this:

> *"Love the Lord your God with all your heart and with all your soul and with all your mind. This is the first and greatest commandment. And the second is like it: 'Love your neighbor as yourself. All the Law and the Prophets hang on these two commandments."*
> **— Matthew 22:37–40**
>
> ✥ **God didn't shrink ten rules into two to make life harder.**
> He simplified the test: Love Him. Love people.

Reading that felt like finding out the test was only two multiple-choice questions instead of ten essay exams.

Not easy—but simple.
It wasn't about flawless rule-keeping.
It was about love.

But I didn't know how to live free yet.
So instead of resting in those two, I doubled down.
Tried to master all ten—plus a dozen more "good Christian" habits for extra credit.

I became a Christian Hermione Granger—armed with highlighters and laminated tabs.

I even gave up secular music and pretended to enjoy the third rerun of that one worship song where everyone claps offbeat.

Inside, I was screaming:
"Look, God! I'm doing all the things! Can I have my miracle now?"

I thought I was being faithful.
Really, I was panicking.
Trying to earn grace.

And you can't.
(I was as disappointed as you are.)

Trying to be your own savior? Exhausting.
I wasn't just tired.
I was spiritually winded.

Running on a treadmill—panting, sweating, but never moving an inch closer to grace.

CHRISTINE PILGRIM

Because underneath it all was a destructive little lie:
God's love is conditional... and I haven't met the conditions.

I believed it.
Lived like it was true.
Thought my infertility, my failures, my heartbreak were proof.

So I made a bargain:
"If I can behave, be holy, and skip enough brownies... maybe God will give me a baby."

That's not theology.
That's desperation.

I was chasing a reward.
God was offering a relationship.

Here's what I finally learned:
God didn't want my performance.
He wanted me.

The broken me.
The unsure me.
The carb-loving, doubt-prone me.

Grace isn't a paycheck for good behavior.
It's a gift—already bought, already sealed.

> *"For it is by grace you have been saved, through faith—and this not from yourselves, it is the gift of God—not by works, so that no one can boast."*
>
> **— Ephesians 2:8–9**
>
> ☙ **Grace isn't a paycheck.**
> You don't earn it, polish it, or prove you deserve it. You just open your hands and receive.

All my striving hadn't brought me closer to Him.
It had distracted me from the truth:
I didn't need to earn love.
I already had it.

Jesus never asked for perfection.
He just asked me to come.

It took years to stop trying to pay Him back for something free.
But when I finally stopped?

Oh, the relief.
The exhale.
That deep, soul-healing rest that only comes when you quit auditioning for love you already have.

I still pray.
I still read Scripture.
I still go to church.

But now I do it from love, not fear.

I'm not trying to impress God anymore.
I'm walking with Him.

And that changed everything.

Because when you stop striving and start receiving, your hands are finally free—
Free from juggling spiritual to-do lists.
Free to grasp the love, peace, and grace He's been holding out all along.

And just when I thought I had finally cracked the grace code, I managed to bungle it in a whole new way. Spoiler: you'll see.

END OF CHAPTER REFLECTION

1. Ever catch yourself hustling for God's approval—like maybe if you pray harder, serve more, or behave better, He'll finally give you what you've been begging for?

2. What's one "spiritual habit" you leaned on to prove you were worthy—when deep down, it was more about performance than love?

3. What would it feel like to quit auditioning for God's love—as if He's Simon Cowell from America's Got Talent, hand hovering over the big red X—and finally just rest in the fact you already have it?

CHAPTER 8

No Such Thing as Too Far Gone

How God Found Me in the Middle of My Worst Decisions

I've made some spectacularly bad choices—
the kind that need a helmet, a waiver, and maybe a therapist on speed
dial.
The kind people shake their heads at and say, "Bless her heart"...
with that tone that definitely isn't a blessing.

You'd think after feeling God's presence—
after that holy cool warmth, like a divine heated blanket fresh from
Heaven's dryer—
I'd never let go.

You'd think I'd march into adulthood like a spiritual superhero.
Bible in hand.
Quoting Scripture.
Converting people in the cereal aisle.

But nope.
I wandered.

Not just *lost my way* wandered.

I packed snacks, made a playlist called *"God Can't Find Me Here,"* and hit the gas.

And don't get me started on my dating life.
I had a talent for finding the wrong men—men who made promises like politicians: loud, charming, and gone when the ballots were counted.

And I stayed.
Way past the expiration date.

I called it love.
It was fear.

Fear of being alone.
Fear that crumbs were the best I'd ever get.

Then came marriage.
One I knew was wrong before I even zipped the dress.
Nothing says "lifelong covenant" like the sudden urge to fake food poisoning and run.
But I said yes anyway.

Because I wanted someone to choose me.
Because I thought smaller jeans finally made me lovable.

Truth bomb:
You can love someone and still know you don't belong together.
You can cry on the bathroom floor and still whisper, *"Maybe tomorrow will fix it."*
But tomorrow doesn't always show up.

So I ran.
Not to God.
Away from Him.

I still believed—just stopped talking to Him.

Instead, I turned to food.
Food never abandoned me.
Never judged.
Never said, *"You're too much"* or *"not enough."*

Ice cream was my emotional support. And chocolate? My ride-or-die.

But food doesn't heal.
It numbs.
And when the sugar high faded, the shame hit harder.

Pain. Eating. Shame. Repeat.

Meanwhile, I was mad at God.
Mad He let me ache.
Mad He stayed quiet.
Mad I had an empty womb and a full fridge.

So I stopped praying.

But here's the thing.
You can ignore God.
Curse Him.
Run as far and as fast as you want.

You'll never outrun Him.

> *"Where can I go from your Spirit?*
> *Where can I flee from your presence?*
> *If I go up to the heavens, you are there.*
> *If I make my bed in the depths, you are there."*
>
> — **Psalm 139:7–8**
>
> ❧ **God doesn't lose track of us.**
> Not in joy, not in heartbreak, not even in the places we'd rather hide. Wherever we run, He's already there.

There is no "too far gone" with God.
Not the hospital room.
Not the lonely car ride.
Not the darkest valley or the highest mountaintop.

He's already there.
Still holding you.
Still loving you.
Still working.

Even in my messiest seasons, He was there.
Every step I took away, He followed.

Sometimes in unexpected kindness.
Sometimes in that quiet whisper: *"You're still Mine."*

That kind of relentless, no-matter-what love?
It changes everything.

And that's exactly where He found me—in the very mess I thought I'd chosen for myself.

END OF CHAPTER REFLECTION

1. Ever hit a point where you thought, "Yep, I've officially worn out God's patience"? What did that season look like?

2. What lies have you caught yourself believing about your worth—maybe from old relationships, failures, or words that still sting (like that boyfriend who treated Axe body spray as a personality)?

3. Can you look back and spot the ways God was still chasing you down—even when you weren't looking for Him?

CHAPTER 9

When You're Tempted to Settle

How God Meets Us in the Middle of "Good Enough"

Some people graduate high school and sprint straight into purpose. I graduated, flipped burgers, and reeked of french fries—complete with fryer burns and breakroom coffee that tasted like melted crayons.

I got my own apartment. Started college.

My sister, Denise? She was out there crushing it—school, career, lipstick that matched her shoes, goals stacked in color-coded tabs.

I admired her.
I envied her.

Meanwhile, I was living on fries and the fragile hope my next paycheck would cover rent *and* toilet paper.

Then came a full-time job offer.
It meant dropping out of college.

Everyone told me not to take it.
I took it anyway.

For a hot minute, it felt right.
Adulting! Paychecks! Hope!
I bought new shoes, organized my purse, and thought, *Maybe I'm finally catching up.*

Then the walls closed in.
No degree.
No ladder to climb.
Just fluorescent lights and an endless loop of *"Is this really my life?"*

Denise moved to Chicago, climbed every ladder in sight, and waved from the top like it was easy.

Meanwhile, I was still calling Mom long-distance to ask how to boil an egg without supervision.

I felt stuck.
Like my story was in black-and-white while everyone else lived in full color.

Eventually, I went back to school, finished my degree, and even earned an MBA. But those in-between years?

Brutal.
Lonely.
One long comparison game I always lost.

My weight yo-yoed the whole time. And underneath it all was a cruel little lie:
If I just lose enough—pounds, baggage, whatever—maybe someone will finally want me.

So I fought back with sheer willpower, Jesus, and a death stare that could make a cinnamon roll flinch.
Shockingly, the cinnamon rolls blinked first—and the weight came off.

Not long after, I got married.

I wish I could say it was a fairytale.
It wasn't.

I knew I'd settled.
But I wanted a baby.
I wanted the life I'd dreamed of since I was five.

I told myself it was good enough.
That maybe "good enough" was all I deserved.

> *"And we know that in all things God works for the good of those who love him, who have been called according to his purpose."*
> — **Romans 8:28**
>
> ❧ **Good enough was never the plan.**
> Even in the heartbreak and the waiting, God was already stitching together a bigger story than the one I thought I needed.

So I stayed.
Even when I cried more than I laughed.
Even when that quiet voice whispered, *"This isn't the life you prayed for."*

One night, I sat on the edge of my bed—heart cracked open, mascara streaked, pajama pants soaked in tears.

And I whispered the prayer I hadn't dared to say in years:
"God... I know I haven't talked to You in a while. But I need You. Please help me."

And just like that—He came.
The same cool warmth.
The same quiet hug.

The same sacred stillness I'd felt as a little girl on the church bus in lace-trimmed socks.

This was never meant to be a one-way monologue of me begging and Him listening politely.
God wanted a conversation.
He wanted me talking—and He wanted me listening.
Relationship is always both.

The problem was, I hadn't figured out how to recognize His voice yet.
I felt His presence, yes.
But hearing Him? That part still felt out of reach.

He was there.
He had never left.
That night didn't fix everything.
But it was enough.

Because sometimes, the miracle isn't a brand-new life.
Sometimes, it's just knowing you're not alone anymore.

And I would need that truth—because the next "no" I got from God? It would be the one that shattered me.

END OF CHAPTER REFLECTION

1. Ever felt yourself settling—job, love, life—just because you were afraid nothing better was coming?

2. Have you ever confused being chosen with actually being cherished? (Yeah... ouch. And nope, flowers on Valentine's Day don't count.)

3. What would change if you really trusted that God hasn't forgotten your dream?

CHAPTER 10

When God Says No

And How His Plans Can Still Be Good

They say if you pray hard enough, sing loud enough, and do everything "right," God will bless you.

So I did.

I prayed like my future depended on it.
I served like I was running for *Christian of the Year.*
I checked every box—twice—just in case God graded on a curve.

And through it all, I begged for one thing:
"Please, God. Make me a mom."

It wasn't a casual wish.
It was *the* dream.

Then came the day my world cracked.

Both fallopian tubes—blocked. Not one, both.
An instant rewrite of my entire future.

But I held on.

God can split seas, raise the dead, make a donkey preach.
Blocked tubes? Easy.

I told myself a baby would fix everything—my marriage, my sadness, my soul.
Reality was too painful, so I kept the dream on life support.

Three surgeries. Three failures. Scar tissue kept coming back, undoing everything the doctors tried.

So I went all in on IVF—last-chance, high-dollar, big-prayer territory. If surgery couldn't fix it, maybe this could.

Science and faith teaming up. This had to be it. And honestly? I thought surely God and science together would be unstoppable.

I reminded God—often—that Hannah begged for a baby and got one.
Surely He could at least copy and paste that miracle for me.
(Yes, I know God isn't a Xerox machine—but still, I asked.)

One night, I lay face-down on the carpet, sobbing so hard my lungs forgot how to breathe.
"Please, Lord. Please. Let me hold my own child."

And deep down, an unwelcome whisper:
This might not work either.

Nope. Not possible. Couldn't be true.

So I kept going.
Shots in the belly. Shots in the hips.
My body became a human pincushion, my prayers just as relentless.

If determination could make babies, I'd have triplets.

Three rounds.
Three failures.
Three heartbreaks that hollowed me out.

God's silence felt deafening.

My body was done.
And for the first time, I said the words out loud:

I will never be a mother.

It broke me in ways I still can't name.

> *"The Lord is close to the brokenhearted and saves those who are crushed in spirit."*
>
> — **Psalm 34:18**
>
> ☙ **God doesn't abandon the brokenhearted.**
> He pulls closer. Right into the ache. Right into the silence.

But here's what I didn't know yet:
Sometimes what feels like the end... isn't.

It's the moment God quietly clears the stage—
because a different kind of miracle is about to walk in.

One that didn't come in a crib.
But would still fill my arms.
And change everything.

And first... He would have to walk me through grief so deep, I didn't think
I'd survive it.

END OF CHAPTER REFLECTION

1. Ever prayed your guts out and felt like heaven stayed silent? How did that change the way you see God?

2. What's a dream you've had to bury—or at least grieve—that you once thought would always be part of your story?

3. Have you ever caught yourself believing your pain was punishment from God? Where did that lie first sneak in—Sunday School flannel graph, a bad sermon, or that relentless inner critic?

CHAPTER 11

Not the End

Why God Still Writes After We Think the Story's Over

The first time I said it out loud, it felt like chewing gravel:
"I don't think I'll ever be a mom."

Saying it felt like carving it in stone.
That was the day the dream died.

And everything went quiet.

I didn't hold a funeral. Didn't wear black.
But something sacred cracked wide open inside me, and I swear I felt it bleed.

After that, I clung to one verse like a kid clutching a blanket after a nightmare:

> *"Sing, O barren one, who did not bear... for the children of the desolate one will be more than the children of her who is married,"* says the Lord.
>
> — **Isaiah 54:1**
>
> ❧ **God's promises don't always follow the world's math.** Where we see emptiness, He sees abundance. Where we see loss, He is already writing a bigger story.

I didn't understand it.
Honestly, I barely believed it.
But I wanted it to mean the story wasn't over.

Still, what I felt wasn't sadness.
It was grief—the kind that sits heavy in your bones.

I grieved a life I'd never live.
A child I'd never hold.

And I was mad.
Not screaming-at-the-sky mad.
More like a quiet, simmering, *"God, why would You do this to me?"* mad.

Why give me this dream only to rip it away?
Why let me beg and sob for years just to say no?

He could've fixed it—one word, one miracle.
But He didn't.

That question stalked me everywhere.
And slowly, my rebuilt faith started to crumble like drywall under a leak.

Was God even real?
And if He was... why did it feel like He'd abandoned me?

I felt forgotten.
And the silence was deafening.

One afternoon, I walked past the baby aisle.
I made it three steps before turning around like a moth to a flame.

There it was—a tiny rainbow onesie.
The kind people buy after a loss, when hope tries again.

I picked it up.
And before I knew it, I was crying—not the cute movie-scene kind, but
the shoulders-shaking, can't-breathe kind.

That's when the church people showed up with their smiles and casseroles.

"God's timing is perfect!" they chirped.

I tried to smile back. I did.
But I also wanted to shove the casserole... well, you know.

It felt like the end of my story.

But it wasn't.
Not even close.

Maybe you've been there too.
Maybe you're there now.

If so, hear me:
God sees you.
God hears you.

And even when the silence feels like a slammed door,
He is still moving pieces you can't see.

Sometimes dreams die.

Sometimes prayers feel wasted.

But with God?
Death never gets the last word.

Resurrection always shows up.
Even if it doesn't look like you prayed it would.

Mine didn't arrive in the way I imagined—
not with a baby in a crib—
but waiting in a hospital hallway.

One end filled with a newborn's cry.
The other with the steady beep of a heart monitor.

I thought resurrection would look like pure joy.
Instead, it came holding hands with heartbreak—
proof that God doesn't only bring life once the dust has settled,
but sometimes right there in the mess.

And soon, I would walk into a hospital hallway where joy and grief held hands so tightly, I couldn't tell them apart.

END OF CHAPTER REFLECTION

1. When you feel forgotten, what changes if you really believe God is still moving pieces behind the scenes? (Even if those pieces feel slower than the DMV.)

2. Is there a part of your story you've stamped "The End" on— like credits rolling on a sad movie—that God might actually be planning to redeem?

3. Where have you seen little flickers of resurrection—life showing up in places you once thought were dead?

CHAPTER 12

When Joy and Pain Hold Hands

How God Shows Up in the Sweet and the Shattering

The hallway was a bridge between two worlds.

At one end, a newborn's cry split the air — high, fierce, demanding to be heard.
At the other, the slow, steady beep of a heart monitor marked each fragile second my brother fought to stay alive.

Upstairs was swaddled hope.
Downstairs was breaking hearts.

Life's beginning.
Life's battle.
Only a staircase apart.

Jim lay pale in a hospital bed, his immune system gone after one more brutal round of chemo.

And yet—he smiled, cracking jokes like laughter itself was medicine.

That was Jim: sunshine in boots, the guy who made optimism look easy—even when life wasn't.

So when leukemia sucker-punched our family, we were the ones reeling.
Jim just squared his shoulders, grinned, and said,
"I'm going to beat this."

And honestly? We believed him.
If anyone could smile cancer into submission, it was Jim.

He had Shannon by his side—his rock.
The girl who'd loved him since high school and still looked at him like
she'd just met her hero.
She could milk cows at sunrise and show up to a wedding looking like
royalty by nightfall.

That's real love—*The Notebook* kind. Messy. Loyal. All-in.
The kind that doesn't flinch when life gets hard.

While Denise and I bolted from farm life after graduation, Jim stayed.
Not because he loved it—because Dad needed him.

That was Jim. Steady. Sacrificial. All heart.

They were just twenty-eight and twenty when they married. But their
love made it look easy.

When they announced they were having a baby, we lost our minds.
A new life.
A new chapter.

Their story was already beautiful—this was the cherry on top.

Then came the diagnosis.
Leukemia.
A cosmic gut punch.
The kind of word that changes the temperature in the room — even if no
one moves.

Watching Jim endure chemo was brutal.
Watching Shannon never leave his side was holy—but gut-wrenching.

It was love in real time—hospital wristbands replacing wedding rings, whispered prayers replacing love letters.

Their faith didn't shake. Not once. Not ever.
Jim clung to Joshua 1:9 like a lifeline:

"Have I not commanded you? Be strong and courageous. Do not be afraid; do not be discouraged, for the Lord your God will be with you wherever you go."

— *Joshua 1:9*

❧ **Courage isn't the absence of fear.**
It's walking into the unknown with shaking knees—because you know you're not walking it alone.

I wish I could say my faith looked like theirs.
It didn't.

While Jim prayed to see his son grow up, I was still angry at God for not giving me one.

Standing in that hospital room, I felt small.
And fake.

Jim and Shannon's faith was the unshakable kind—rooted, immovable.
Mine was the see-saw variety—up when life was good, crashing when it wasn't.

Years earlier, in my "all-in" faith season, I'd convinced them to come to church with me.
They grabbed hold of Jesus and never let go.

I didn't know then they'd be the ones holding me up someday.

The day their son was born split my heart in two.
Upstairs: new cries, swaddled hope, tiny fingers curling around Shannon's.
Downstairs: quiet machines, antibiotics dripping into Jim's veins, his hand too weak to hold his baby for more than a minute.

Jim and Shannon convinced the medical team to wheel him down so he could be there for little Nate's birth.
Jim was determined not to miss the important things.
And they made it happen—even though he was sick enough to be in a hospital bed fighting for his life.

Joy and heartbreak braided together—inseparable.

It felt holy.
And cruel.

Still, Jim smiled and cracked jokes.
Still, he encouraged us—even as his strength slipped away.

And Shannon stayed—present. Unshaken. Tender.
The kind of love that doesn't run from the dark.

Just when the air in that hospital room felt too heavy to breathe... the phone rang.
Bob, our youngest brother, was a perfect bone marrow match.

The moment the doctor told us, the air shifted.
We laughed. We cried. Hugged so hard we could've cracked ribs.

It felt like God Himself had just walked into the room—miracle tucked under His arm.
Some people would've called it luck. I called it God showing up.

We talked about everything Jim would get to do now.
Teach Nate to fish.
Take Shannon to the beach.
Ride tractors without getting winded.

The transplant worked.
Day by day, color returned to Jim's face.
His voice grew stronger. His laugh—louder.

We watched hope march back into our family like it owned the place.
It unpacked its suitcase.

And for a while, we believed it would.
We could almost taste normal again—Sunday dinners, family trips, Jim chasing Nate across the yard.
We started making plans.

We didn't know hope was already packing its bags.

That it would slip out quietly.
And when it left—
it would knock the wind out of me.
And it would take Jim with it.

END OF CHAPTER REFLECTION

1. Ever watched someone else's faith stay rock-solid while yours felt like it was unraveling at the seams?

2. What does trusting God even look like when nothing adds up and your prayers feel like they're hitting a ceiling?

3. Can you think of a moment when love showed up so real, so tangible, it felt like God Himself had just walked in?

CHAPTER 13

Faith on the Floor

Holding On to God When Loss Knocks You Flat

The day hope left—it didn't slam the door.
It slipped away in the night.

Hope is reckless. It sneaks in when you swore you were done with it. And
for a while—we let it.

We pictured holidays.
Backyard football games.
Laughter spilling into the kitchen.

We let ourselves believe again.

But cancer doesn't play fair.
It doesn't care how many prayers you've prayed or how many times
you've already beaten it.

It came back.
This time—with backup.

Still—Jim fought.
We fought.

Another transplant was possible.
And once again, Bob stepped up.

Two brothers. One fight.
A bond deeper than blood.

We prayed like our lives depended on it—because his did.
We believed.
We begged.

A second transplant gave us hope.
But cancer returned—fiercer this time.

This time, Jim was tired.
Not nap-tired.
Soul-tired.

One quiet visit, he looked at me.
Gentle eyes. Faint smile.

"Thank you for bringing me closer to God," he said.
"I don't want to die—I want to see my son grow up. But I know where I'm
going. And I know I'll see you again."

Then he talked about Nathan. Little Nate.
His miracle boy.
His everything.

He just wanted time—to toss a ball.
Teach him to drive.
See him grow into the man God made him to be.

And God gave them some.
Between treatments and transplants, there was time to build a home.
Time to watch Nate grow and to draw closer to God.

Time to say the words that needed saying.

While Shannon was pregnant, doctors warned Jim might not live to see Nate born.
But he did.

Diagnosed at thirty.
Lived until thirty-five.

Before he died, Jim told Nate four things:

1. Believe in God.
2. Always be kind.
3. Be good to your mom.
4. Don't forget to have fun.

He added, "Every good and beautiful thing is created by God above. God is love."

And if time ran out?
He prayed Nate would grow up knowing God—so one day, he could find him again.
The one thing Jim wanted most was to see Shannon and Nate again—someday—in Heaven.

That was his prayer.
Not just healing here.
Reunion there.

Even now, it rips me open.
But that moment cracked something hard in me—bitter, angry, controlling.

And in that crack, something warm slipped in.
A whisper. A promise: *You'll see him again. Hold on.*

I remember one day not long before the end—just the two of us, parked on the couch watching *Happy Gilmore* for the hundredth time.
Jim knew every line and wasn't shy about saying them a split second before Adam Sandler did.

His laugh—loud, ridiculous, contagious—filled the room.
For a few minutes, there was no cancer. No chemo.
Just two siblings laughing at a stubborn golf ball that wouldn't go in the hole.

That was Jim.
He found joy in the middle of hard places.
Joy and heartbreak braided together—right to the very end.

Shannon was by his side when he went home to Jesus.
She was always by his side—talking, comforting, making sure he knew how much he was loved.

We never think we're hearing someone's last words when they're spoken.
But looking back, maybe Jim knew.

He kissed Shannon goodbye.
Then he said:
"Thank you, God, for everything."

Even in his last breath—he was still praising.
Still believing.
Still looking forward to Home.

> *"I have fought the good fight, I have finished the race, I have kept the faith."*
>
> — **2 Timothy 4:7**
>
> ❧ **A life of faith isn't about never stumbling.**
> It's about finishing—scarred knees, weary heart, but still clinging to God at the end.

He knew where he was going.
And he wanted us all there with him someday.

And then... he was gone.
One day he was laughing.
The next—the silence was deafening.

Grief hit like a freight train.
Anger barreled in right behind it.

I didn't scream out loud.
I had to be strong—for Shannon.
For little Nate.
For our parents.

But inside—I was yelling at God.
Why him? Why now?
Why take this good, kind, faithful man?

Jim believed.
He prayed.
He trusted with all he had.
And still—he died.

That's when I learned a brutal truth.
Sometimes faith isn't a feeling.

It's a choice.

Choosing to believe when everything in you wants to quit.
Choosing to trust when nothing makes sense.
Choosing to keep walking with God—even when your heart is shattered.

Faith isn't always loud.
Sometimes it's quiet. Steady. Barely visible—but still there.
Sometimes it just whispers: *Stay.*

God never promised a pain-free life.
But He promised to be in it with us.

> *"We also rejoice in our sufferings, because we know that suffering produces perseverance; perseverance, character; and character, hope.*
> — **Romans 5:3-4**
>
> ❧ **God doesn't waste pain.**
> He turns pressure into strength. Heartbreak into hope.

When Jim died, a part of me died too.
But something else was born.

I became softer.
More compassionate.
Able to sit in someone's pain and simply say, "I get it. You're not alone."

And no—believing Jim was "with Jesus" didn't erase the ache. The empty chair at holiday dinners still gutted me every time. But it did keep me from drowning completely.

We don't always get answers.
But we do get God.

His comfort.

His presence.

His promise that this pain is not the end.

> *"He comforts us in all our troubles, so that we can comfort those in any trouble with the comfort we ourselves have received from God."*
> — **2 Corinthians 1:4**
>
> ❧ **Your survival can become someone else's lifeline.**
> What nearly broke you might be the very thing that helps someone else hold on.

Here's what loss taught me: the scar you wish you didn't have may one day be the scar that helps someone else keep standing.

One day—Satan will be no more.

No more cancer.

No more goodbyes.

No more prayers ending in silence.

Until then—we hold each other up.

We walk each other home.

And we cling to a hope bigger than death.

I miss my brother every single day.

But I know where he is.

I know I'll see him again.

And I know, without a doubt, he's whole.

No more needles.

No more pain.

Just Jesus.

And joy.

The kind Jim never lost—now complete in His presence.

But me?

I was left in the ache.
Left staring at the empty chair.
Left trying to convince myself that hope was still bigger than grief.

I wanted to believe death didn't get the last word.
But when the house went quiet, when the holidays came hollow, when the nights felt endless—
faith didn't feel like fire.

It felt like silence.
And I was about to drift farther from God than I ever had before.

END OF CHAPTER REFLECTION

1. Have you ever hit something so painful it left you asking "Why?" — whether you asked it to God, the ceiling, or just into the air? What helped you breathe through it?

2. When life guts you—do you pull away from faith, people, or hope altogether? Or do you find yourself leaning in closer? What makes that choice feel impossible sometimes?

3. Could the very scar you hate be the thing that helps someone else hang on?

CHAPTER 14

The God Who Waits

How Drifting from God Happens Quietly—
and How to Find Your Way Back

I thought I was holding it together.
Smiling. Functioning. Folding laundry like a pro.
Inside? I was unraveling like a cheap sweater in a dryer set to "volcano."

After Jim died, I scavenged for scraps of good in the grief.
Sunsets seemed brighter.
Friends made me laugh when laughter felt impossible.
I counted what I still had—not just what I'd lost.

Shannon stayed close.
She and Nate came for every holiday.
It made Christmas less hollow.
Like Jim was still there—in stories, in Nate's grin, in Shannon's quiet strength.

But outside of holidays, life didn't pause for my grief.
Bills came. Grocery lists grew.
And the cracks in my own world kept widening.

Marriage is supposed to be a soft place to land—
inside jokes, bad TV, burnt toast eaten with someone who loves you.
Mine looked fine from the outside.
It wasn't chaos. Just... lonely.

I loved him. I tried.
But somehow, we lived side-by-side without really meeting in the middle.
We had moments—he could be so effortlessly charming.
But I wanted more than flickers. I wanted steady light.

So I told myself what "good wives" say:
Love is sacrifice.
Marriage is hard work.
If I pray harder... wait longer... even learn to bait a hook (though I hate worms)... maybe it'll feel like love.

But I wasn't just tired.
I was disappearing—
one silent dinner, one skipped conversation at a time.

It's exhausting to fake *fine* while Googling, *Is it normal to cry in the shower this much?*

I didn't yell at God this time.
Didn't plead. Didn't bargain.
I just turned the volume down.
On prayer. On worship. On hope.
Until there was nothing left to hear.

Spiritual drifting isn't always loud.
Sometimes it's quiet exhaustion—a soul running on fumes while life keeps spinning.
I didn't run from God.
I just stopped turning toward Him.

I functioned like a mascara-wearing Roomba—bumping into walls, spinning in circles, pretending I had a plan.
Underneath? Hollow.

Coffee didn't fix it.
Even twelve Target throw pillows—clearance-priced—couldn't fix it.

What I missed... was God. The presence I didn't notice but couldn't escape.

> *"Where can I go from your Spirit? Where can I flee from your presence?"*
>
> **— Psalm 139:7**
>
> ❧ **We run. We hide. We build walls.**
> And still, God shows up—uninvited but never unwelcome.

I may have gone silent.
But He never stopped speaking.

Even when I cried behind closed doors.
Even when I whispered, *How did I get here?*
Even when I felt too broken to pray—He stayed.

Not glaring.
Not lecturing.
Just waiting.

God doesn't panic when we wander.
He doesn't stamp FAILED on our story.
He waits—with grace, with kindness, with eyes that see the whole picture, even when all we see is a mess.
Not with crossed arms and a cosmic foot tap, but with open hands.

Looking back, I see it now—

a golden thread in the mess.
Even in the dark.
Even in the doubt.
Even when numbness pretended to be peace.

God wasn't punishing me.
He wasn't abandoning me.
He was guiding me.
Gently. Quietly. Patiently.

Waiting for me to whisper:
I miss You.

It wasn't fancy. Just honest.
But something cracked open.

That ache in my chest?
Not just sadness.
It was homesickness for God.

"The Lord will fulfill His purpose for me;
Your love, O Lord, endures forever."

— **Psalm 138:8**

❧ God's purposes don't expire.
His love doesn't run out. Even when we waver, His plans hold
steady.

Even when I didn't love myself, He did.
Even when I thought I'd ruined everything, He said, *I'm not finished*
with you.
Even when I had nothing left, He gave me Himself.

God doesn't wait for you to get it together.

He meets you in the unraveling.

In the silence.

In the moment you finally ask, *Are You still there?*

And His answer?

"I never left."

But if He never left...

Why did it feel like the one door I'd begged Him to open
was about to slam shut in my face?

END OF CHAPTER REFLECTION

1. Ever found yourself drifting—not in a big, dramatic way, but in the quiet, slow fade you barely noticed?

2. Have you ever called numbness "peace," just because it hurt less than honesty?

3. What would change if you stopped trying so hard to fix yourself and simply let yourself be loved—as you are, not as you think you should be?

CHAPTER 15

What Felt Like No

When God Closes a Door You've Been Praying to Walk Through

You can convince yourself of almost anything when you feel unworthy.
I once convinced myself I was lucky just to be tolerated—like real love
was too much to ask for.
(It's not.)

Low self-esteem is a quiet thief.
It doesn't kick down the door.
It slips in with a whisper:
*This is as good as it gets. Be grateful. Don't expect more. You don't deserve it
anyway.*

So I settled.
Not for chaos.
Just for a life that felt smaller than the love I dreamed of.

And instead of turning to God, I turned to easy fixes.
More food.
More numbing.
(Duct tape does not fix everything. I checked.)

Then, in the middle of the ache, God handed me three plot twists.
Three kids.

Not biologically mine—my husband's from his first marriage.
They crash-landed into my life with juice boxes, Velcro shoes, and peanut
butter fingerprints on every available surface.
They hugged me like I was the hero of their Saturday morning cartoons.
I loved them before I knew what hit me.

They already had a mom. A real one.
I never wanted to step into her place.
I just wanted them to feel safe. Loved.
Two weekends a month—that was my window.

That was my prayer: *Let them feel loved while they're here.*

Even with my own dream of motherhood aching in my chest, I opened
my heart.
I braided hair.
Kissed scraped knees.
Laughed at knock-knock jokes that made zero sense.
I baked cookies.
The cookies were fine.
The kids? Amazing.

For a while, I thought maybe this was it—God's plan for me.
Not to have my own child, but to love someone else's.
And honestly? That felt holy.

But it also felt incomplete.
Because there was always the ache.
The quiet grief no one else could see.

I wanted to hear "Mommy" and know it was for me.

I wanted a child to look into my eyes and say, without words, *You're my whole world.*

Sometimes the ache blindsided me.
In the grocery store.
At the park.
In the baby aisle at Target—where I swear I never meant to end up but somehow always did.

I'd smile at other moms.
Then cry later in my car.
Happy for them.
Heartbroken for me.

Then one night, at my parents' kitchen table, came a plot twist I didn't see coming.

Both Shannon and Denise had gotten remarried and moved forward after Jim's death.
Shannon leaned in, grinning.
"I have an announcement."

We expected a new house.
Or a puppy.
But nope. Pregnant.
Cue squeals, hugs, happy tears.

And then Denise chimed in: "Me too."
Both of them. Pregnant. At the same time.

I smiled like a good sister.
Inside? I shattered.

The bathroom lock clicked—louder than it should have.
My back pressed against the wall, solid and cold, as I slid to the floor.

Lavender hand soap mocked me from the counter, all calm and pretty while I was falling apart.
I pulled my knees to my chest.
And the heartbroken sobs came hard and fast.

*"God, this is not fair.
Why would You let me carry this dream so long if You're never going to give it to me?"*

Faith dangled by a single, fraying thread.
But like always, I wiped the tears, fixed my face, and pretended I was fine.

Later, Denise whispered that she'd miscarried. Twice.
She had two older boys from her first marriage, but never carried another pregnancy after that—not with her new husband, not ever.

Guilt hit like a sucker punch.
I'd been so buried in my own pain, I hadn't seen hers.

And Shannon—months later—held a newborn girl in her arms.
She named her Faith.
The name was perfect.
But for me, it was another twist of the ache I carried.

We all carry something, don't we?
Invisible grief.
Private heartbreak.

Some of us bleed behind locked doors.

Nobody escapes life without scars.

> *"When you go pass through the waters, I will be with you; and when you pass through the rivers, they will not sweep over you."*
> — **Isaiah 43:2**
>
> ❧ **God never promised calm seas.**
> But He did promise we won't go under.

And maybe... just maybe... God wasn't punishing me.
Maybe He was protecting me.

Because if I'd had a child with the man I was married to, I would have stayed.
I would have sacrificed myself in the name of being a "good mom."
I would have endured things no woman should quietly endure.

But God knew.
He knew I'd never walk away if a child was in the picture.
So in His mercy—not His anger—He closed that door.
At the time, it didn't feel like mercy. It felt like a cosmic prank. But looking back, I see it differently.

Still, I struggled.
I numbed with food. Ice cream doesn't judge—but the shame always tagged along.

The weight came back.
The shame tagged along.
And I stayed mad at God.

I wanted answers.
Why the dream had to die.
Why the ache stayed.
Why the waiting never ended.

But looking back, I see it now:
God didn't walk away from me.
I walked away from Him.

And even so... He waited.
Not with crossed arms.
Not with tapping feet.
But with the porch light on.
Coffee brewing.
Door still open.
Welcome mat at the door.

> *"Even to your old age and gray hairs, I am He, I am He who will sustain you. I have made you, and I will carry you; I will sustain you, and I will rescue you."*
>
> — **Isaiah 46:4**
>
> ♪ **Too old? Too broken? Too far gone? Nope.**
> God says: *I've got you.*

I didn't know the next season would take me somewhere even lonelier—and eventually, straight into ruins I never wanted to revisit.

END OF CHAPTER REFLECTION

1. What lies about your worth have you carried around—lies that need to be swapped out for truth (or at least challenged)?

2. Ever felt overlooked—like blessings, opportunities, or good breaks were being handed out to everyone else but you? What did you do with that ache?

3. What if that closed door in your life wasn't rejection at all—but mercy in disguise?

CHAPTER 16

Restoration in the Ruins

Why God Sometimes Starts Rebuilding in the Places You'd Rather Forget

The day I learned my step kids' mom and her second husband were having twins—through IVF, the very same thing I'd tried and failed?
It felt like a cosmic prank.

Twins.
She already had three kids. Soon she'd have five.
And me? Still empty-handed.

"God," I whispered, jaw clenched. *"This cannot be Your idea of fair. You give her twins—and I can't even get one?"*

Silence.
A big, echoing, holy nothing.

But even in the wreckage, I felt the nudge: *You have three children to love.*
At the time, that whisper didn't feel holy—it felt cruel. But it stuck.

So I did.
I made pancakes.

Watched TV shows I never would have picked myself.
Sat through board games where the rules were more... "optional" than not.

Those kids owned my heart before I could stop it.
But I was just Christine. Not "Mom."
And I wasn't trying to be.

They already had a mother, and I respected that.
I just wanted them to feel chosen—every single time they walked through that door.

Every other Sunday night, when they left, the house filled with a silence that broke me twice.

Somewhere in that ache, I stopped praying.
Stopped talking to God at all.
If He was listening, He wasn't answering.

So I threw myself into work.
The office didn't care about my empty womb or my broken heart.
They just liked my "get it done" attitude.

I had no degree. But I'd taken exams, earned some fancy initials after my name, and hustled hard.
I climbed as far as I could—until my manager said, "Christine, you're killing it—but without a degree, you're stuck."

Ouch.
But true.

I should've stayed in college the first time.
Instead, I'd quit to escape that greasy fast-food job and wound up in an administrative role that promised "opportunity"... and led nowhere.

So here I was.

Late thirties.
Back in college.
Surrounded by students who thought ramen was a food group and all-nighters were a competitive sport.

I reminded myself: These years will pass whether I do this or not.

And they did.

I earned my degree.
Lost 100 pounds.
Fought for a healthier me.

When I crossed that graduation stage, I wept.
Not for the paper.
For the proof: I didn't quit on myself.

Then I signed up for an MBA because... why not?
The time would pass anyway.

But while I was transforming, my marriage stayed stuck.
Lonely.
Heavy.
Unchanged.

I prayed.
I compromised.
I stayed longer than I should have.

And finally... I left.

Christians aren't supposed to get divorced, right? At least that's the vibe I picked up. But staying would've killed me faster than leaving.

Divorce wasn't the magic relief button I'd hoped for.

Nights still ended in sobs. Days carried guilt like a shadow. Every "what if" replayed on loop.

But sometimes the bravest thing you can do is walk away from what's slowly killing you.

I ran from my marriage.
And I ran from God.

But here's what I didn't see then:
He never ran from me.

He met me in the wreckage—and started rebuilding.

But the first thing He rebuilt wasn't my faith.
It was my understanding of where God really is when the silence feels unbearable.

> *"The Lord is close to the brokenhearted and saves those who are crushed in spirit."*
>
> — **Psalm 34:18**
>
> ❧ **When your heart feels shattered, God doesn't back away.** He sits with you in the ruins and starts the quiet work of putting you back together.

I thought the ruins meant the end.
But what I didn't know yet was that silence was waiting for me there too—and it nearly convinced me God had left for good.

END OF CHAPTER REFLECTION

1. Have you ever gone through a season where everything felt silent—like your prayers, your plans, or even life itself wasn't answering back? What did you do with that silence?

2. What guilt, shame, or regret still clings to you—like a weight you can't seem to shake?

3. What if the ruins in your story—the very places you'd rather forget—weren't the end at all, but the starting point of something new?

CHAPTER 17

When God Feels Silent

When Silence Doesn't Mean Absence

After the divorce, the questions didn't trickle in.
They stormed the gates like emotional SWAT.

Not the sweet, *ponder over coffee* kind.
The kind where you're your own hostile witness, cross-examining your faith with dramatic flair:
If God is real... then what in the actual heck is this mess?

I wasn't shaking my fist at heaven.
I was on the floor. Broken.
Wondering how you can pray your guts out and still feel like God's voicemail is full.

I'd ticked every spiritual box I knew how to.

And what did I get?
A shattered heart.
An empty nursery.
A marriage that felt like slow emotional suffocation—just enough charm sprinkled in to keep me hoping.

But real love doesn't make you guess.
It doesn't vanish and reappear like a bad Wi-Fi signal.

Still, I stayed.
Because leaving felt like performing open-heart surgery on myself... with
a spoon.
And not the good kind.
One of those flimsy plastic ones from a gas station.

I kept hoping this time would be different.
It wasn't.

And while I was crying into my pillow, the questions piled up:
- Where was God?
- Why didn't He step in?
- Why let me dream of motherhood if He was never going to let it
  happen?

And it wasn't just my marriage.
Losing my brother Jim—the rock of our family—wrecked me in ways I
still can't name.
We prayed. We begged. We believed.
And he still died.

Faith started to feel like a bad joke.
Church songs made me cry.
Prayers felt fake.
Faith felt like pretending.

And I was so tired of pretending.

Yet even in my doubts.
Even in my tantrums.
Even in my rage-quit prayers—God didn't move.

I couldn't feel it then.
At the time, I would've rolled my eyes if someone told me He was there.
But now, looking back, I know it's true.

Now I know—He stayed.

Quiet.
Still.
Near.

Because here's the thing:
God doesn't live in church buildings or only show up when your Bible reading streak is on fire.
The day I said "yes" to Him, He moved in.
And He's not the kind of roommate who bails when the dishes pile up.

He didn't leave when I doubted.
He didn't roll His eyes when I stopped praying.
He didn't say, *Well, she's a mess. I'm out.*
He just waited.

"If we are faithless, he will remain faithful, for he cannot disown himself."

— **2 Timothy 2:13**

⸙ Even when we're a disaster, God doesn't flinch.
His love isn't performance-based. He stays—even when we're convinced He won't.

I used to think silence meant absence.
Now I know it sometimes means comfort.
The kind that doesn't need words—just presence.

The kind that sits with you in the ruins and whispers, *I know.*

I still wrestle.
I still ask why.
But now I know my questions don't scare Him off.

Because faith isn't never doubting.
It's choosing to keep reaching for God, even when you're not sure He's reaching back.

He always is.
He doesn't shame the doubter.
He meets them.
Every single time.

Just like He met Thomas. You know—the doubting disciple who flat-out said, "I won't believe it unless I see the proof."
If the disciples had group nicknames, Thomas would've been Doubter Guy. And Jesus didn't kick him out of the band.

Just like He meets me.
Just like He's waiting to meet you.

Because the truth is—
He never walked away.
We just finally opened our eyes and saw He'd been there all along.

But realizing God was still with me was only the beginning.
Because rock bottom was waiting for me—
and it would become the last place I ever expected to meet Him.
And that's where the story turns.

END OF CHAPTER REFLECTION

1. Ever been convinced God was silent—and only later realized He'd been there the whole time?

2. What's the unspoken thing you've been too scared—or maybe too angry—to actually say out loud?

3. How would it shift things if you really believed you weren't alone—even when you're doubting, spiraling, or rage-quitting faith altogether?

CHAPTER 18

When Rock Bottom Becomes Holy Ground

How Rock Bottom Became the Beginning

Divorce isn't just a break.
It's a freefall.

And when you land?
There's nothing there to catch you.

Even when it's the right choice, it still feels like a funeral.
Not just the death of a marriage—
the death of every dream tied to that life.

I thought leaving would feel like freedom.
The deep breath.
The windows down.
The dramatic drive into a future that was supposed to cue swelling violins
and end credits.

But when the dust settled?
Guilt moved in.

Not the mild, *Oops, I forgot to water the plant* guilt.
The heavy kind.
The kind that unpacks a suitcase in your soul and says, *You failed. Again.*

I still showed up.
Did the job.
Smiled at neighbors.
Held my life together with coffee and concealer.

Inside, I was one giant bruise.

Therapy helped.
(Go. Seriously. It's a game-changer.)
It gave me words, strategies—
and the reminder that imagining throwing a shoe at your ex doesn't mean
you're not healing—it just means you're human.

But peace?
Nowhere to be found.

Memories could wreck me without warning.
One day in the grocery store, a box of Eggo waffles made me cry over lost
Sunday mornings.
Divorce is weird like that.

Then came the night I cracked wide open.

Alone on my couch.
Curled around a throw pillow like it could keep me from shattering.
No TV. No noise. Just me, silence, and the unraveling.

And then it happened.

The sobs showed up—hiccupping, unstoppable—
and with them, my most desperate prayer:

"God... if You're there... if You even care... I need You. Because I can't do this anymore."

Not pretty. Not polished.
Just mascara streaks and raw honesty.

Something shifted.

Just stillness.
A quiet presence.
Not an audible voice—
more like a steadying calm settling deep inside me,
as if God Himself was gently placing a hand on my shoulder and saying,
You're not alone.

This wasn't the unmistakable, "I know that's Your voice" moment I longed to know.
This was softer.
A soul-deep reassurance.
A quieting of the storm inside me.

It wasn't instant healing.
It wasn't a miracle in one night.
But it was enough light in the dark to keep breathing.

Now I see it clearly.
That pain wasn't punishment.
It was permission.

Permission to stop pretending.
Permission to break.
Permission to come home.

He didn't cause the pain.
But He refused to waste it.

He used it to pull me closer.
Back to Him.
Back to myself.
Back to something sacred.

When I think about my step-kids now, I see it differently.

Maybe I wasn't meant to be in their lives forever.
But for a season, I could be a soft landing when everything tilted sideways.
And in return, they gave me something too—the imprint of their laughter,
their stories, their little hands etched into my heart.

We're a thousand miles apart now, but they're still with me.

It wasn't the life I prayed for.
But it was the life God used.

And sometimes, that's the bigger gift.

Because pain will tear you open.
But not just to wreck you.
It makes room—
for healing, for grace, for a redemption story you didn't see coming.

Somewhere in the rubble, I realized—
This wasn't the end.
Not even close.
It was the beginning of the life I was always meant to live.

And in the wreckage, rock bottom became holy ground—the place where
I stopped running.
My new beginning.

> "The Lord will fight for you; you need only to be still."
>
> — **Exodus 14:14**
>
> ❧ **Rock bottom isn't the end.**
> It's the place God meets you, steadies you, and begins the fight
> you can't win alone.

I thought holy ground would make me untouchable.
Turns out, the enemy loves a woman on the mend—
and he knew exactly how to knock on my door next.

END OF CHAPTER REFLECTION

1. Ever lived through something you swore was "the end"—only to realize later it was actually the beginning?

2. Can you remember your own rock-bottom moment—the one where everything cracked open? What shifted after that?

3. What are you white-knuckling right now that maybe—just maybe—you don't have to carry alone? (Besides the remote and a bag of chips.)

CHAPTER 19

Flirting with Doubt and Dating the Devil's Assistant

When Loneliness Opens the Door to the Wrong Voices—
and How God Keeps Knocking Anyway

The enemy is sneaky.

Not innocent-or-playful sneaky, like a kid hiding behind the couch. More like a cartoon villain twirling his mustache while plotting a trap you don't see coming.

He doesn't show up when you're spiritually on fire—Bible open, coffee steaming, highlighters locked and loaded.
Nope.
He waits until you're exhausted.
Emotionally wrecked.
Spiritually running on stale crackers and sarcasm.

Then... he slides in.

Satan isn't God. Not even close.
He doesn't know your future—he just panics thinking about it.

So he does the only thing he can: whispers doubt until you start questioning your own mind.

And that's where I was.

Rock bottom.
Heart shattered.
Brain tangled like Christmas lights in July.

Cue the psychic impulse.

At first, I laughed.
"A psychic? Please. Bible-Camp Christine says hard pass."

But that night?
The silence was deafening.
The ache in my chest—a fifty-pound kettlebell.

I thought, *What if this random stranger knows what God won't tell me?*

So... I called.

"Hi," he said.
"I'm The Eye. I see all."

Just The Eye.
Like a bad magician's stage name.
Or a knockoff Marvel villain.

I half expected him to tack on, "*...for $49.99 a minute.*"

His voice was smooth. Mysterious.
I pictured him jingling twenty bracelets—like a one-man tambourine band.

At first, it felt magical.

He said things that sounded true: "You've been through something hard."
No kidding. Sherlock would be proud.

Looking back, I realize I gave him breadcrumbs of my pain, and he handed them back in glitter, calling it divine wisdom.

What didn't show up after that call?
Peace. Joy. Clarity.
Just confusion—plus the urge to send him an invoice for emotional damages.

Now I know why God says:

> *"Do not turn to mediums or seek out spiritists..."*
> — **Leviticus 19:31**
>
> ❧ **Stop hunting for answers in dark places.**
> I'm not hiding. Come to Me.

But I wasn't listening yet.

Enter: the charming atheist attorney.
(Cue dramatic organ music.)

He was smart. Funny. Generous.
Fancy dinners. Jewelry. Trips.

Finally—someone carrying the weight instead of me.

For a minute, I thought maybe this was healing.

Then one night, fork in hand, he asked:
"You don't really believe in God, do you?"

"Um... yes, I do."

He shrugged.
"I'm an atheist."

And went back to his steak like he hadn't just sucker-punched my soul.

Red flags?
They were flapping like parade banners in a hurricane.

But I told myself: *Maybe I can fix this. Maybe he just hasn't met the right Christian.*
Basically, I was out here dating the devil's assistant.

He sounded like a podcast host with all the answers.
Made the universe sound like a random accident—
no design, no purpose, just chaos pretending to be order.

People make things up all the time.
The Tooth Fairy. Santa Claus. (Sorry if I just ruined Christmas for anyone.)
At some point, we all find out they were just stories.

Could this be the same?

And slowly, his doubts started sounding like mine.

Maybe faith is just a fairy tale.
Maybe this whole God thing is something people made up—passed down to give meaning to the mess.

I started to wonder: *Could he be right?*

What I didn't realize was I was standing in a spiritual ambush.

That gnawing in my gut?
The Holy Spirit, whispering: *Sweetheart, come home.*

But the rollercoaster was messy.

Charm. Confusion. Diamonds. Drama.

He even gave me a necklace with three diamonds—"yesterday, today, tomorrow," he said. A promise for all time.

Two days later, he broke up with me.

Apparently, "tomorrow" had a cancellation policy.

Finally, I'd had enough.
No fireworks.
No big sign from the sky.
Just a quiet, stubborn knowing deep in my soul:
I couldn't keep shrinking myself to fit someone else's belief system.

Now, looking back, I don't just see the pain—I see the protection.

God never left—
even when I dialed the psychic.
Even when I tried to date away the doubt.

He waited. He watched. He kept the light on.

Because once you belong to Him, you belong forever.
No matter how far you run—
if you're on the phone with a psychic or dating the devil's assistant—
He still remembers who you are... and He never stops coming.

I didn't know it yet, but God was already bringing someone into my life
who would love me like He does—
quietly, faithfully, without conditions.

And this time, it wouldn't be a rescue from loneliness.
It would be the start of real healing.

END OF CHAPTER REFLECTION

1. Ever hit a season where you started wondering if God was even real—or if faith is just Santa Claus for grownups?

2. Have you ever chased answers in all the wrong places—psychics, relationships, distractions—and ended up more confused than when you started?

3. Looking back, can you spot where God was quietly protecting you, even when you were convinced He'd checked out?

CHAPTER 20

From Atheists to Answered Prayers

What One Quiet Man and One Desperate Prayer Can Teach Us About Healing

I'll be honest—I was trying to fill the void. To prove I was still wanted. That's when Miles walked in.

At first, he was just Miles.
But soon, I realized he was different.

The last guy was an emotional rollercoaster.
Miles? An emotional porch swing.

Quiet. Kind. Steady.
The kind of man you could lean against and just... breathe.

A summer night swing—dependable, never jerking you sideways.

Which is hilarious, because in real life he thrives on rollercoasters and sharks.

(Apparently porch-swing calm doesn't apply at amusement parks... or aquariums.)

The man is also a die-hard Michigan State fan. I couldn't tell a touchdown from a free throw—but I still ended up in MSU t-shirts on game days.

With Miles, there was no drama.
Just calm. Just safe.
And yes... tall, dark-haired, and handsome. The kind of handsome that sneaks up on you when he smiles.

Funny too—always slipping in a one-liner at the exact moment I needed it. Like the time he smirked: "People act like sharks are dangerous, but after the Black Friday stampedes you've been through? Sharks would probably be scared of you."

He wasn't a rom-com hero with grand gestures and choreographed speeches.
He was more like the "brings-you-coffee" guy. The "watches-the-credits" guy. The "assembles-your-2 a.m.-impulse-buy-furniture" guy.

He tells me I'm beautiful—mostly with that quiet twinkle in his eyes. And once, with quiet conviction, he said I deserved more than I'd ever been given in the past.

Who does that?
Apparently, Miles.

But here's the thing: leaving chaos doesn't mean leaving pain.
I still dragged it everywhere—
a backpack full of bricks: guilt, shame, failure, second-guessing.

I smiled on cue.
Laughed at the right times.

The guilt didn't scream anymore. It whispered—at night, in the car when a song hit too close.

If emotional suppression were an Olympic sport, I'd be on a Wheaties box.

You failed. You're not who they think you are.

That's the thing about guilt—it never makes sense.
It just squats where grace belongs and refuses to leave.

Even with Miles, I hid it.
I didn't want him to see me worrying about my ex-husband's bills.
Didn't want him to see the ghosts of a marriage I once begged God to save.

And yes, I worried about my ex—because for years, I'd taken care of him and felt responsible for him.
The same man who drained me dry.
Who made the mess.
Who left me picking up shards.
And still—I lay awake wondering if he was okay.

But God had a rescue plan already in motion.
Not just Miles.
Healing.
The kind you don't see coming.

One night, bone-tired of pretending, I prayed—for the first time in months—
"God, I don't know how to stop hurting. Please help me."

Not polished. Not pretty.
Just desperate.

And I swear, Heaven leaned in.

Slowly, things shifted.
Truth found me in unexpected places.
Of all things, a verse I'd memorized years ago barged back into my
thoughts—like my brain had been holding onto truth long after I stopped
believing it mattered.

"I'm still here. I haven't changed. I'm not done."

People spoke words I didn't know I needed.
And peace—tiny, hesitant—slipped in and whispered, *You're not alone.*

I buried the grief like a lead balloon in my chest.
I didn't want Miles to run.
Didn't want to be the "can't get over it" girl.

But God knew.

And Miles? Oh, Miles was different.
The loyal kind. The text-you-back-and-mean-it kind.

He didn't try to fix me.
Didn't toss advice like confetti.
He just stayed—
steady, kind,
making room for tears, silence,
and pajamas-and-grief days.

In all that quiet love, I caught glimpses of God's heart.
The God who stays.
The God who doesn't flinch at tears or silence.
The God who doesn't walk away.

Shame still lingered—made itself comfy, feet up, remote in hand.

Then my sister dragged me to a women's retreat—
an awkward step that felt like spiritual bailing before I even got started.

I didn't know it then, but God was already plotting a rescue.
Not with fireworks.
Not with skywriting.
Just a weekend in Chicago.
A church full of strangers who hug first and ask questions later.
And a sister who refused to let me drift any further.

I thought I was signing up for bagels and small talk.
God had other plans.

END OF CHAPTER REFLECTION

1. Have you ever carried guilt long after God had already forgiven you? What does it look like when grace wants to move in, but guilt keeps hogging the couch (and probably drinking all the Diet Coke)?

2. Who has God brought into your life—maybe quietly, maybe unexpectedly—to help you heal in ways you didn't even know you needed (and probably wouldn't have signed up for if you had a choice)?

3. And what about today? Is there a prayer—even a simple, messy whisper—you could offer to let God step into the places that still hurt?

CHAPTER 21

Turns Out, God Can Use Sisters, Speakers, and Surprise Huggers

The People You Least Expect Might Be the Ones Who Walk You Home

My sister can spot a spiritual meltdown from fifty paces.
No burning bush required—just that laser-eyed sibling radar.

The second I walked in, Denise looked at me like I was hiding contraband.
She didn't need the details.
She just knew: I'd drifted so far from God, I might as well have applied for citizenship on a different continent.

How much she understood of my knot of doubt, grief, and stubbornness? Not sure.
But she has a sixth sense for this stuff.
Maybe even a seventh.

After a few gentle nudges—and, let's be honest, some *less* gentle ones—she talked me into a women's retreat at her Chicago church.

I told myself it would be low-key.

Stretchy pants. Good bagels. A little Jesus talk. Nothing weird.

Spoiler: That was just the holy appetizer.

Chicago gave me carbs and conversation.
Wisconsin later? That would be the miracle feast.

But that weekend, I was running on fumes.
Pretending I was fine.
Tired of carrying questions with no answers.

We walked into the church and sat at a round table with women who hugged you before learning your name—women who probably crocheted Proverbs in their spare time.

I smiled. Made small talk.
But inside? I was duct-taped together.

One real question, and I might've unraveled completely—
tears, truth, mascara streaks and all.

Then the speaker began.
Her topic?

Psychics.

Of *all* things she could've chosen—faith, forgiveness, tithing—she landed on that.
I froze.
I almost choked on my complimentary mint.

Was this planned?
Had someone tipped her off?
Coincidence? Or was God aiming straight at me?

I tried to act unbothered.
Nodded like, *Wow, what a fascinating topic... for someone else.*
Inside? Full internal panic.
Cue the theme music from *Law & Order: Psychic Crimes Unit.*

But then—something unexpected.
I felt seen.
Not just by the speaker—by God.

Like He whispered, *I still see you. I'm still here.*

Something cracked open that day.
No stage lights.
No applause.
Just a flicker of hope:

Maybe God hasn't given up on me.
Maybe He still wants me—with all my mess.

That weekend, Denise and I got honest.
I admitted my faith was hanging by a thread—
some days, I wasn't even sure I believed at all.

She didn't hit me with a sermon.
No "just pray harder" grenades.
She listened. Really listened.

And for the first time, I learned her full story.
I always thought she was like a skater gliding across fresh ice—smooth,
effortless, untouched by cracks.
But I'd never seen what was underneath.

She'd walked through fire—
divorce, raising two boys alone, finding love again... only to lose him to a
sudden heart attack at forty.

It shattered her.
And this time, she didn't hide the ache—she let me see it all.

Something beautiful happened in that honesty.
I could finally stop pretending, too.

Later, God brought Paul into her life.
Gentle. Steady.
A man with quiet faith—
not flashy words—just prayers, walks beside her, and the willingness to
help rebuild.

Eventually, she married him—and watching their life together was like
watching redemption in real time.

Watching them, I saw more than a happy couple.
I saw hope.
Proof you can lose everything—and still be found again.

God doesn't rescue us just once. He keeps coming. Over and over.

Denise? God used her—this once-perceived-perfect sister—to reach me.
Not with force, not with judgment—but through realness.
Through late-night calls. Honest conversations. Silent hugs.

She didn't drag me back to God.
She walked me home.

It wasn't just sisterhood anymore.
It was sacred.
It was God saying, *You're not too far gone. You can come home, too.*

But that weekend only cracked the door.
Next came a phone call, a Chicago heatwave,
and an AC unit that shouldn't have worked—
until it did.

END OF CHAPTER REFLECTION

1. Is there someone in your life God might be using to gently guide you back to Him?

2. What part of your story—even the messy, duct-taped-together parts—might God want to use to help someone else?

3. Have you ever had a moment that felt like God was speaking straight to you? What did it awaken in you?

CHAPTER 22

Rotisserie Christians and a Divine AC Unit

Why the Smallest "Coincidences" Might Be the Miracles You've Been Missing

By now, Denise wasn't just "into church."
She was basically on staff—minus the paycheck.

Small groups. Volunteering. Probably had her own pew and personalized offering envelopes.
But something was different this time—beautiful, quiet, unshakable.

When we talked, I could hear it.
A softness.
A calm.
A peace that hadn't been there before.

She was getting close to God again.
And maybe—just maybe—hoping I'd follow.

Then came the phone call.
One of our usual sister chats—

updates sprinkled with "you won't believe what just happened."
But this one stopped me mid-sip of Diet Coke.

She was planning a garden party for the women at her church.
Think Pinterest on steroids—fruit punch, flowers, snacks too pretty to eat.
She'd been excited for weeks.

Until... the AC died.

Not on a breezy spring day.
In the middle of a Chicago heatwave so intense you could taste the humidity.

She panicked.
"I couldn't cancel," she said. "Not with older women coming—one with a heart condition. I wasn't about to roast them alive."

So she did the only thing left.
She prayed.

I could picture her pacing—hands on hips—pleading:
"Lord, this is Your party. You know these women. You know they can't be sittin' around here like a bunch of rotisserie chickens. If this thing's gonna happen, You've gotta fix it. I've got nothing."

An hour before guests arrived, Paul gave it one last try—wiggled wires, glared at the unit, maybe smacked it with a screwdriver.

And then—boom.
It worked.

Not a polite puff of air.
A full-on Arctic blast.

Guests came. They laughed. They prayed. They sipped punch without fainting.
It wasn't just a cool breeze—it felt like heaven cracked a window just for them.

Then, at 2:00 p.m., as the last guest walked out the door—
The AC died.
Completely.

Days later, the repairman shook his head.
"There's no way this thing should've worked. A critical part's burned out. This thing was *dead.*"

It was literally impossible that it ran that day. But it did.

Denise told me the story as casually as reading a shipping label.
But I could hear it—she believed God had duct-taped her AC together with supernatural power, just long enough for His daughters to meet.

I sat in silence.
Part of me wanted to call it coincidence—machines do weird things.
Another part—the part still aching for something real—whispered: *What if she's right?*

Denise didn't preach.
Didn't try to convince me.
She just let the story hang there.

And something cracked inside me—
not a wave of clarity, just a tiny crack in the wall I'd spent years building.

I didn't have answers.
But for the first time in a long time, I had a thought I couldn't shake:
Maybe He's real. Maybe He cares. Maybe He's closer than I think.

And if He was?
I wanted to know.

That story wouldn't let me go.

Then Denise sent an invite I wanted to delete:
a Wisconsin retreat.

I went anyway.

I didn't know it then, but Wisconsin would be the place the walls cracked wide open,
and I'd have to decide if I was all in or done for good.

END OF CHAPTER REFLECTION

1. Have you ever had a moment that felt like more than coincidence—like the universe was winking at you?

2. Have you ever had a "God story" of your own, even if you didn't call it that at the time?

3. What would it look like for you to stay open to God's presence in the unexpected—and let yourself hope for a miracle in your own life?

CHAPTER 23

The Weekend I Almost Didn't Go

The Battle Between Your Excuses and the Invitation That Could Change Everything

If God had a marketing department, my sister Denise would've been the regional manager.
Custom flyers. Follow-up calls. Zero unsubscribe button.

Her latest campaign?
"Operation: Drag Christine Back to Jesus."

Target strategy: a women's retreat in Wisconsin.
Three days. Lots of worship. Probably scented candles and "mountaintop moments."

She called it a spiritual recharge.
I called it a perfectly good excuse to stay home in sweatpants.

My list of reasons to say no was award-worthy.
Busy.
Running on fumes, running from faith.
Even my coffee maker was one meltdown away from filing for disability.

And spiritually?
Flatline.
The kind where you don't even bother charging the paddles.

The last thing I wanted was to be trapped in a building with women belting out worship songs while I sat there wondering if God had blocked my number.

But Denise doesn't quit.
"I'll pay for your plane ticket," she said. "Just come."

Classic Denise—making a way where there is no way, occasionally with holy guilt-trips baked in.
She believed this retreat mattered.
She believed *I* mattered.

So, with zero excuses left, I packed a bag and got on the plane.

She picked me up in Chicago.
The next morning, we crammed into a car with a few church ladies—
the kind who carry worship playlists, Yeti tumblers, and enough snacks to survive the apocalypse.

Somewhere between the highway miles and sanctified trail mix, my walls started to crack.

The retreat center was simple. Tucked near Lake Michigan.
The kind of place that doesn't shout. It whispers.

For the first time in forever, my chest loosened.
Calm. Still. Almost sacred.

But my brain? Still sprinting marathons.
Work was moving from Lansing to Grand Rapids.
My choices?

A commute that would slowly kill my soul.
Or uproot my life—and maybe lose Miles in the process.

Neither option sounded like peace.

So I whispered a desperate little prayer:
God, if You're planning on talking, now's the time.

The rooms were... cozy.
A twin bed shoved against the wall—basically a padded shelf with a blanket. Fine. Navy SEAL training disguised as a retreat.

At 2 a.m., I discovered its hidden spiritual gift: launching you straight to the floor if you roll too far right.
Apparently the retreat budget covered Bibles, not guardrails. Or helmets.

Later, I wandered downstairs and found a circle of women talking.
Not small talk.
Real talk.

They weren't just talking about God.
They were swapping stories about hearing Him.

Not burning bushes or neon signs.
Just nudges.
Peace in grief.
Clarity in chaos.
Moments where they knew He'd been steering.

And here's the thing: they weren't weird.
No one was humming. Nobody floated.
These were Target-shopping, crockpot-owning women—
and yet they talked about God like He picked up their kids from school.

Something in me cracked open.
I blurted the question that had been eating at me:
"But how do you *know* it's God? Not just your own thoughts?"

One woman leaned in, smiling like she knew a secret.
"You just know," she said.

Cool. Helpful as a screen door on a submarine.
I nodded, pretending I got it.
Inside, my brain screamed: *That's exactly what people say when they don't know!*

Still... something about them stirred me.
The way they didn't just *talk about* God—
They *talked to Him.*
Like He was right there. And He was talking back. At least to them.
To me? Radio silence.

And oh, how I wanted that.

Then Denise's phone rang.
Our brother, Bob.

Bad news.
Mom and Dad had been in a car accident.
Both in the hospital.

My stomach dropped.

Bob said they'd be okay. Just bumps and bruises.
But maybe I should come home.

Denise took a breath.
Looked straight at me.

"I have a strong feeling they're going to be okay," she said.
"I think God wants us to stay."

She wasn't dismissing it.

She was locked in on something deeper.
"I think you're supposed to be here," she said. Calm. Certain.
"I think God has something for you this weekend."

And somehow—even in the middle of fear and chaos—
I believed her.

Not with certainty.
But with a flicker.

Maybe—just maybe—God was about to speak.

> *"Come near to God and He will come near to you."*
>
> — **James 4:8**
>
> ❧ **God isn't waiting for perfect prayers.**
> He just wants real ones—and He'll always meet you there.

But that first night, the silence stung—
and set me up for the day everything changed.

Which, for the record, means "Operation: Drag Christine Back to Jesus"
was officially working.

END OF CHAPTER REFLECTION

1. Have you ever almost said "no" to something—only to realize later it was exactly what you needed?

2. Can you relate to being flat-out spiritually exhausted—but still having that tiny flicker of curiosity about what God might say if He actually spoke?

3. If God really could speak to you—personal, clear, just for you— what would you want Him to say?

CHAPTER 24

The Night I Whispered to God

*One Twin Bed, a Desperate Prayer, and the
Silence That Made Me Ask Again*

That night, I climbed into my tiny twin bed and pulled the blanket over me.
It had the texture of a hotel comforter that had survived one too many industrial washes—scratchy, stiff, but pretending to be cozy.

Down the hall, someone coughed like they'd swallowed a kazoo.
Sleep? Not happening.

My brain was running laps.
What if this whole weekend was just emotional tourism? What if I went home as lost as I came?

I curled up, trying not to fall off the world's smallest mattress.
Pretty sure it was designed for a middle school sleepover, not a grown woman in spiritual crisis.

But the real reason I couldn't sleep wasn't the kazoo cougher.
It was the women downstairs.

The way they talked about hearing from God—like He actually answered.
Not in clouds or lightning bolts. Just in everyday whispers.

Was that real?
Could He actually speak to people?
Because me? I'd never heard a thing.
It felt like I'd been left out of a cosmic group chat.

And yet—I wanted it.
Not vague hints. Not coincidences.
Words. Real words.

A whisper. A flicker.
Honestly? A Post-it note would've been enough.

So, I prayed. Quiet. Nervous. Desperate.
"God... if You're real, please speak to me."

I waited.
Held my breath.
Listened hard.

Nothing.
No voice. No goosebumps.
No divine podcast dropping from the sky.

Just the hum of the fan and a squeaky bedframe begging for WD-40.

Hope reached out.
Came back empty.

Maybe God didn't want to talk to me.
Maybe I was too skeptical.
Too broken.
Too... me.

I pulled the covers tight and tried to swallow the disappointment.
It felt like being the only kid at camp who didn't get a care package.

But just before sleep dragged me under, a thought floated up.
Not mystical. Not booming.
Just a quiet nudge in my tired heart:

Ask again tomorrow.

And somehow, I knew I would.

I fell asleep still waiting.
Morning brought coffee, questions, and a gut-punch of envy—
and a deeper hunger I couldn't shake.

And yes—the kazoo cougher was still alive and well.
Apparently, even God lets some mysteries linger.

END OF CHAPTER REFLECTION

1. Can you relate to wanting to believe—but feeling like doubt has you stuck in quicksand? What does that "quicksand" look like in your story?

2. Have you ever asked for a sign, a word, or even just a flicker of something real—then sat there wondering if the silence was your answer?

3. If God could lean in and tell you one thing right now—just for you, no churchy filters—what's the sentence you most ache to hear?

CHAPTER 25

Am I the Only One Not Hearing Him?

Wondering If God Speaks... and Why I Couldn't Hear Him

The next morning, Denise and I shuffled into the cafeteria.
Linoleum floors. Overcooked bacon. And the faint smell of coffee that tasted like it had been brewed sometime during the Clinton administration.

The room buzzed with bright-and-early risers who seemed perfectly content to spend their weekend away with God. Meanwhile, I had questions ricocheting around my head like loose change in a dryer.

I wasn't even awake yet—barely upgraded from zombie to human—but the question was already burning a hole in my brain. So I blurted it out.

"Denise... do you ever actually hear God speak to you?"

She smiled the kind of smile that said she probably saved Jesus a seat at her kitchen table every morning.
"Yes," she said, calm as ever. "He speaks to me through His Word—the Bible—and sometimes I sense Him in my thoughts."

I squinted at her. That was not the answer I was looking for.
"But how do you *know* it's Him?" I pressed. "Like... what if it's just your own brain making stuff up?"

She took a slow sip of coffee, calm in a way I wished I could be.
"It's not like hearing words out loud," she said. "It's more like a sensing in my spirit."

Lovely. Meanwhile, I couldn't sense anything but absence.

Still, that absence didn't erase the stubborn little ember in me.
Somehow, it kept flickering.

If God was real, I needed Him to prove it.
Not because I wanted to test Him—
but because I was barely hanging on.

Later, in the meeting room, a woman named Kim got up to speak.
Her topic? The sinful woman with perfume, tears, and a religious crowd throwing shade.

I tried to stay casual. Maybe plan a fake bathroom escape.
But then she started talking about shame. About guilt.
About the heavy stuff you carry when you're convinced you're too broken to be loved.

And suddenly—boom.
That woman in the Bible? She was me.

I'd been lugging around guilt like designer luggage filled with bricks.
Looks expensive. Feels crushing.

The divorce. The doubts.
That one psychic call we don't talk about.
It all whispered the same thing: *You broke something God won't fix.*

Part of me believed it.
Part of me thought this pain was permanent.

But Kim's message—Confident Hope (which I was sure applied to everyone but me)—chipped at that lie.
Grace. Forgiveness.
A love big enough to start over.

And for the first time, I didn't just want peace.
I wanted freedom.
Freedom from the doubts that stalked me.
Freedom from the silence that kept convincing me I was forgotten.
Freedom from the fear I'd disappointed God too many times to be worth saving.

But the question still haunted me:
If God was speaking... why couldn't I hear Him?

Was I too broken?
Too deaf?
Had I missed some heavenly deadline?

It seemed like everyone else was getting divine whispers with their scrambled eggs—clear, steady, certain.
Meanwhile, I was talking to the ceiling.
Whispering prayers into the air.
Hoping somebody—anybody—was on the other end.

I hated admitting it, but I was jealous.

The other women talked to God like He was sitting at the table with them—coffee mug in hand, nodding along.

Certain. Confident. Secure.

And me?
I felt like the kid who missed the school bus.

Late to faith. Late to answers.

I didn't need fireworks. Or angels.
I just needed a word. Any word.

This doubting girl was desperate.
And I was about to ask again.
Even if silence was all I got.

I thought maybe I'd missed my chance—that God had given His best words to everyone else.

But then the silence broke.
And once it did, nothing in my life was ever the same.

> *"My sheep listen to my voice; I know them, and they follow me."*
> — **John 10:27**
>
> ❧ **Even when you feel deaf to His whispers, God hasn't forgotten how to call your name.**

END OF CHAPTER REFLECTION

1. Ever lugged guilt so heavy it felt like maybe you'd maxed out God's grace limit?

2. What's one lie you've carried around about yourself—maybe for years—that God might be dying to cross out and rewrite?

3. Ever feel like God's handing out heart-to-hearts at every other table while you're stuck talking to the ceiling (and the ceiling's not even polite enough to nod)?

CHAPTER 26

The Night Heaven Broke My Silence

What Happened When I Finally Heard His Voice

I didn't expect it that day.

Not after years of silence.

Not after every unanswered prayer.

Not after whispering, *God, are You even real?* into what felt like a cosmic voicemail box.

But then it happened.

God spoke.

And in that moment, the silence shattered.

And the God I had doubted became the God I couldn't deny.

Earlier that day, I wandered into the tiny bookstore.

The usual—devotionals, bookmarks, mugs promising you mercies new every morning.

I wanted one book and one book only:

How to Hear God in 10 Easy Steps (Even If You're a Mess Who Packs Snacks Instead of Faith).

Shocker: it didn't exist.

So I grabbed something about discerning God's voice and hugged it like it might start glowing if I squeezed hard enough.

Then came "quiet time." Five full hours.
No phone. No small talk. Just me, God, and my brain—wired like a toddler hopped up on Skittles.

Honestly? It felt like being locked in a room with all my insecurities and zero snacks.

So I headed down to the lake and sank into the grass.

Still water. A soft breeze. Birds chirping like they were auditioning for a Disney contract.
If Heaven had an opening line, this was it.

"Lord," I whispered. *"I want to hear You. Please. I'm listening."*

And then... nothing.
Just the birds. The breeze.

Eventually, the chill chased me back to my room.
Hope dropped straight through the floorboards.
Maybe I just wasn't one of those people who ever got to hear Him.

Later, lying on my bed, I tried again.
This time, desperate.

"God... if You're real, please speak to me."

Over and over, I whispered it.
"I believe. I believe."

But truth? I wasn't sure I did.

Why could everyone else hear Him like He was sending divine text messages, while I sat here wondering if Heaven had marked me Do Not Disturb?

And then—

It happened.

I don't remember falling asleep.
One second, I was out cold.
The next—BOOM.

I shot upright in bed like Heaven had just plugged me into a power outlet.
Not scared. Not confused. Just... *awake.*
Every hair on my arms standing up.
Heart pounding like it was trying to escape my ribcage.

It felt like the ceiling ripped open and God Himself poured into that tiny dorm room.

I scrambled for the notebook on the desk like my life depended on it.
And my hand—without hesitation—started flying across the page, faster than my brain could process:
- *Go to Grand Rapids.*
- *That's where your promotion is.*
- *Quit thinking about Lansing. I've cleared the path.*

And then... silence.

But this time? It wasn't empty.
It was thick. Holy. Electric.
Like God had just leaned over the edge of eternity, dropped His words into my lap, and then dropped the mic.

I froze, staring at the notebook like it might burst into flames.

Did that just happen?
Was that GOD?
Speaking. To ME?

It wasn't thunder. No Morgan Freeman cameo.
But it wasn't my normal thoughts, either.
These words were sharper. Clearer. Heavier.
They didn't just pass through my mind—they landed. Like they'd been aimed straight at me.

> "Call to me and I will answer you and tell you great and unsearchable things you do not know."
>
> — **Jeremiah 33:3**
>
> **⟐ God isn't dodging your prayers.**
> He answers when you call—even when you least expect it.

Now, I know—if you're a skeptic, this sounds like the kind of thing people say right before they end up on a Netflix documentary. But for me? There was no denying it.

And I couldn't help but think—why now?
Why not years ago when I was ugly-crying on the bathroom floor surrounded by Kit Kat wrappers and broken dreams?

But somehow... I just knew.
It was Him.

The God I'd doubted, tested, accused of ghosting me...
just broke His silence.
With me.

And suddenly, I didn't just want to cry.
I wanted to run down the hallway yelling, "GUYS! HE TALKS!"

Later, I found Kim.
"I heard Him!" I blurted. "God talked to me!"

She smiled like honey.
"That's wonderful." She paused. "Now... have you ever asked Jesus to save you?"

I blinked.
"Yes. Probably a hundred times. Still not sure my application got approved."

Deep down, I was afraid I hadn't done it right.
That I hadn't been enough.

But Kim prayed with me.
And this time, something clicked.

Peace flooded the room like sunlight.
And I knew—Jesus already did it all.
No tests. No hoops.
No spiritual obstacle course.

Just a gift.
All I had to do was say yes.

That night, I didn't just hear His voice.
I got adopted.

For the first time in forever, I went to bed knowing:
I am His.
And He is mine.

I thought hearing His voice would be the ultimate gift.
But that same night? God went one step further—
and ripped out a pain I'd carried for years.

And pointed me to a queen with a plan.

END OF CHAPTER REFLECTION

1. Have you ever wished God would just go ahead and say *something already*—not in vague coincidences, but in a way so clear you couldn't miss it?

2. What's the thing that makes you wonder if He'd ever actually speak to you—*the* doubt, the guilt, the "maybe I'm just too much of a mess" thought?

3. Do you feel sure you belong to Jesus—or is there still a part of you quietly wondering if you missed a step somewhere?

CHAPTER 27

When God Rips Out the Pain You've Carried for Years

How One Night, One Prayer, and One Ancient Queen Changed Everything

The day had been long.

Beautiful. Exhausting.

My face hurt from smiling.

My soul whispered, *Something just happened.*

I closed my door and leaned against it like a movie character in a dramatic ending scene.

I was saved.

Actually saved.

This time, no question marks.

Me—the skeptic. The doubter. The girl who once wondered if God's voicemail was full.

Now officially stamped *Team Jesus* for eternity.

It felt like God had thrown a warm blanket over my shoulders.

Not a scratchy retreat-center blanket. A holy, just-out-of-the-dryer kind.

And then my brain barged in.
Cool. Great. But... now what?

I wanted more.
Not just salvation. Not just a one-night holy sparkler show.
I wanted to *keep* hearing Him.
Not someday. Not maybe. Always.

So I did what any brand-new believer who doesn't know what they're doing would do.
I dropped to my knees and prayed.

"God, I love You. Thank You for saving me. Thank You for speaking to me. I want to keep hearing You."

And then—
The emotional ache.
That heavy, dragging weight I'd carried for years—it lived in my chest like an unwanted Airbnb guest who refused to check out.

I didn't understand why it was still there.
Why, after therapy, after prayers, after years, it clung like duct tape you can't peel off.
I was over it.
So over it.
But apparently—it wasn't over me.

"God," I whispered, *"please take this emotional pain. All of it. I believe You can. I believe You will. Please... just take it."*

I wasn't holy.
I wasn't dramatic.
I was just... *done.*
And sometimes, done is the best place for a miracle.

And then—something happened.

Like, for real.

The emotional pain started lifting.
Slow. Deliberate.
Up and out of my chest.
I could feel it leaving.
Floating toward the ceiling.
Like Heaven had turned on a giant vacuum cleaner in my soul.
Sucking every ounce of grief right out of me.

Up. Out. Gone.

Like God Himself reached in, grabbed the emotional pain, and yanked it out—like a chirping fire alarm battery at 2 a.m., or a bad appendix nobody's sad to see go.

Gone.
Poof.
Bye-bye baggage. (And believe me, no one was more shocked than me.)

And listen—I know how this sounds. If someone else told me their grief floated toward the ceiling like a balloon, I'd have smiled politely and Googled "therapist near me." But this wasn't made-up. I felt it.

I froze.
Did God just perform emotional surgery with zero anesthesia?
"Uh... thanks?" I whispered. *"Also, wow."*

For the first time in years, my chest felt light.
Like someone had cracked open a window inside me.

I pressed my hand to my chest, almost expecting to feel the grief return.
But it didn't.

The ache that had been my shadow? Silent.

> "Jesus replied, 'I tell you the truth, if you have faith and do not doubt...
> you can say to this mountain, 'Go, throw yourself into the sea,' and
> it will be done.'"
>
> — **Matthew 21:21**
>
> ☙ **Even shaky faith in a strong God can move what feels
> unmovable.**

I grabbed my Bible.
Flipped through the tabs my sister Denise had stuck in there like sprinkles
on a cupcake.
And my eyes landed on one word.

Esther.
Read it.

Why Esther? I had no idea. But I turned the page anyway.
And wow.

Esther wasn't just a beauty queen in a tiara.
She was fierce. Smart. Strategic.
A woman who knew when to wait quietly and when to step out boldly.
And when she did—she changed everything.

Suddenly, I knew.
This wasn't just *her* story.
It was mine.

Through Esther's story, it felt like God was saying:
Quit hiding. Step forward. Let them see you.
Move to Grand Rapids.
Work where you can be seen.
Stop waiting for life to come find you.

> *"When he saw Queen Esther standing in the court, he was pleased with her... 'What is it, Queen Esther? What is your request? Even up to half the kingdom, it will be given you.'"*
>
> — **Esther 5:2–3**
>
> ❧ **Courage opens doors fear can't touch.**
> Step forward. Let grace meet you there.

I closed the Bible and whispered into the dark,
"God, if this is You... I'm listening."

And I felt it again.
That holy shift. That knowing.
This wasn't random.
This wasn't my own pep talk.
This was Him (and believe me, I couldn't explain it away).

For the first time ever...
I wasn't just reading the Bible.
The Bible was reading me.

And I was finally hearing Him.

END OF CHAPTER REFLECTION

1. Have you ever begged God to just take something painful away already? What happened when you asked?

2. What weight have you carried so long it feels like part of your identity—and could this be the moment God wants to lift it?

3. Where might God be whispering, "S*tep forward"* in your life right now? What would courage look like in that place?

CHAPTER 28

When God Cancels Your Flight to Deliver a Message

How a Storm, an Old DVD, and an Ancient Queen Confirmed My Next Step

In forty-eight hours, God had flipped my life like a pancake.
Now I was sitting in the airport, clutching a sandwich so soggy even Jesus wouldn't multiply it, doing my best not to cry.

The retreat was over.
Big hugs. Promises to "stay in touch."
Translation: the occasional Facebook like.

But it felt holy—like God had left fingerprints on my soul.
We drove back to Chicago in a haze.
My heart felt cracked open.
Grace poured in.
Peace. Clarity.
A giant scoop of *You're not crazy—you're being called.*

Then—bam.
Storm. Flight canceled.

Airline agent with a face like stone:
"Next flight? Tomorrow afternoon."

Translation: Go find a toothbrush because you're not leaving this city.

I sighed—not panic, just that weird calm you get when you know God's
up to something.
Sure, part of me wanted to rush home. Check on Mom and Dad after the
accident.
But deep down, I knew.
They'd be fine.
God had other plans.

I called Denise.
She didn't hesitate.
"On my way."
Ride or die. Snacks included.

The next morning, I wandered her house like a stray cat.
I spotted a shelf of leadership books practically shouting, *Yes, I've done
every Bible study twice.*
I asked if I could read one.

She waved on her way out. "And there are leadership DVDs too."

DVDs.
What year was this?
I half expected a VCR to crawl out of the closet.

But whatever. I popped one in, coffee in hand.

Instead of leadership tips or bullet points about "vision casting"... boom.
Esther.

I nearly spit coffee everywhere.

147

My jaw dropped.
My heart kicked up like someone had just yelled *Surprise!*

Of all the Bible stories, this guy picked Esther.
The same story God pushed on me at the retreat.
The one that whispered, *Step up. Be seen.*

This wasn't coincidence.
This was God grabbing a bullhorn and shouting through a DVD player
from 2003.
A holy mic drop.

But the timing was too exact. It felt like God had hacked the DVD player
just to prove a point.

Tears blurred my eyes.
Was my flight canceled just for this?
Felt like it.

The speaker said Esther waited. Prepared. Positioned herself.
The king noticed.
The timing was right.
The door opened.

And it hit me—hard.
This wasn't just her story.
It was mine.

Time to stop hiding.
Time to quit hoping someone would notice.
It was time to step up, go west, and show up where God was calling me.

Grand Rapids.
That's where I needed to be.

This wasn't ambition.
It was obedience.

And yeah, I worried about Miles.
I'd finally found a good man—real love, safe love.
Part of me worried—was I about to blow up the best relationship of my life for some half-baked Grand Rapids dream?
I didn't want to lose him.

But God wasn't asking me to choose.
He was asking me to trust.

So yeah, my flight got canceled.
But this wasn't an accident.
It was an appointment.

A leather couch.
A lukewarm coffee.
Apparently an old 2003 DVD player.
And a God who refused to let me miss His message.

Because that's just who He is.
And little did I know, that canceled flight was only the first of many detours God would use to rewrite my story.

END OF CHAPTER REFLECTION

1. Have you ever had a delay or detour that felt annoying in the moment—but later you realized it was divine timing?

2. Is there a decision you keep circling—not just pressure, but maybe God trying to nudge you forward?

3. Where might God be whispering, "Quit hiding. Step up."—and what would courage look like there?

CHAPTER 29

When God's Directions Don't Come With a Map

The Crossroads Between Love, Logic, and a Long-Distance Move of Faith

> *"Trust in the Lord with all your heart and lean not on your own understanding..."*
>
> **— Proverbs 3:5**
>
> 🦋 **Sometimes faith feels less like a GPS and more like driving with the headlights barely on—but still moving forward.**

I was half-awake, sipping coffee in pajamas I wouldn't wear to check the mail. Yet here they were, starring in my spiritual awakening.

That's when I noticed the Tree of Life picture on my wall. Again.

Denise had given it to me years ago. It had always just... hung there. But that morning, it felt alive.

The words under the branches read:

"Go to church. Take time for prayer. Find your purpose and do it the best that you can."

I blinked.
"Okay, God," I muttered. *"That's oddly specific."*

It had been years since I'd stepped inside a church.
Apparently, God was done being subtle.

So I started searching. Asking around. Googling. Praying.
Finally, I found one.

No fog machines. No "Holy Ghost Glow Party" sermon series.
Just Jesus, the Bible, and kind people who didn't pounce on visitors.

It was awkward at first.
I walked in alone, scanning for a seat that didn't scream, *Hi, I'm new. Please don't hug me.*
But I kept going. Week after week.

And slowly, my heart shifted.
God showed up in those pews like He had reserved a front-row spot just for me.

Then came the nudge.
Not even a nudge—a shove.

God wanted me in Grand Rapids. For work.

Cue the panic.
The drive was long.
Gas prices were rude.
And I had a halfway-decent social life in Lansing.

Still, I couldn't shake it. The retreat message echoed: *Go.*

So I talked with my manager.
"Okay," I said. "I'm ready to work in the Grand Rapids office now."

Just like that, the first domino fell.

So I commuted. Every. Single. Day.
120 miles round trip. From Lansing to Grand Rapids.

My beloved Trailblazer was not built for this life—I was singlehandedly keeping Michigan's gas stations in business. Pretty sure they were planning a statue in my honor.

So I downsized.
New smaller car. Better gas mileage. Bonus? CD player.
Game changer.

That's when I discovered a CD set—basically a cinematic version of the Old Testament, with actors so convincing it felt like they were living in my car.
It was dramatic. Powerful.
Basically, Marvel's Avengers meets Genesis.

I was hooked.
Somewhere between Exodus and Leviticus, I started yelling at Moses in my car.
Drivers passing me probably thought I was either holy or unhinged. Possibly both.

But even with all that Scripture soaking in, I wanted more.
A breakthrough. A promotion. A burning bush, maybe.

Instead? Crickets.
No raise. No recognition. Just gas receipts.

Doubt whispered, *Did I get this wrong?*

But deep down, I knew I hadn't.

Then winter hit.
Every commute felt like auditioning for *Ice Road Truckers: Michigan*—
except no paycheck and definitely no camera crew.

One frozen night, jaw clenched, white-knuckling the wheel, I heard it.
That same still, small voice from the retreat:
*Move to Grand Rapids. Do not be afraid. Everything will work out as planned. I
have cleared the path for you.*

I blinked.
Was that God? Or just me trying to avoid another frostbitten commute?

But it came again.
Calm. Certain.
Move. I've already gone before you.

And my heart sank.
Because moving meant leaving Miles.

Miles—the good guy I'd prayed for.
Steady. Kind.
The one who texted me on bad days and laughed at my worst jokes.

Now I was supposed to just... go?
"God, what if I lose him?" I whispered.

But the answer stayed the same:
Trust Me. Everything will work out as planned.

Telling Miles was awful.
I blamed the drive, the snow, the distance. My voice cracked anyway.

He looked at me and said softly,

"I'm not going to stop you from doing what you need to do. But... I don't want you to leave."

Ouch.
Direct hit to the heart.

That one sentence weighed more than 120 miles of gas receipts.

I wanted to shout, *Forget obedience! I'll stay!*
But I couldn't.

Miles didn't know God's voice yet.
Saying, "So... God told me to move," would've sounded like I'd been sniffing paint fumes.

So I moved. Alone.
We stayed together long-distance.
Weekends. Texts. Phone calls.
Stretched love.
Not easy.

And still—no promotion.
No recognition.
Just silence.

Doubt whispered louder.
Maybe you messed up.

But I knew better.
The enemy twists truth into confusion.

So I fought back.
I chose faith.

> "And without faith it is impossible to please God, because anyone who comes to him must believe that he exists and that he rewards those who earnestly seek him."
>
> — Hebrews 11:6
>
> ✍ Faith isn't about having it all figured out—it's about showing up, shaky knees and all, and still believing God meets you there.

And this wasn't my plan anymore.
It was His.

Obedience didn't just change my zip code.
It changed my life.

But God wasn't finished.
When He really wants to get your attention? He says it twice.
And the second time would leave me undone.

END OF CHAPTER REFLECTION

1. Have you ever felt God nudging you toward something that made zero sense on paper—but you couldn't shake it anyway? What did you do?

2. Has fear, uncertainty, or even love for someone ever delayed your obedience to God? What helped you finally move forward?

3. If God were to confirm something for you—say it twice, in two totally different ways—what would you want Him to repeat so you knew it was really Him?

CHAPTER 30

When God Speaks Twice
So You Don't Miss It

How a Quiet Lake, a Sister's Prayer, and One Unmistakable Confirmation Changed Everything

When my sister invited me to another women's retreat, I said yes faster than a toddler grabbing a cookie—or me grabbing ice cream at midnight.

I was spiritually parched.
Not cucumber-water parched.
More like desert-wandering, lips cracking, questioning-God's-existence parched.

My soul had been doing somersaults of doubt.
My prayers? Sounded like voicemails to a God who'd muted notifications.

I needed Him.
Not in a sunsets-are-inspiring kind of way.
I wanted goosebumps. A message so clear I couldn't miss it.

The retreat center was the same as last time.

Ah yes, the twin beds—back again, creaking in judgment, like, *"Still no husband? Guess it's just us tonight."*
And of course, women armed with color-coded prayer journals and highlighters of holiness.
Some of them had more highlighters than a Staples clearance bin.

It felt safe. Sacred. Slightly cheesy.

I grabbed my Bible, my journal, and my sweatshirt-that's-basically-a-blanket, and headed to the lake.
The air was crisp. The water calm.
Birds chirping and waves crashing like they were auditioning for a Nicholas Sparks movie.

I waited. Listened.
Wind. Birds. Waves. Nothing else.

I sighed.
"Hello? God? It's me again. Feel free to interrupt."

Nothing.
Just a giant blue sky and me, trying not to fall apart in front of the birds.

I laid back in the grass. Whispered,
"I'm here. I believe. Please... say something."

And then, without warning, without thunder or lightning—He did.

Not loud. Not dramatic.
But real.
Straight to my soul:
You and Miles will be married. Listen to Me. Bring Miles, his daughter Maddie, and his mom Judy closer to Me.

I shot upright like someone had dumped ice water on me.

"Wait—married? As in toothpaste-sharing, bill-splitting, the whole forever kind of married?!"

Miles and I weren't even in the same city.
His daughter barely spoke to me.
His mom was polite but guarded.

And yet, God just dropped a wedding prophecy in my lap.

If you're skeptical, trust me—I was too. I half expected a hidden camera crew to jump out and yell, "Gotcha!"

I grabbed my journal.
Scribbled like a frantic court stenographer at a UFO trial.

Later, I found Denise.
We snuck into a quiet room.

And I cracked open.
All of it came out. The jealousy. The pain.
Years of baggage rattling like a busted-wheel suitcase.
"I always thought you were perfect," I said. "Smart. Confident. Everything I wasn't. I always felt... less."

She didn't flinch. "Christine," she said softly, "my life hasn't been perfect. I fought hard for every bit of this."
In that moment, my rival turned human.

We cried. The messy, mascara-streak, hiccup kind of cry that feels holy when it's over.

Then Denise dropped a bomb.
"I prayed for you today," she said.
"I sensed God saying you'll be a light in the darkness—and He'll use you to bring Miles, Maddie, and Judy closer to Him."

I froze.
My jaw hit the floor.

I mean, I could've brushed it off as coincidence if she had only mentioned Miles and Maddie—safe bets, right? But Judy? Specifically naming his mom? That was too much. Too exact. That was God.

I nearly dropped my Bible.
"WHAT did you just say?"

She repeated it. Word for word.

I shoved my journal at her like it was Exhibit A in the trial of *Is God Actually Talking to Me?*
"Denise. That's exactly what He told me this morning!"

We sat there in stunned silence.
Two sisters. Two messages.
One God who doesn't believe in mixed signals.

And in that moment, I knew.
I wasn't making this up.
I wasn't imagining Him.
He speaks. He confirms.

And when it's really important?
He says it twice.
And I had no idea how much that "twice" would change everything.

END OF CHAPTER REFLECTION

1. Have you ever begged God for a sign—and nearly fallen over when He actually gave it? What did He say, and what did you do?

2. Who's the person you've spent years comparing yourself to—and what might shift if you saw them through God's eyes instead of your own?

3. Have you ever heard the same message from God twice—through completely different people or places? How did it shake your faith (or steady it)?

CHAPTER 31

When Faith Looks Like Pancakes Before Church

How Small Yeses, Sunday Breakfasts, and God's Timing Led to a Proposal

After the retreat, God's instructions were crystal clear.
Hearing from God feels amazing.
Like a divine hug for your soul.

But obeying?
That's where things get messy.
Especially when what He asks feels like free-climbing Mount Everest in flip-flops.

God said: *Bring Miles, Maddie, and Judy closer to Me.*

Great plan. Holy plan.
Zero idea how to do it.

I'd invited Miles to church before.
He always declined—kind, thoughtful, but unmoved. Like trying to push a boulder with a feather.

Still, he never mocked my faith.
Never rolled his eyes when I whispered prayers over coffee or dashed off
to retreats with a highlighter bright enough to land planes.
He just stayed on the sidelines. Watching. Waiting.

That retreat message tugged at me, though.
It wasn't just my word—Denise had sensed the same thing I heard.
Confirmation is beautiful.
But it doesn't make obedience convenient.

One night I whispered,
"God, I want to obey. I do. But this mountain is huge.
And my hiking boots are from the Target clearance rack."

Silence.
But the lake breeze memory came rushing back.
I had my marching orders.
Time to strategize.

Enter: Operation Jesus & Flapjacks.

Miles loved breakfast food more than most people love oxygen.
So instead of, "Want to come to church?"
I tried, "Want to get pancakes Sunday? We can swing by church first."

He shrugged. "Okay."

Okay? Just like that?
I tried to act casual, but inside I was screaming, *Did that just work?!*
It felt like winning the lottery and fitting into old jeans—at the same time.

Honestly, I'd prayed, begged, and even tried subtle guilt trips—and none of
that worked. And now... pancakes did it? If that's not divine intervention,
I don't know what is.

That one Sunday turned into two.
Then three.
Church and The Flapjack Shack.
Worship and waffles.
Hymns and hash browns.
He didn't bolt. Didn't look bored.
Once, he even closed his eyes during a worship song.
A full-on miracle, people.

When Maddie was with us, she came too.
She told me she didn't believe in God.
"My mom doesn't believe, so I don't either," she said with a shrug.

I didn't push.
I just wanted her close enough to hear, if God decided to whisper.

And honestly—I got it. If you don't believe, church can feel like a bunch
of strangers singing karaoke to Someone you're not sure exists.

She told me later she knew I was a Christian the first day we met.
She even told her mom.
That led to their first-ever talk about faith.

Her mom admitted someone she loved had died.
"If God was real, He would've saved him," she said.

I got it.
My brother Jim had died praying.
Sometimes grief leaves more questions than answers.

So I didn't hand Maddie a neat, churchy response.
I just let her questions sit with mine.
And I prayed that someday, somehow, God would show up for her too.

Meanwhile, I was still living in Grand Rapids, commuting to Lansing to see Miles.
Lots of miles for Miles.
Worth every one.

One Sunday, after pancakes and hugs goodbye, something shifted.
He held me longer.
Eyes wet. Silent.

Panic set in.
Was he breaking up with me?
Or just tired of driving all these miles for me?
"Do you think I'm going to leave you?" I whispered.

The look in his eyes told me everything.
Fear. Love.
A lifetime of holding on tight to people who didn't stay.

I cupped his face.
"I'm not going anywhere. I love you."

That moment wasn't flashy.
It wasn't a movie scene.
But it was holy.

Weeks later, Miles asked me and Maddie to dinner—it was his weekend with her.
We pulled up to the place where we'd had our first date.

Over burgers and small talk, he got up, walked around the table, and dropped to one knee.

Time froze.
My heart malfunctioned.

He held a little velvet box that looked like angels had personally guarded it.
"Christine," he said, voice shaking,
"I love you. I want to spend my life with you. Will you marry me?"

Even the restaurant noise faded, like heaven had hit the mute button.
For a second, I just blinked at him—mouth open like a goldfish trying to remember how to breathe.

"Yes," I finally whispered.
Tears. So many tears.

And underneath all of it, I knew—this wasn't just Miles' question. It was God's answer.

Maddie was crying too.
"These are happy tears! And I've been keeping this secret for months!"

Miles laughed.
"It wasn't months."

"It felt like months," she huffed, hands on her hips.

We laughed. We cried.
We hugged and laughed until my cheeks hurt, tears mixing with joy.

Later, Maddie told me she'd helped pick out the ring.
The proposal may not have been a surprise,
but the joy of it still felt like a miracle.

And in my heart, I heard it again.
Not in words. Just that holy knowing:

You and Miles will be married.

God had said it.

I had believed it.
And now—here it was.

Because when God writes a love story,
it doesn't feel rushed or random.
It feels like pancakes and pews and whispered prayers stitched into everyday life.

Until one day, you look up and realize—
You're standing in the middle of a miracle.

And God was just getting started.

END OF CHAPTER REFLECTION

1. Have you ever said yes to God in some small, ordinary way—only to watch it snowball into something unexpectedly beautiful?

2. What's one thing God might be nudging you to step into right now—even if it feels scary, inconvenient, or uncertain?

3. Can you look back on a season and see how God was secretly connecting the dots the whole time?

CHAPTER 32

The Left Turn That Led to a Holy Detour

When God's "Not Yet" Is Just Training for a Bigger Yes

Before Miles and I were even married, God started talking about real estate.

Not marriage. Not ministry.
A house.

"You and Miles will buy a home together."
Not might. Not if you're good little Christians.
Just—*will*.

When God says something that clear, you don't argue.
You don't overthink it—you just listen.

Now, I know saying "God told me" can make people look at you like you announced you just spotted Bigfoot in aisle five at Kroger.
So let me clarify.

It wasn't an audible voice.
No Morgan Freeman narration.

Just that bone-deep knowing—so sharp, so precise, I couldn't pretend it
was just me.

And then—again.
The same words.
The same steady certainty.
So clear I couldn't ignore it if I tried.

Sometimes I still wonder,
"Was that You, God... or just me over-caffeinated and under-hydrated again?"

But when it's really Him? Oh, He makes sure you know.
He doesn't whisper once and hope for the best.
He'll whisper it again. And again.
Through a sermon.
Through a stranger's words.
Even through a bumper sticker that feels a little too on-the-nose.

Denise calls it "a sensing."
I call it God waving heavenly flags:*"Girl. I've told you already. Let's go."*

So when God whispered about a house, I believed Him.

I pictured weekend pancakes in our kitchen.
Maybe a window that made every morning feel like a Disney sunrise.

It felt like more than a house.
It felt holy.
Like God handing us a pen and saying, *"Go ahead. Write the next chapter."*

Then came the nudge.
Driving through Lansing, I heard it: *Turn left.*

Why? There was no Starbucks that way.
No Target.

Not even a half-decent strip mall.

But I'd learned not to ignore those whispers.
So—I turned.

Down the street were a row of plain duplexes.
Nothing fancy. Nothing grand.

But months earlier, I'd fallen in love with one online.
It was big. Roomy. Had space for us and a rental unit.
Perfect—except for the price tag that screamed,
"Girl, not in this decade."

So why was I here?

That night I told Miles.
He gave me the look.
Miles doesn't leap.
He tiptoes—probably with a spreadsheet in one back pocket and a backup plan in the other.

But with a cookie bribe, I got him to drive with me.

The first few duplexes practically screamed, "please don't"—peeling paint, shutters hanging on for dear life.

Miles shook his head.
"Christine, that one needs a tetanus shot."
"That one needs a bulldozer."

We were about to bail when—boom.

Behind a hedge big enough to hide a marching band sat the duplex.
The same one from online.
But this time?

A foreclosure sign.
Half the price.

Cue holy goosebumps.

If you're skeptical, I get it. A foreclosure at half-price sounds like HGTV producer bait. But standing there in real life, it felt like God winking at me.

We called a realtor.
Made an offer.
Prayed like crazy.
And waited.

We didn't get it.
Door slammed shut.

I wanted to cry.
Or eat a donut and name it "Disappointment."

God had led me there—so why the big NO?

But now I get it.

The house wasn't the miracle. It was just the rehearsal for trust.

God wasn't trying to give us a home that day.
He was teaching us how to hear Him.
How to follow the whisper—even when it leads to a no.

Because sometimes the miracle isn't what He gives.
It's what He teaches while you're waiting.

That detour wasn't about the duplex at all. It was training wheels for the next step—one that would start with heartbreak before it turned into a gift.

END OF CHAPTER REFLECTION

1. Have you ever taken a turn that felt random in the moment—but later realized God had set the whole thing up?

2. What did you learn from a door that looked wide open—then slammed shut?

3. Can you think of a time when the real miracle wasn't getting what you asked for, but what God showed you in the waiting?

CHAPTER 33

When God Says "Not That One" and Then Hands You the Keys Anyway

How a Closed Door, a Quieter Yes, and a Little House of Grace Changed Everything

The phone rang.
I answered like a woman holding a balloon made of hope—one squeeze from popping.

It was our realtor.
"I'm sorry," she said. "HUD accepted another offer."

Pop.

I didn't cry. I just blinked.
Like someone deleted the last page of my favorite book.

Wait... what?
God told me to turn left. There was a parting hedge! A foreclosure sign!
This was supposed to be it.

Instead, it felt like I'd followed divine breadcrumbs straight into a glass door.

It felt like walking straight into invisible glass.

Had I made it up? Imagined God's voice? Or was I just guessing the end of the story like a kid at bedtime?

Faith walked with a limp that day.

But underneath the fog of disappointment, a whisper surfaced:
This is part of it too.

It didn't make sense. It didn't feel good.
But it felt holy.
Like God smiling softly and saying, *"Relax. That was just the warm-up."*

And here's what I've learned:
God doesn't waste steps.
Not even the ones that bruise you.

His path is wobbly stepping stones across a river—
one no, one not yet, one soggy sock at a time.

"I will instruct you and teach you in the way you should go; I will counsel you and watch over you."
— **Psalm 32:8**

He's not handing you a map and waving goodbye.
He's walking it with you.

A few days later, I went back to the foreclosure listings.
Still scrolling like a woman desperate for closure, I spotted it.
A little three-bedroom foreclosure.

Not a duplex. Not fancy. Not "HGTV ready."
But affordable. Simple.
Full of potential.

It looked like pancakes on Sunday.
Like Maddie's laughter bouncing off freshly painted walls.

"Let's go see it," I told Miles.

From the second we pulled up, it felt different.
The yard wasn't a jungle.
The house didn't scream *RUN*.
It whispered, *Take me home.*

Inside? A little tragic.
The bathroom vanity had clearly stormed out in a fit of rage.

But the bones were solid.
The heart? Still beating.

We toured a few others just to say we did.
But honestly? Everything else felt like awkward first dates after meeting
your soulmate.

Look, I know how unhinged it sounds to call a foreclosure my soulmate
house. But that's how clear it felt.

I prayed one of those borderline-unstable prayers:
"God, if this is it, swing these doors wide open.
If it's not, slam them shut so hard I forget what backsplash even is."

And then—everything clicked.
Offer accepted. Papers signed. Doors opened like butter on warm toast.

We stood in the empty living room, grinning like two people with zero idea what they were doing—but kind of loving it.

The house came with nothing.
No fridge. No stove.
The bathroom vanity and sink were missing too—
because who doesn't love brushing their teeth over a bucket?

Which meant full HGTV mode.

We bought shiny new appliances—
finally, a kitchen that looked less like a campsite and more like a home.

We painted every wall.
Scrubbed every inch.
Chose a backsplash that caught the morning sun like hope in tile form.

And somewhere in that dust and joy, it hit me:

This wasn't just a fixer-upper.
It was redemption.

This house had been forgotten.
Overlooked.

So had I, once.

But God rebuilds what the world tosses aside.
He breathes life into broken things.
Leaves fingerprints on every inch.

The duplex? That was the setup.
A holy stepping stone.

Because if God hadn't told me to turn left—

and if I hadn't stumbled on that foreclosed duplex—
I never would've started looking for a foreclosure at all.
And I would've missed the house God had planned for us all along.

And this house of grace would soon have front-row seats to one of our biggest faith battles yet.

END OF CHAPTER REFLECTION

1. Have you ever followed a path that felt so right—only to have the door slam in your face?

2. Can you think of a time when disappointment turned out to be a setup for something better?

3. What "stepping stones" has God used in your life—little yeses, random detours, even soggy-sock moments—that led you somewhere you never expected?

CHAPTER 34

When Your Faith Looks Good On the Outside But Feels Wobbly On the Inside

How God Meets Us in the Middle of Doubt—and Refuses to Let Go

Life in Lansing finally had a rhythm.

Church on Sundays. Brunch after.

Maddie sitting with the youth group—curious, but cautious. Like someone testing the pool water with one toe. Never fully jumping in.

And me? I was trying.

Really trying.

To go deeper with God.

I had an hour-long commute each way.

Two options: complain about traffic or turn my car into a chapel. I chose the chapel—with Tim Hortons detours, because coffee and donuts? Basically communion.

I listened to the Bible on CD.

Yes, CDs. Shiny discs I loaded one at a time.
My car even had a cigarette lighter—basically a time machine on wheels.

But those words?
They soaked in.
Jesus filling the car.
Sunlight spilling through the windshield.
Scripture coming alive somewhere between exits 90 and 67.

I finished the New Testament, then started the Old again.
Stories I thought I knew hit different.
Verses I'd read a hundred times felt like brand-new treasure.
And I remembered all the ways God had shown up for me.

But something was off.

On the outside, I looked like I had my spiritual act together.
Church? Check.
Bible? Check.
Worship playlist? On repeat.

But inside?
There was a quiet hum of unease.
A whisper I couldn't shake: *You're still doubting.*

And I was ashamed.

How could I still struggle with this?
I had seen miracles.
Heard God's voice.
Watched Him move mountains with my name on them.

And still, at night, I'd whisper:
Why do I doubt? Why can't I just believe like everyone else? What's wrong with me?

That's when the enemy crept in.

Not fireworks or pitchforks—just stray thoughts that sounded like my own:

Maybe you imagined it. Maybe it was coincidence. If God was real, wouldn't He make it more obvious?

My faith felt like wet cement—and the enemy was stomping through it in muddy boots.

Paul warned us the enemy would use lies like this.

> "But I am afraid that just as Eve was deceived by the serpent's cunning, your minds may somehow be led astray from your sincere and pure devotion to Christ."
>
> — **2 Corinthians 11:3**
>
> ❧ **Faith doesn't need to be complicated.**
> Stay close to Jesus. The noise will try to pull you away—but He is enough.

I wasn't doubting because I didn't care.
I doubted because I did.

I wanted to believe with everything in me.
But faith in an invisible God? Not easy.
Especially for someone wired like me—equal parts heart and head.

I wanted intimacy with God.
And a notarized affidavit confirming His presence.
Which—let's be real—would've cleared this whole thing up for believers and doubters alike.

So I searched. Again.
Theology books. Articles.

Late-night YouTube spirals where science and faith didn't throw punches.

I didn't want to doubt. I just wanted to know.
And even after everything He'd done, I still found myself whispering:
God, are You really there?

But I kept it inside.
Miles was still growing in faith.
Maddie was just dipping her toes in.
So I smiled. Nodded. Sang worship songs.

And one night, I cracked.

Sat on my bed.
The house quiet.
Air heavy with questions.
I whispered:
"God... why can't I just believe?
Show me something—anything—to prove You're real."

I waited.
No lightning.
No angel holding a banner outside my window.
Not even a flicker of the bathroom light.

Just... silence.

Or so I thought.

Looking back, He was answering me.
Not with skywriting—but with presence.
With patience.
With steady grace.

> "O LORD, you have searched me and you know me. You know when
> I sit down and when I rise; you perceive my thoughts from afar...you
> are familiar with all my ways...you hem me in—behind and before;
> you have laid Your hand upon me."
>
> **— Psalm 139:1–5**
>
> ❧ **God doesn't just know about you. He knows you.**
> Completely. And He never leaves. Even in doubt. Even in the
> dark.

He wasn't disappointed in my doubts.

He understood every tear.

Every 2 a.m. spiral.

And He already had a plan to blow my doubts out of the water.

God wasn't asking me to fake faith.

He was inviting me to bring my mess to Him.

Because tested faith—the kind that's shaken and rebuilt?

That's the kind that lasts.

The kind that can stand in a storm.

Little by little, He kept showing up.

Sometimes subtly.

Sometimes boldly.

Always lovingly.

Eventually, as you will see later in my story, I stopped asking for proof.

Because I knew.

Not with my eyes.

Not with my ears.

But deep in my soul.

And that proof I begged for?

Oh, He had a plan for that.

Spoiler alert: unforgettable—and definitely not subtle.

END OF CHAPTER REFLECTION

1. Have you ever found yourself doubting—even while begging God to help you believe?

2. What lies sneak in when your faith feels shaky, and how have they tried to pull you off course?

3. Looking back, where can you see God being patient with your questions—quietly steady even when you were spiraling?

CHAPTER 35

When God Flips Your Script

The Plot Twist You Didn't Ask For—But Might Just Need

Christmas came and went.

The lights got boxed up.

Candles burned to stubby ghosts.

The cookies? Gone. (Okay, fine, I ate them—pajamas, midnight, Hallmark movie I pretended to hate but didn't.)

Then reality arrived. Michigan winter.

Not the cute snow-globe kind.

This was snowbanks taller than preschoolers, wind slapping your face like, "Try again, sunshine."

Roads so iced over I half-expected penguins to waddle by.

Every morning I white-knuckled it, 60 miles to work. Then did it again to come home.

Tried to be grateful. My inner cheerleader hit the megaphone:

"At least you have a job! A car! At least you didn't fishtail into that ditch like the guy behind you just did!"

The truth? I hated every frozen mile.

My job was in Grand Rapids.

But Miles and Maddie were in Lansing.
We bought our house in Lansing because that's where Maddie was.
And Miles had made it clear from day one:
"I won't leave my daughter. Not for anyone."

See, Miles grew up with an empty chair where his dad should've been.
He vowed Maddie would never wonder if she mattered. And I believed him.

He showed up for every play, scraped knee and math meltdown.
Fatherhood wasn't default—he chose it.
She mattered. And I loved that about him.
But it didn't thaw my windshield, or my dreams.

I'd shelved my MBA dreams— leadership roles, promotions, a career like my sister's.
Because a promotion probably meant moving.
And as long as Maddie was in Michigan, so were we.

Instead, I sat behind a desk, gray skies, Lean Cuisine on my lap, watching the clock and wondering if this was it—my big "calling."

I wasn't bitter—just... tired in places I didn't know could get tired.

Love had anchored me in Lansing. I didn't regret it.
But there was that quiet ache:
Could I ever live both callings—career and love—in the same zip code?

And then God hit the divine plot twist button.

One day, I got a text from Miles: "Call me when you get a chance..."
Stomach drop. You know that text. Either "Let's book a cruise" or "The world's on fire and I forgot marshmallows."

I called.

His voice was calm.
"My ex got a job offer."

Pause.

"Where?"

"San Antonio."

San Antonio. Texas.

I blinked so hard, I almost dislodged my contact.

No way Miles was letting Maddie move to Texas.
Unless... he didn't get a choice.

What followed was a custody battle we never saw coming.
Long. Emotional. Draining.
Every update felt like whiplash—one day hope, the next heartbreak.

I know some people would say, "Well, that's just life—messy custody battles happen." And they do. But for me, it wasn't just legal paperwork. It was my entire future dangling on a thread.

Looking back, God wasn't panicked.
He wasn't scrambling for Plan B.
He'd already seen it coming.
While I was sobbing into coffee,
He was gathering the pieces:
my waiting, Miles' heartbreak, Maddie's future—
and weaving a larger story.

This wasn't just about a move.
It was about trust.
It was about surrender.

It was a reminder: when God rearranges your life, He isn't reducing—He's expanding.

Because here's what I've learned: When God flips the script, He's not erasing your plan—
He's rewriting it into something bigger.

And what happened next?
It wasn't just lawyers and courtrooms.
It was Maddie, caught in the middle, saying something so simple—and so heartbreaking—
that it rerouted our entire future.

END OF CHAPTER REFLECTION

1. Have you ever pressed pause on your dreams for someone you love? How did it shape you—for better or harder?

2. When life flips the script without warning, what does trusting God actually look like for you in the middle of it?

3. Can you think of a time when an unexpected twist ended up leading to something bigger or better than you could've planned?

CHAPTER 36

When God Says "Go" Into the Unknown

Trusting His Lead Even When You're
Still Holding a Snow Shovel

Michigan winter was still throwing a tantrum.
Snowbanks pretending to be mountains.
Driveways doubling as CrossFit death traps.

And right in the middle of that frozen mess... Maddie arrived.

She came in quiet this time. Cocoa. Silence.
Then, softly, like words made of fragile glass:
"My mom said we're moving to Texas."

The air froze harder than the driveway.
I glanced at Miles. His shoulders dropped. His eyes went still.

Then Maddie whispered,
"I don't want to go. I want to stay where my dad is."

That night, after she went to bed, Miles sat in silence.

No TV. No music. Just the hum of the furnace and his heart breaking.

Finally, he said, "I need to talk to her mom."

He tried. He pleaded. He pointed out Maddie's whole world was here—friends, school, family.

It felt like arguing with a brick wall in cowboy boots.
Texas was happening.

And suddenly, we were in it.
The legal maze. The wait. Emotional exhaustion disguised as custody proceedings.

But the hardest part? Watching Maddie's hope shrink.

One night, curled up on the couch, she whispered,
"I just wish things could stay the same."

She loved her mom. She loved her dad just as much.
And she didn't want to choose between them—or leave him behind.

Something rose up in me then.
This wasn't just a court case. It was a heart case.
She needed fighters. Not lawyers. People. Family.

And then I heard it. Quiet. Steady.
A whisper in my spirit:
"Go to Texas with her."

I froze. Was that God—or just me, emotional and already Googling cowboy hats?

Let's be honest—if you'd told me a year earlier I'd be considering Texas because of a whisper, I would've laughed and handed you directions to the nearest padded room.

But the words wouldn't budge.

So I asked, "Maddie... would it help if your dad went to Texas too?"

Her eyes lit up like someone switched on the sun.
"Well... yes. It would."

And before my brain caught up, I said it:
"Then if you're going to Texas, we're going to Texas."

That smile? Pure sunshine. Holy sunshine.

I didn't know how it would happen. But I knew the Who.

That night, laptop open, prayers flying faster than my typing—I searched the internal job board at my company.

Nothing in San Antonio. My heart sank.

Then—bam. Austin. Dallas.

One management role in Austin practically screamed my name.

Geography is not my spiritual gift. Google rescued me: Austin was an hour and a half from San Antonio. Close enough to show up.

I looked at Miles dead serious:
"I'm going to get this job."

He gave me The Miles Look—the one that says, "I love you, but you're a little unhinged."
Then he smiled. "Okay, Dear."

My resume looked like it was typed by a caffeinated squirrel using Word 2002.

And yes, even I wondered how on earth a clunky Word doc and a prayer were supposed to change our future—but stranger things have happened.

I rewrote it, added some power verbs, hit submit like launching a prayer rocket.

Then came the waiting.
And the waiting.

But in the silence, I heard it again:
"Hold steady. I'm not done."

> *"The LORD is good to those who wait for Him, to the soul who seeks Him."*
>
> — **Lamentations 3:25**
>
> ✍ **Waiting feels like doing nothing.**
> But sometimes it's where God does His best work.

I didn't know how it would end. But I knew this:
The seed had been planted.
And God? He was already making room for roots to grow.

And little did I know—what sprouted next would shake everything we thought we knew about faith, family, and calling.

END OF CHAPTER REFLECTION

1. Have you ever felt God nudging you in a direction that made zero sense at the time? What did you do with it—ignore it, wrestle it, or leap anyway?

2. What "impossible" situation has forced you to loosen your grip and fully surrender to God?

3. Can you look back and see a moment where God was already laying the groundwork—long before you even knew what you'd need?

CHAPTER 37

When the Weeble Wobble Stopped Bouncing Back

How God Shows Up in Hospital Hallways, Hard Conversations, and the Prayers We Didn't Think We Knew How to Pray

The Weeble Wobble—those egg-shaped toys that wobble but don't fall down—always bounced back.
That was our nickname for Dad. The Weeble Wobble.

Quadruple bypass? Bounced.
Cancer? Wobbled.

We joked he practically had a hospital punch card—one more stay and he'd earn a free sandwich.

But this time felt different.

Chaos already swirled around me—custody hearings, job hunting in Texas, sanity dangling by a thread—when my phone rang.
It was my brother Bob. His voice sounded tight, like he was trying not to break.

"Christine... Dad's in the hospital again. It doesn't look good."

My first thought? Again?

The Weeble Wobble always bounced back.
Every time.
Part of me shrugged. He'll be fine. He always is.

But something deeper whispered: *This time is different.*

Dad had paid the long-term price for surviving prostate cancer.
Radiation zapped the disease—but left silent, hidden damage, brutal in
its persistence.

I flashed back to a night years earlier—me rushing from work into the
fluorescent hallway of despair.

Dad lit up when he saw me. "I'm so glad you're here."
He couldn't pee. His belly ballooned. Pain etched his face.

Then—my tough, stoic, "pull-a-breech-calf-out-of-a-cow-before-dinner"
Dad—he cried.
He whispered, "Christine... please, pray with me."

I wasn't exactly a prayer warrior then—more like a toddler stacking
spiritual blocks. But Dad never wavered. So we prayed.

"God, help me. Please help me get through this."

My heart cracked.

I marched to the nurses' station, where they were chatting like it was a
Starbucks break.

"Excuse me," I said sweetly—
with the kind of smile that curdles milk.

"My dad's in severe pain and hasn't peed in hours. Someone needs to help him."

A nurse offered a lazy, "We'll be in soon."

I snapped.

"Listen, Sharon—and yes, I see your name tag. If someone isn't in that room in two minutes, I will scream, file a complaint, and make sure this never happens again. What's your last name?"

That worked.

A nurse bolted after me. Catheter in. Bag filled instantly—like a busted fire hydrant.

Dad squeezed my hand.
"See, Christine? God helped me. We prayed... and He helped me."

And sure, the skeptic in me wanted to argue that it was the nurse, not God. But looking back, the timing was too sharp to dismiss.

Back then, I called it coincidence. Now I see it was training—God teaching me how to pray, one hallway crisis at a time.

God sent me. I was the answer to Dad's prayer—and I didn't even know it.

That fluorescent-lit hallway, the pain melting into relief—
that moment was holy.
Grace in an unexpected place.

Now Bob's words echoed in my kitchen.

I wanted to believe this was another Weeble Wobble moment—a bounce back.
But my heart already knew the truth: This time, he might not get back up.

I wasn't ready.

We always assume there will be more time. But sometimes, time runs out—and faith shows up when you least expect it.

This time, it didn't feel like God bouncing us back. It felt like He cracked the toy open and started rewriting the story.

END OF CHAPTER REFLECTION

1. When have you brushed something off, only to realize later your gut already knew the truth?

2. Can you think of a time when you unknowingly became the answer to someone's need or prayer—even if you didn't realize it at the time?

3. Who has been your Weeble Wobble—the one who always seemed to bounce back? How did their resilience impact your faith?

CHAPTER 38

When God Plans the Wedding

Pulling Off a Three-Week Miracle with One Prayer, a Clearance Rack, and a Best Friend Who Refused to Panic

Weddings are supposed to be romantic.
Florals. Pinterest boards. Slow-motion twirls under fairy lights.

Mine started in a hospital room—with pudding, a stubborn father, and a ticking clock.

The second I walked in, I knew something was wrong.
Mom sat beside Dad's bed, spoon in hand, face trembling as she tried to be strong.

"He won't eat," she whispered.

I reached for his hand. It was cold. Thin. Breakable in a way that made my stomach turn.

"What's going on?"

No answer. Just tears.

I called Bob from the hallway.

"It's cancer, Christine," he said quietly. "Colon cancer. Bad. It's spreading. We'll know more tomorrow."

Cancer. Again.

But this time, it didn't sound like another round of *Dad bounces back.* It sounded final.

Back in the room, Dad forced his usual smirk.
"Oh, I'll be fine. Just need my pills. Maybe some surgery."

Classic Dad—brave, stubborn, and willing to try anything. Prayer. Vitamins. Apple cider vinegar. Wheatgrass. The man would've juiced a lawn if someone swore it cured cancer.

Then, out of nowhere:
"When are you two getting married?"

I wiggled the ring at him.
"Just waiting for the right time."

He raised an eyebrow. "Well, you're not exactly a spring chicken anymore."

I laughed. Brutally honest as always.

Then he leaned closer, voice soft.
"Don't wait. Get married now. I want to see it. My church."

The doctors interrupted—clipboard faces, quick checks that didn't feel routine at all.
One caught my eye, tilted his head toward the hallway.

"Your dad doesn't have long," he said quietly. "Maybe a few months. Maybe weeks."

The air left my lungs.

"Do you think he has at least three weeks?" I whispered.

A pause. "Maybe."

That was all I needed.

First call: Denise. "It's bad. Come tomorrow."
Second call: Shannon.
"Three weeks. Dad wants to see us married. Can we pull it off?"
She didn't even blink.
"Girl, please. Who do you think you're talking to?"

If Jesus had called twelve women instead of twelve men, Shannon would've been team captain.

Within hours, she had a plan—dress shop, invitations, flowers. Boom.

She found two hot-pink bridesmaid dresses for Maddie and Faith. The only two left, on the clearance rack. Exact sizes. Zip. Spin. Grin. Perfect fit.

Some would shrug it off as coincidence. But standing there watching those girls twirl, it felt like more than luck. It felt like favor.

And somehow, she even tracked down the exact same dress in her size online.
It arrived faster than a pizza and fit like it was made for her.

This wasn't a Pinterest wedding. It was a holy hustle.
Three weeks. One miracle. A thousand whispered prayers.

What felt rushed and messy at the time turned out to be God's timing all along—giving Dad a front row seat, and me a memory I didn't know I'd cling to.

And somehow—God and Shannon—stretched every penny until it sparkled.

If you gave that girl a loaf of bread and a coupon, she'd cater a royal banquet and still have change left for flowers.

Shannon still lived in my parents' small town, and that girl had connections.
Vendors didn't just give her discounts—they acted like they were in on a divine secret.

When the cake arrived, I cried.
It wasn't just cake.
It was love stacked in three tiers, frosted with miracles.

It looked ordinary to anyone else—but to me, it was proof God was in the details.

Deep down, I knew—this wasn't just Shannon's brilliance.
It was God, throwing holy confetti over the whole thing, whispering, *"See? I've got this."*

Later, I held Dad's hand.
"Dad... we're getting married."

His eyes lit up. "Good. God wants that. I like Miles."
Then he squinted.
"But you're doing it in my church, right?"

"I don't even know who to call."

He grinned. "Delores."

Ah yes, Delores—the organist, encourager, and unofficial church cheerleader from when I was a little girl.

That night, I knelt beside my bed.
"God, if this is for Dad... if this is for You... make a way."

And I remembered:

> *"And my God will meet all your needs according to His glorious riches in Christ Jesus."*
>
> **— Philippians 4:19**
>
> ♪ **God's provision isn't stingy.**
> He meets needs out of abundance, not leftovers.

When you think you don't have enough time, money, or hope—He's already on it.

I didn't know what tomorrow would bring.
But I knew this much:
God had the guest list.
And He was already decorating the aisle.

> *"There is a time for everything, and a season for every activity under the heavens... a time to weep and a time to laugh, a time to mourn and a time to dance."*
>
> **— Ecclesiastes 3:1,4**
>
> ♪ **Joy and sorrow don't live in separate worlds.** Scripture reminds us they often walk hand in hand.

God wasn't just planning a wedding. He was giving us one last dance before the goodbye I didn't want to face.

END OF CHAPTER REFLECTION

1. Have you ever had to move fast—make a bold decision in the middle of heartbreak or crisis? What did you do?

2. Is there someone you want to honor before it's too late? What's one tangible way you could show them love right now?

3. Can you remember a time you cried out for help—maybe to God, maybe just into the silence—and something or someone showed up in a way you never saw coming?

CHAPTER 39

Fifty Bucks, a Best Friend, and a God Who Leaves Nothing to Chance

The Story of How a Clearance Rack Dress, a Bargain Reception, and a Perfectly Timed Miracle All Fell into Place

How much does a miracle-fueled wedding cost?
Apparently, fifty bucks and a Shannon.

The hospital room was quiet.
The steady beep of machines mixed with the soft shuffle of nurses.
Dad lay still, his hand in mine, his chest rising slower than yesterday.

A knock.

A man stepped in—glasses, kind smile, voice like warm tea.
"Hi, I'm Pastor Herb."

Dad lit up like they'd been best friends since kindergarten.

Then Herb turned to me.
"Anything I can do?"

Without thinking, I blurted, "Dad wants Miles and me married in his church."

Herb nodded. "I'd be honored to officiate. You can use the church. Fifty dollars."

Fifty. Five-zero. Less than a dinner out. Less than a Target run.
God was coupon-clipping on my behalf.

I'd just eyed a $900 chapel. For that price, I half-expected it to come with stained glass, live doves, and a harp soundtrack on demand.

And since we'd already blown our budget on Maddie's upcoming spring break Disney trip, a last-minute wedding fund wasn't exactly in the ledger.

That's when Shannon arrived—not just in person, but in full-on miracle mode.

Shannon worked her magic and booked a reception hall for twenty bucks—five minutes from the church.
Pretty sure she paid in banana bread and a wink.

Invitations? Clearance aisle, printed in hours.
Family? Mobilized like we were staging a holy flash mob.
Caterer? Somehow, she scored us a full dinner for all the guests for the price of a Happy Meal. And honestly, it tasted better too.

If Shannon had been in charge of the loaves and fishes, everyone would've left with dessert and a to-go box.

Every time something fell into place, Shannon and I looked at each other and whispered, "This is really happening."
And God whispered back, *I know.*

I thought God was just covering a wedding. Turns out, He was teaching me something bigger—that if He cared about the details, He'd cover the impossible too.

Then came the dress.
Cue dramatic music and questionable lighting.

One dress made me look like a haunted Victorian ghost.
One came with shoulder pads bigger than a linebacker in full gear.
One made me look like a frosted cupcake with trust issues.

Finally, Shannon took my hands.
"Christine. You deserve a dress that makes you feel beautiful."

So I prayed a tiny prayer:
God, please help me find a dress. And please don't let it cost more than my first car.

We didn't need couture. We needed something that made me feel beautiful.
And preferably not made of fabric that could double as a shower curtain.

We found it online—thumbnail photo, blind faith.
We rushed the shipping, braced for tears.

It arrived. Soft. Simple. Beautiful.
It fit perfectly. No sewing. No contortionist moves to zip it.

I twirled in front of the mirror and—for the first time in a long time—felt like a bride.
A clearance-rack, God-delivered princess.

Some people would call it luck—a clearance-rack score and a perfect fit. But standing there in that dress, I couldn't shake the sense that God was grinning, whispering, *"Even this detail matters to Me."*

If he's that generous, of course He can cover a dress, a church, and a perfectly timed fifty-dollar miracle.

But miracles don't stop pain—they carry you through it. And while the wedding came together, Dad was quietly coming apart.

And here's what hit me:
God's will doesn't mean easy. It means possible.

And when it feels like the wind's at your back? That's not luck.
That's God clearing the path before you stumble.

Shannon—Director of Miracles and Bridal Logistics.
Compensation: eternal blessings.

Because honestly?
Fifty bucks and a Shannon isn't just enough for a wedding.
It's enough for a miracle.

But while miracles stacked up around me, another truth pressed in: Dad's body was coming undone. And soon, the real goodbye came knocking.

END OF CHAPTER REFLECTION

1. Have you ever seen the details line up so perfectly that "coincidence" didn't even stand a chance? Could it have been more than luck?

2. When has life surprised you with something that almost felt playful—like a perfectly timed gift or miracle?

3. Have you ever had something work out so perfectly you wondered if it was just good timing—or something bigger at work?

> *"He who did not spare His own Son but gave Him up for us all—how will He not also graciously give us all things?"*
>
> **— Romans 8:32**
>
> ❧ If God gave us His very best, His own Son—why would He hold back anything else we truly need?

CHAPTER 40

A Goodbye Wrapped in Grace

When God Answers Differently Than You
Hoped—But Exactly How You Needed

When I told Dad we were getting married in his church, his whole face
lit up.
Not a polite grin. Full-on sunshine breaking through a storm cloud.

For a moment, it gave him life.
That last piece of unfinished business? Clicked into place.

The next day, everything changed.

At the hospital, a nurse pulled me aside.
Quiet voice. Kind eyes.
"Your dad only has a few days left."

It hit like a tsunami.
I just wanted him to see me in the dress. At the wedding.
To know he was part of it.

But deep down, I knew.

The next morning, Mom called.
"They're moving your dad to hospice. Can you come?"

Hospice—
A door slowly closing.

"I'm on my way."

When I arrived, he looked asleep. Breathing shallow.

Then his eyes flew open. "I'm alive!" he yelled. "I thought I was dead—but I'm alive!"

I laughed through tears.
"Yes, Dad. You're alive. We're here."

He turned, wide-eyed.
"Are you coming with me?"

"I am," I promised. "Every step."

As they wheeled him down the hall to go to the hospice facility, he introduced me to the staff like I was the guest of honor.
"This is my daughter. She's coming with me."

Sweet, but also slightly alarming. As in, wait—where exactly are we going, Dad?

It floored me.
Not that he said it—but how he said it.
"This is my daughter." With pride.

Growing up, I was often called the "laziest kid" in the family—half joke, half not.
That label stuck like gum on a shoe.

But in that hallway? He saw me. Claimed me. He was proud of me.
It was all I ever wanted. And it was enough.

Later, nurses tucked him into hospice.
I heard him whisper,
"I love You, God. I love You, God."
They said he might not wake again.

I leaned over to Mom.
"What was one of Dad's favorite songs?"

She didn't pause.
"The Old Rugged Cross."

Of course it was.
A hymn older than sliced bread.

I pulled out my phone, whispering,
"Please let there be a version between banjo stampede and off-key soloist."

Found one. Played it.
Then played it again.
And again.

Every chorus felt like a prayer.

Mom leaned close.
"It's okay," she whispered. "You can go now. No more pain. You're going to Jesus."

Bob took her home for a break.
I stayed.

Leaning close, whispering words I'd carried my whole life:

"Dad, I love you. I forgive you. We're good now. You can go to Jesus."

At some point, I dozed off.
When I woke, he was still there.

I didn't want Mom to miss it.
"Dad, I'll be right back. Getting Mom. Be right back."

Halfway out of her driveway, my phone rang.
The hospice nurse.
"Your father has passed away."

It shattered something in me.

"Mom... I'm so sorry. He died alone. I promised I'd be there."

She held my hand.

"He's not alone, Christine. He's with Jesus now."

She was right.
But it still felt like I'd broken my word—the last word I wanted to break.

When we got back, I braced for the stillness of death.
Instead, I heard music.
Soft worship music.

"Has this been playing long?" I asked.

The nurse nodded.
"Several hours."

"Was it playing when he passed?"
"Yes."

Peace rushed in.

He didn't die in silence.
He died surrounded by praise.
Carried home by worship.

I thought the goodbye was only grief. But it became a setup for something deeper—learning that God doesn't just show up in joy, but in the ache too.

And sure, someone could call that coincidence—that a playlist happened to be running. But to me, it was God's way of saying, *"I was here. I never left him."*

Not alone.
Not abandoned.
Held.

Another nurse said gently,
"Some people wait until their loved ones step out. Maybe that's what your dad needed."

Maybe she was right.
Maybe that was his final gift.

God didn't answer my prayer the way I wanted.
But He did answer.
With mercy. With music.
With a goodbye wrapped in grace.

We held Dad's funeral in that little country church—the one with creaky wooden pews, red carpet, sunlight slanting through stained glass, and the faint smell of old hymnals.

It was the same church where, just a few weeks later, I walked down the aisle to marry Miles.

Since Dad wasn't there to walk me, Mom took my arm.

Step by step, she held me steady. But I could feel him smiling on us as we moved forward—
his love just as present as the sunlight streaming through the windows.

Dad's seat was empty.
But his presence... I felt it in the hush before the music started, in the way the light seemed to linger on the altar.

God had promised we'd be married.
And we were.

Before we knew Dad was sick, we'd already planned Maddie's spring break trip.
Miles' mom, Judy, was coming with us. Disney World and Universal Studios.
Everything was booked and paid for—and it just happened to fall a few days after our wedding.

I smiled at Miles and said, "Well... looks like we're honeymooning with your mom."

Because nothing says newlywed romance like holding hands on *It's a Small World* while your mother-in-law eats Dole Whip in the seat beside you.

Honestly, you could call that awkward. And it was. But it was also healing—God stitching laughter into fresh grief in a way no travel brochure could've promised.

And you know what?
It turned out to be the most magical, God-ordained honeymoon I could have imagined.

Somehow, in the middle of fresh grief, there was laughter—real, from-the-belly laughter.
And I like to think Dad saw it.

I like to think Jim saw it too—both of them smiling from Heaven, glad we hadn't forgotten how to find joy even with the ache still fresh.

Florida sunshine on our faces, the smell of popcorn and sunscreen in the air.
Roller coasters screaming overhead—it all felt like God pressing His hand over my heart and saying, *"See? I'm still here. There's still beauty."*

I thought goodbye was the mountain. I didn't yet know the valley ahead would demand even deeper trust.

END OF CHAPTER REFLECTION

1. Have you ever had the chance to bring peace or comfort to someone in their final moments? How did it change you?

2. If you've lost someone close, what memories or last words rise to the surface and stay with you?

3. Looking back, what brought you comfort in your grief—a song, a moment, or even unexpected laughter? Could that have been God's way of meeting you there?

CHAPTER 41

The Miracles That Began to Cement My Faith

When You're Still Waiting, Still Wondering, and God's Already Setting the Stage

We came home from our honeymoon glowing.

Bags stuffed with sandy flip-flops. Half-eaten granola bars. Hearts full.

The wedding had been a miracle.
Dad was gone, but his spirit felt close.
I was sure God had stacked the deck for us this time.

Then—bam.
Reality showed up like a nosy neighbor with a leaf blower.

Bills multiplied. Job leads vanished.
Court papers still glaring: "You thought this was over? Cute."

The Austin job?
Total radio silence.
Not a no. Not a yes.

Just digital tumbleweeds.

One night, Miles dropped his keys, looked at me, and asked,
"Any word yet?"

I sighed. Dramatically.
"Nope. But God's not about to let Maddie go to Texas without us."

I flung an arm over my face.
"He knows my heart. And my hatred for Michigan winters.
If it's not a job, it'll be holy teleportation.
Either way, I'm getting us to Texas."

Waiting became a full-time job.
Refresh. Refresh. Smack laptop. Repeat.
If job-board cardio counted, I'd have had Olympic abs.

We'd prayed. We'd planned.
We looked like conspiracy theorists with too much red string.
But it stayed heavy. Unresolved.

Meanwhile, Maddie's mom had already gone to Texas.
New job. Her husband soon joining her.

It was already April. Maddie would be leaving Michigan when school
ended in June.
The train was moving—with or without us.

One night, Miles sat beside me on the bed.
Quiet. Tired. Heavy.
"Even if we win," he said softly, "Maddie still loses a parent.
I hope you're right about this job. We can't fail her."

He was right.
She didn't need pixelated Skype love.

She needed us there. In person. Daily.
So Texas it was.

Faith said *Go.*
Logic said *You're insane.*
We packed anyway.

Here's the truth:
My faith wasn't cement—it was Silly Putty.
Stretchy. Fragile. Picking up every stray fear.
One minute hope, the next panic.
Basically, I was the wobbly shopping cart of faith—looked fine until you
tried steering it straight.

And the enemy? Oh, he saw all of it.
Because he knew the danger wasn't my doubt—it was what would happen
if I stopped doubting.
If I ever really believed—down to my bones—that God was speaking to me?
I'd be unstoppable. The devil would need a vacation.

Listen, if I find a mascara that survives a Hallmark movie marathon, six
people get a text.
If Miles likes my chili, the internet hears about it.
So imagine what I'd do if I knew—*knew*—God was real and working in my
life?
Game over for the enemy.

> "Put on the full armor of God, so that you can take your stand against
> the devil's schemes."
>
> — **Ephesians 6:11**
>
> ✒ **God doesn't send you into battle in flip-flops.**
> He gives you armor for a reason.

One night, I sat on the edge of the bed and finally got real.
"Lord... I'm tired.
I'm trying to believe, but I need help.
If this Texas job is from You, open the door.
I need to know You see us."

And no, it's not like He has an email filter for "only polished prayers."
Even the messy, desperate ones go straight to the top of the stack.

> *"Cast all your anxiety on him because He cares for you."*
> — **1 Peter 5:7**
>
> ❧ **God's inbox is open 24/7.**
> He actually wants your messy prayers.

So I did something radical.
I let go.
Not perfectly, but enough to unclench my fists.

I handed it over.
Prayed.
Waited.

Then—boom—another job posting popped up.
Same organization in Austin. Different role.

I applied.
Waited.
Still nothing.

But God wasn't ignoring me.
He wasn't ghosting me.
He was just doing His thing—lining up puzzle pieces I didn't know existed.

I thought the silence meant God had left me hanging. But it was a setup—He was moving pieces I couldn't even see.

> *"But the Lord is faithful, and he will strengthen you and protect you from the evil one."*
>
> — **2 Thessalonians 3:3**
>
> **You're not unprotected.**
> God's got you covered.

But God wasn't just setting up job listings and interviews.
He was about to show up in the most ordinary place—with a whisper that changed everything.

END OF CHAPTER REFLECTION

1. Have you ever thrown up one of those raw, no-script prayers—just you and your messy heart on the table? If so, what happened?

2. Can you relate to waiting for something you couldn't control—when the silence felt unbearable? What helped you keep holding on?

3. Looking back, have you ever realized things were quietly lining up—pieces falling into place you didn't even know were missing? Could that have been God at work?

CHAPTER 42

The Still, Small Voice

When God Speaks Without Thunder—
and You Finally Learn to Listen

After what felt like a lifetime of refreshing my inbox, it finally happened.
I had a reason to pack a suitcase.

A work conference. Jekyll Island, Georgia.
Once a year, others in my role flew in from across the country.

The goal? "Socialize and share ideas."
The reality? Hugs that lasted two seconds too long and the same, "Can you believe it's been a year?"

But this time felt different.
Something was in the air.
Heaven was plotting.
And I had no clue what was coming.

There was a guy there I'd met once, years ago.
Genuine. Down-to-earth.
The kind of guy who remembers your name even if you're not a big deal.
Now he had clout.

On the last night, I spotted him in the lobby of the restaurant.
That's when it hit me.
The nudge.

Tell him your story.

My stomach did the Macarena—because apparently, I'm stuck in the '90s.

Could've just been nerves, right? That's what I told myself. But the feeling wouldn't leave.

So, I walked over like someone about to jump into freezing water—terrified, but no turning back.

"I hope you don't mind me sharing something personal..."

And then it all came spilling out.
The two Austin jobs I had already applied for—but no reply, just absolute silence.
Maddie moving.
Our desperate plan to follow.

He just nodded. Calm. Steady.
"I'll make some calls."

That was it. No pep talk. Just quiet confidence that made me believe he meant it.

Apparently, he did.

The next day after I got back from the conference? My phone rang.
It was HR.
Job one? Gone.
Job two? Wide open.

Interested in an interview?
Um...YES!!

I nearly launched my laptop in the air and broke into a one-woman
praise dance right in my office area.

The phone interview went shockingly well.
So well they invited me to Austin for an in-person interview.

Cue immediate panic spiral.

What if I blow it?
What if this was my one golden ticket and I totally mess it up?
What if I ruin everything?

That night I cracked.
"God, I'm scared. I cannot mess this up. Please, please help."

Then, mid-toothpaste, it happened.
Not out loud.
But crystal clear in my spirit: *"Read Proverbs 27."*

I froze, toothbrush dangling like a confused walrus. Pretty sure Crest
wasn't designed for holy encounters.

But there it was again: *"Proverbs 27."*

I spit, rinsed, grabbed my Bible.
My hands were shaking as I turned the pages.

I didn't know what I was about to read—only that God Himself had sent
me here.

> "Do not boast about tomorrow, for you do not know what a day may bring. Let another praise you, and not your own mouth; someone else, and not your own lips."
>
> — **Proverbs 27:1–2**
>
> ❧ **Tomorrow isn't promised.**
> You don't need to hustle for approval. Let God and others do the talking for you.

Goosebumps.

I had no idea what that verse said before I read it. None.

If you think I'd memorized Proverbs to whip out the perfect verse for my life—nope. I was just as shocked as anyone.

This wasn't me. This was Him.

The verse literally said, "Let another praise you." And it was like God was whispering, *Stop trying to prove yourself. Let Me handle it.*

The next day, I asked my Managing Partner for a recommendation letter.
He didn't just say yes.
He also offered to call the hiring manager himself.

Then, one by one, six more leaders stepped up—to write letters for me.
Some I asked. Others volunteered like it was a holy recruitment drive.

It was like a holy LinkedIn endorsement parade.
Only better, because they spelled my name right.

Every letter was personal.
Not the generic "team player" nonsense.
They wrote about my heart. My grit. My work ethic. My character.

Each one felt like God whispering, *"See? I told you I've got this."*

And here's the kicker:
I thought God wanted me in Grand Rapids to get a promotion there.
But maybe that was never the point. Maybe it was just the setup—to prepare me for something bigger.
If I hadn't transferred, none of this would've happened.
I wouldn't have worked with most of these people.
Wouldn't have had their support.

God had been stacking the dominoes long before I even knew there was a game.

When I flew to Austin, I packed a folder full of letters.
And a suitcase full of shaky faith.

I handed those packets over with a nervous smile and a whispered prayer:
"God, if this is Your plan, fling this door wide open.
If it's not... maybe just close it softly. No slammed fingers, please."

Something had shifted.

One quiet night, toothpaste and all...God spoke.
Not with fire. Not with thunder.
Just a still, small voice.

And for the first time?
I really, truly believed He was right there.

But God wasn't done. In an airport security line, one whisper turned my shaky faith into unshakable certainty.

END OF CHAPTER REFLECTION

1. Have you ever felt that nudge to share your story—even when every part of you wanted to stay quiet? What happened when you did?

2. Has God ever surprised you with a quiet word in the most unexpected place—the kind of moment you might have dismissed as instinct or coincidence, but later realized was Him?

3. Where do you find yourself hustling to prove your worth—and what might it look like to let God be the one who speaks for you instead?

CHAPTER 43

The TSA Whisper That Blew My Mind

When God Parted Traffic, Cleared Security, and Spoke Straight to My Heart

The miracle started somewhere between my sweaty palms and a TSA line that looked like a Black Friday sale at Kohl's.

I flew into Austin the night before the big interview.
Hopeful.
Nauseated.
I'd rented a car and prepaid for gas— one small, forgettable choice.

I didn't know it yet, but that tiny choice would become part of the miracle chain.

That night, I stood at the hotel window.
"God, I'm scared.
What if they don't like me?
There are a lot of other candidates.
Miles and Maddie are counting on me.
Please... show me what to do."

The next morning—I wore my best "please hire me" smile.
A brand-new professional suit.
Praying I wouldn't sweat through my blouse.

Then there was the interviewer who could've won a gold medal in poker.
I couldn't read her at all.
I wasn't sure she liked me.
I walked out thinking, *Well... there goes Texas.*

By the time I shook the last hand, I was late for my flight.
I bolted for the car.

Straight into Austin traffic.
Bumper to bumper.
Brake lights to the horizon.

I prayed again. *"God, please help me make this flight."*

Traffic parted out of my lane like Moses had just relocated the Red Sea
to Austin.
It was like God Himself said, *"Girl, I got you. Floor it."*

I flew to the rental return.
Prepaid gas got me out in seconds.
I grabbed my carry-on—roller bag dragging behind me like a sleepy
toddler—
and sprinted toward the terminal like my entire future depended on it.

At the kiosk, I punched in my confirmation number like I was launching
missiles.
Grabbed my boarding pass.
And crammed it into my purse without even looking at it.

Then I saw it.
The longest TSA line I'd ever seen.

Think Disneyland meets DMV meets the entire cast of *Les Mis* lining up for bread.
Pretty sure I saw someone selling popcorn halfway back.

My stomach dropped.
I was toast.

And then I heard it.
Not out loud.
But deep in my spirit.
"Look at your ticket. You have TSA PreCheck. You do not have a line."

I froze.
I had never signed up for TSA PreCheck.
Didn't have it on my ticket when I flew in.

"God... was that You?"

It came again. Calm. Steady.
"Look at your ticket."

And that's when the panic hit.
What if I looked... and it wasn't there?
What if this "voice" was just my own desperation dressed up as faith?

My hand hovered over my purse like it was a live grenade.

My entire faith was hanging in the balance—right there, ten feet from the security line.

Finally—deep breath.
I reached in.
Fumbled through Chapstick. Loose change.
Then... paper.

My pulse shot up.
I froze, like yanking it out too fast might cancel the miracle.

Slowly, dramatically—Oscar-worthy slow—I pulled out the boarding pass.

And there it was.
Bold. Glorious.

TSA PRECHECK.

I gasped. But the miracle wasn't the shortcut line. The miracle was the whisper. God had spoken—and for the first time in my life, I really knew it was Him.

This was 2014.

And I know what you're thinking—it sounds impossible. But here's the kicker: years later, I learned about a little-known TSA program called Managed Inclusion. Sometimes they slipped non-members into PreCheck to clear traffic jams. It began in 2014 and ended in 2015, and hardly anyone knew it existed.

Back then, I knew TSA PreCheck existed, but I'd never signed up, never used it, and had no idea a secret program like that could've landed me in the fast lane. That thought never even crossed my mind.

Which is why that whisper—the one that told me to look at my ticket— still stops me in my tracks.

Even if PreCheck randomly showed up on my ticket, nothing explains how I heard that whisper before I even looked. I didn't know it was possible. But God did.

That whisper? That was God.

> *"My sheep listen to my voice; I know them, and they follow me."*
> — **John 10:27**
>
> ❧ **God's voice isn't just for prophets or pastors.**
> He speaks to His kids—and yes, even in TSA lines.

I walked straight to the empty PreCheck line.
Through in minutes.
My gate right in front of me.

The real miracle wasn't making the flight.
It was that I'd heard God's voice—
and recognized it.

From that moment on, there was no turning back.
My doubt died in that airport line. God is real—and I knew it.

After I landed in Michigan, I whispered,
"Thank You, Lord. Please don't stop talking to me."

And then I heard Him again:
"You will get the job. You will be moving to Texas. Do not worry. I have cleared the path."

When I got home, I told Miles,
"I'm getting that job. Start packing—we're going to Texas."

Then I spilled the whole story—
traffic parting like the Red Sea,
the whisper at the airport,
the boarding pass,
the miracle PreCheck.

I told it with so much wonder, he couldn't help but believe me.
It sounded unbelievable—
but I saw it in his eyes.
He wanted it to be true.
And deep down, he knew it was.
He smiled, shook his head, and gave the classic Miles line: "Okay, Dear."

And a few days later, the call came.
The job was mine.
A promotion.

If I hadn't moved to Grand Rapids...
If those leaders hadn't written those letters...
If I hadn't trusted the still, small voice...
I wouldn't be heading to Austin.
I wouldn't be writing this story.

God had orchestrated every detail.
He cleared the path.
And I followed His voice.

The job was secured. Texas was calling.
But faith doesn't stop at answered prayers—it deepens when the real adventure begins.

And Texas? Oh, Texas had surprises—but not the kind that come wrapped in gift bags.

END OF CHAPTER REFLECTION

1. Have you ever had everything line up so perfectly that "coincidence" didn't even stand a chance—it had to be God?

2. Has God ever worked through something ordinary—or even a system you didn't know existed—to remind you He was with you?

3. Can you think of a time you followed a little nudge, not knowing where it would lead—and it ended up changing everything?

CHAPTER 44

Trading Snow for Sunshine

When God Says "Go," Sells Your House in a Blink,
and Hands You a One-Way Ticket to Trust

We didn't walk into that courtroom to fight.
We walked in to wave the white flag.
To surrender.
To peace.
To something bigger.

Hand in hand.
Hearts pounding.
Not with dread this time—just a suspicious calm.

This wasn't war anymore.
It was a holy exhale.

> "Let the peace of Christ rule in your hearts."
>
> — **Colossians 3:15**
>
> ♪ **Not fear. Not frantic control. Peace.**
> The kind that takes over like it owns the place—and keeps you
> steady, even in chaos.

Our attorney stood.
Dropped the plot twist to end all plot twists.
We weren't fighting Maddie's relocation to San Antonio.
We were moving to Texas, too.
Austin, to be exact.

Because if you're going to uproot your life, you might as well do it
somewhere with breakfast tacos, sunshine, and a possible Matthew
McConaughey sighting at the grocery store.
Alright, alright, alright.

The judge blinked.
Definitely not what she expected.
She was braced for another fight. Instead, she got surrender. God flipped
the script.
She looked at Miles.
"If you're willing to uproot your life to be close to your daughter... then
your daughter deserves more of you."
Boom.
Gavel down.
Love won.

Miles got more holidays. More summer weeks.
More of the beautiful, ordinary days you never write on a calendar but
feel in your bones.
Case closed. Hearts full.

As we walked out of the courthouse, the air felt lighter.
We weren't fighting anymore.
We were following.

There was just one little issue.
Austin wasn't cheap. Paying Texas rent and a Michigan mortgage?
Cute. As in: impossible.

So I prayed.
Not desperate this time—just steady.
"Okay, Lord. You said go.
We're going.
But You'll need to sell this house fast."

And wow, did He deliver.
That house flew off the market like it had just been blessed by Chip and Joanna Gaines.
We listed it. Within days—offers. Not one, but two. God didn't just sell our house fast—He showed off.

And remember that duplex we were sure was "the one"—and crushed when it slipped away? Turns out, it would've been a financial disaster. Our realtor said selling it would've been like a root canal without anesthesia—slow, painful, expensive.

Basically, God saying, "Trust Me. You don't want this mess."

That's what a good Father does—protects you, even when you don't see it.

And that's exactly what we felt.

We found a two-bedroom apartment in Austin.
Online. Sight unseen.
Not fancy. Not big. But just right.

We sold what we could.
Packed what we couldn't part with.
And bubble-wrapped the rest like it was going to be jostled by a pack of angry gorillas.
The only thing not bubble-wrapped? My sanity.

Our last night in Michigan, I stood in the empty living room.
The walls still echoed with laughter, late-night talks, and whispered prayers I once thought bounced off the ceiling.

We hadn't even lived there that long.
But looking back, I can see it now.
This house wasn't random.
It was a setup.
God gave us just enough time to make it beautiful.
Then sell it.
The profit became the down payment for Texas.
What felt temporary to us?
Strategic to Him all along.
It wasn't random. It was just the setup—God lining up Texas long before we packed a single box.

Even the middle of the floor had memories—
that's where I taught our dog Bentley his circus tricks.
Rescued under a bridge.
Smartest dog in America. Point a finger—"Bang Bang!"—and he'd drop like a shaggy cowboy in a Western. Honestly, Bentley had more tricks than I did.

Bentley adored Miles.
And of course, Bentley was coming with us.
Thankfully, the new apartment allowed genius-level dogs.

Honestly, Bentley seemed more prepared for Texas than I did.

I pressed my hand to the wall.
Said goodbye to the me who had lived there.
The me who was still learning to trust.
Then I whispered one more: *"Thank You."*

We walked out the front door.
Not just toward Texas.
Toward a new season.
Toward the kind of faith that packs up everything, trusts the GPS named Jesus, and just goes.

We thought the hard part was over.
We thought the battles were behind us.

Spoiler: We thought we were heading into sunshine and tacos. Instead, Texas held blessings, battles, and plot twists big enough to make Bentley drop mid-trick.

END OF CHAPTER REFLECTION

1. Ever made a move that felt impossible—then watched God work it out better than you planned?

2. When has a "no" in your life turned out to be God's protection in disguise?

3. How do you know when peace is really from God—and not just wishful thinking?

CHAPTER 45

Jalapeños, Jesus, And a Girl Who Chose Faith

Finding Home, Fighting for Hearts, and Watching God Plant Seeds That Refuse to Die

We arrived in Austin with two things:
A two-bedroom apartment.
And a mountain of bubble wrap.

"Okay, Lord," I prayed as we dragged in boxes.
"We're here. Now what?"

Austin greeted us with blazing sun, endless traffic, and construction cones arranged like abstract art exhibits.

But in the middle of the heat and chaos, it felt like God was handing us a reset button.

The apartment wasn't fancy.
But it was ours.
Cold air. Fresh paint. No mysterious odors left behind by previous tenants.
It felt like a holy reset.

Bentley plopped down by Miles' recliner like, *Yep, this is home now. Someone bring me a snack.*

Miles wasted no time becoming Road Warrior Dad.
Every weekend, he drove to San Antonio for Maddie.
Football games. Marching band competitions. Talent shows.
The man could've gotten a NASCAR sponsorship—except with fewer pit crews and more trumpet solos.

We'd pull into the school lot and see Maddie wave, her trumpet flashing in the sun. And just like that, the miles melted away.
Watching Miles beam in those bleachers?
That wasn't just a proud dad moment.
That was a miracle with a marching band soundtrack.

Soon, we found a church that felt more like a family reunion than a building.
We joined a small group—the kind of people who pray with you, bring casseroles, and also know how to wield jumper cables.

Miles immediately claimed the kitchen like a Food Network finalist.
Think Guy Fieri—only with better hair and far fewer flame-covered shirts.

Sausage-and-cheese stuffed jalapeños. Beef and broccoli so good it deserved its own Yelp page.
Miracles and marinades, baby.

By small group night, we were a potluck machine.
Miles brought the flavor.
I brought dessert (nobody beats me... except maybe my mom).
And the paper plates.
Because no one wants to wash eight people's dishes on a Tuesday night.

Everyone else brought their specialties—casseroles, dips, and that one mystery dish nobody could pronounce but everyone ate anyway.

There were three other couples in our small group: Matthew and Jenni, Tim and Liz, and Scott and Yolanda.

From the very first night, it felt like family. The kind of people who make you laugh until your cheeks hurt—and then pray with you like it's second nature.

Our group wasn't just about Bible study and casseroles.
We hit the streets together, too—packing up gift bags of essentials and heading downtown to the homeless shelters.
Maddie came with us, wide-eyed and willing.
It was holy in its ordinariness—watching her hand out socks, toothbrushes, granola bars.

She was learning what I was still learning: helping others the way Jesus did doesn't always look grand. Sometimes it just looks like showing up.

And Jenni? She quickly became my instant Austin soul sister.
I loved her smile and her laugh.
We prayed.
We laughed until we cried.
We survived Black Friday together—two caffeinated raccoons in yoga pants hunting for deals.

That small group gave us roots in Austin. Friends who prayed with us, fed us, and reminded us we weren't alone.

But the biggest miracle wasn't the apartment.
Or the church.
Or even those heavenly jalapeños.

It was Maddie.

Every other weekend, she came to church with us.
Quiet. Watching. Listening.
But she was there.

One night, curled up on the couch, she said, "I need to talk."
She told me again why her mom had stopped believing—how someone she loved had died, even after desperate prayers.
And how that broke her faith.

I met her eyes and asked what I'd asked God a thousand times:
"Why is there so much hurt?"

We flipped to Ephesians 6.
Talked about spiritual armor—not swords and shields, but truth, peace, faith.

> *"Put on the full armor of God, so that you can take your stand against the devil's schemes."*
>
> — **Ephesians 6:11**
>
> ❧ **God doesn't hand out plastic shields.**
> His armor is the real thing—strong enough for a fourteen-year-old with questions and a heart ready to believe.

Then I told her what I'd learned the hard way:

"This world is loud and dark sometimes. Bad things happen—not because God isn't good, but because there's real evil at work here. Satan is roaming around, trying to mess up our lives.
Trying to use his schemes to keep us from trusting Jesus."

"That's why God gives us armor. Protection for when life feels like it's falling apart.
And one day? This fight will end. Death won't win forever."

"God always hears you," I added.
"Even when the answer hurts. Sometimes we won't understand until Heaven.

Sometimes He lets us see sooner."

Something softened in her eyes.
A seed planted.

> *"He who began a good work in you will carry it on to completion until the day of Christ Jesus."*
>
> **— Philippians 1:6**
>
> ❧ **God doesn't plant seeds just to abandon them.**
> He keeps watering until they grow.

Weeks later, Maddie stunned us with five little words—
words that almost made us drop our forks:
"I want to be baptized."

Holy ground, right there between the mashed potatoes and green beans.
It didn't **look** holy—but it was. God Himself had pulled up a chair at that table.

But reality hit.
She was fourteen now.
Her mom had the final say.
And she said no.

The word hung in the air. Maddie's shoulders slumped. And just like that, our holy dinner-table moment turned into a spiritual plot twist nobody wanted.

I reached for her hand and waited until her eyes met mine.
"You already belong to Him," I said softly.
"Baptism is beautiful, but Jesus already claimed you."

She blinked away tears, jaw set with determination.

"I'll do it when I'm eighteen."

I grinned through my own tears.
"And we'll be in the front row—cheering like it's the Super Bowl."

Because faith had already taken root.
Fierce. Beautiful.
Growing in a girl brave enough to believe—even when life gave her every reason not to.

And God?
He was just getting started.

We thought Maddie's faith was safe. But a tug-of-war was coming—one that would test every prayer we'd ever prayed and prove just how far God would go to fight for her.

END OF CHAPTER REFLECTION

1. Have you ever found yourself asking the same hard question Maddie asked—"Why *do bad things happen to good people?*" How has your perspective shifted as you've walked with God through your own pain?

2. What does it look like to really show up for someone you love—even when it's inconvenient, even when it costs you something?

3. Can you think of a time when someone you love took even a tiny step toward faith—and it stirred something in you too? How did their courage shape your own walk with God?

CHAPTER 46

Texas, Tacos, and Tug-of-War

When the Fight Isn't Yours Alone—Standing Firm, Letting God Lead, and Watching Him Write the Next Plot Twist

We moved to Texas for a promise.
What we didn't realize?
That promise came with tacos, triple-digit heat, and a plot twist the size
of... well... Texas.

Life was finally settling.
Me, Miles, and Maddie—same state, same air, same chaotic highways.

I started my new job.
It was actually going well.
We were breathing again.
Well... mostly.

The apartment?
Cute at first.
Now? A shoebox with neighbors who thought midnight Zumba was a
lifestyle.
Air vents delivering mystery smells I never ordered.
And a pantry so small, cereal-box Jenga became a legitimate sport.

I craved a house.
A porch swing.
A backyard.
Space for Bentley to chase his tail without ricocheting off the furniture.

But Austin's housing market?
Pure gladiator arena.
We'd find a house, fall in love...
Gone before we even made it to the front door.

House hunting in Austin? Like trying to adopt a unicorn while fifty other people are waving cash.

After heartbreak #76, I slammed the laptop shut and sighed.
"Okay, God. I get it. It's a no. For now."

Then the phone rang.
Miles answered.
His face went pale—like the phone had just announced we were tributes in the next Hunger Games sequel.

His ex-wife had lost her job in San Antonio.
She planned to move back to Michigan—with Maddie.

"You moved her across the country," Miles said, jaw tight. He paused. "And now you're taking her back?"

We were stunned.
We'd just built a life here.
Maddie had friends. A school she loved. A band she adored.
She was finally asking questions about God.
Faith was starting to take root.

And now this—like someone yanking up a brand-new sapling.

Going back to Michigan?
Not an option.
No jobs. No plan. No boots for scraping snowdrifts.
And zero desire to leave 75-degree Decembers.

We couldn't go back.
And we weren't about to let her go.

So we stood our ground.
Back to court.

Only this time, we weren't fighting to stay in Michigan.
We were fighting for Maddie to stay in Texas.

Maddie's mom wasn't thrilled. And her stepdad—who, by the way, never
even moved to Texas—wasn't exactly cheering us on either.

But we weren't fighting them.
We were fighting for her.

Our Bible study group became a mini army.
Prayers poured in.
People reminded us that God shows up in courtrooms too.

Miles poured out his heart every night.
Terrified of losing her again.

One night, his voice cracked as he whispered, "I can't do this again. I can't
lose her."

I squeezed his hand.
"This isn't our battle. It's His."

And God didn't show up with lightning bolts or burning bushes.
He showed up with peace.

The kind that sneaks in quietly.
The kind that holds you steady when everything's shaking.

> "And the peace of God, which transcends all understanding, will guard your hearts and your minds in Christ Jesus."
> — Philippians 4:7
>
> ❧ Peace that doesn't make sense still makes you steady.

Skeptics might say it was just determination or inner grit.
But I knew better—that calm wasn't mine.
It was borrowed peace, and it came straight from Him.

We didn't know what the judge would say.
But we knew Who had the final word.

So we stood.
Shaky but stubborn.
Broken but brave.
Believing love would lead the way.

And what God had planned next?
Let's just say...
Texas-sized miracle incoming.

I thought the courtroom would be the battlefield.
But God had already drawn up His playbook—and He was about to call the first play during a college football game.

END OF CHAPTER REFLECTION

1. Have you ever tried to bulldoze your way into something—forcing doors open, white-knuckling your way through, convinced you could make it happen—only to realize God was quietly saying, "Not yet"? What shifted when you finally let go?

2. When life yanks the rug out—circumstances, people, or even your own fears—what keeps you steady? What's your anchor when everything else feels wobbly?

3. Sometimes the fight isn't for us. It's for someone we love. Have you ever stood your ground for somebody else? Where did your strength come from in that moment?

CHAPTER 47

The Night God Called the Final Play

How a Football Game, a Whispered Promise, and a Living Room Victory Lap Taught Me to Trust Him for the Win

I didn't think a college football game would change my life.
But one December night, between a touchdown and a popcorn avalanche, God whispered something I'll never forget.

First, you need to know this about Miles: the man bleeds green.
He graduated from Michigan State, and Spartans football isn't a hobby—it's a personality trait.

December 5, 2015. Big Ten Championship Game.
Recliner tilted like a throne, snacks stacked like a fortress, eyes locked on the TV as if the fate of the free world hinged on a first down.
He was yelling at the quarterback.
Arguing with refs who couldn't hear him.
Coaching from the couch with the confidence of a man certain ESPN would air his wisdom—if only they knew.

Passion level? Nuclear.

I was one bad call away from filing a noise complaint... on my own husband.

So I retreated to the bedroom like a refugee escaping a sports war zone.

In the quiet, the yelling from the living room felt almost comical. But underneath it, sadness crept in—not about football, but about Miles. The fear of losing Maddie again, of walking through that heartbreak twice.

I whispered a prayer that felt almost too small to bother God with.
"Lord, I know it's just a game... but could You let Michigan State win? Just give Miles a win tonight?"

And then I heard it.
Clear. Firm. Like He'd been waiting for me to ask.

Just like Michigan State will win tonight, that's how you will win in court.

And trust me, I get it—football prophecy? Really? Even I questioned it for a second. But then it came again, calm and steady. I'd never heard anything so clear. Not my thought. Not a pep talk. God.

I sat there frozen. Then tiptoed back to the living room and sank into the couch like nothing happened.

"How much time's left?" I asked.
"Not much," Miles groaned. "We're toast."

But I knew better.

Final minutes. Michigan State got the ball.
First down. Another. Another.

Miles paced, barking at the screen like he had a direct line to the quarterback's helmet.

Then—BOOM.

The stadium erupted on TV, but it might as well have been our living room.
Crowd roaring. Band blaring. Commentators losing their minds.
End zone. Touchdown. Seconds left. Spartans win!

Miles launched off the couch like a firework.
"YES! GO GREEN!!"

He fist-pumped. Chest-bumped imaginary teammates. Nearly did a Lambeau Leap onto the coffee table.

I just smiled quietly. Because I already knew.

For the fact-checkers: this is 100% real. December 5, 2015. Michigan State versus Iowa. Big Ten Championship. Twenty-two plays. Nine minutes. With just 27 seconds left, LJ Scott barreled into the end zone—dragging what felt like half the Iowa defense with him. Michigan State 16, Iowa 13. Last-second touchdown.

Could you call it coincidence? Sure. But what are the odds that God had already whispered it to me minutes before it happened? That's not luck—that's a promise.

It felt like God had strapped on a headset and called the final play Himself.

When Miles finally collapsed into the recliner, breathless from his living room victory lap, I said, "God told me Michigan State would win. And that's how we'll win in court."

He blinked. "Or maybe the Spartans are just good?"

I grinned. "Nope. A promise."

That night wasn't just football.
It was heaven whispering, *I've got this.*

And whenever doubt tried to sneak in later, I went back to that moment. Because when God whispers? He wins.

And if I ever forget?
There's still a popcorn kernel—forever wedged in our couch cushions—to remind me.

But God's promises don't always unfold like a touchdown. Sometimes they come wrapped in a loss—only to reveal a miracle hiding in the word *however.*

END OF CHAPTER REFLECTION

1. Have you ever had God speak right into your heart—at a time or place you didn't expect? Maybe even in a moment that felt too ordinary—like folding laundry, sitting in traffic, or watching a football game?

2. Can you remember a time when God gave you reassurance before a hard season? How did that moment steady you when everything else felt shaky?

3. Where in your life right now do you most need to hear God's voice—and simply trust what He says?

CHAPTER 48

The God of the "However"

When a Courtroom Loss Turned into a Texas-Sized Miracle—Exactly the Way He Said It Would

Same courtroom.

Same judge.

Same "I might throw up in my purse" feeling.

Déjà vu—but this time, it felt like God Himself had already stepped into that courtroom ahead of us.

And the stakes? Sky-high.

We'd flown back to Michigan for the hearing.

Michigan. In January.

Just in case we needed a reminder of the cold, gray stuff we'd left behind for Texas sunshine.

Because the case had never been officially transferred to a Texas court, it stayed under the same Michigan judge. She already knew Miles' history—and that he was willing to do whatever it took for Maddie to have access to both of her parents.

Maddie was thriving—friends, routine, faith blooming.
And now a single gavel bang could rip it all away.

I sat behind Miles and his attorney, next to his sweet mom, Judy.
Across the room, Miles' ex-wife smiled like she was already hanging a
"Welcome Home, Maddie!" banner.

Earlier over lunch, I'd clutched my coffee like a flotation device.
"Judy," I whispered, "this sounds crazy, but during the Michigan State
game, God told me, 'Just like they'll win tonight, that's how you'll win in
court.'"

She gave me a kind nod. I couldn't tell if she believed me—or was just
being kind. But I didn't care.

I knew what I heard, and I was hanging onto that whisper like it was my
only parachute.

The judge started reading her decision.
Calm. Even. Deadly serious.

Then—gut punch:
"I find that the plaintiff has just barely proven that the domicile should
be changed to Michigan."

Wait. WHAT?

My ears buzzed.
The fluorescent lights blurred.
My stomach swan-dived to my shoes.

We... lost?

Had I made this up? Mistaken desperation for God's voice?

And trust me, I was already bracing for the skeptic inside me to scream, "*See? You just made it all up.*"

I looked at Miles—shoulders slumped, jaw tight.
Judy went still beside me.
Across the aisle, the ex-wife looked like she'd just won the Showcase Showdown on *The Price is Right.*

But God... You said!

And then—

"However..."

Y'all.

That single word hit me like caffeine straight to the soul.
Best. Word. Ever.

I wanted to stitch it on a quilt, hang it over the mantle, maybe even tattoo it on my forehead.
Forget baby names—our next dog? *However.*

Imagine yelling, "However, sit!" at the dog park.

We all straightened in unison.

The judge went on.
"We must consider what's in the best interest of the child..."

One factor after another—pointing toward Texas.
Every sentence a breadcrumb on a holy trail.

Finally, the line that made my heart stop—in the best way:
"I find that the best interest of the child is to remain in her current school district in San Antonio."

BOOM.

The opposing attorney shot to her feet.
"Wait—are you saying the plaintiff won—but the child stays in Texas?"

"Yes," the judge said, cool as ever. "The child must remain in her school.
Therefore, domicile cannot be executed."

Translation?
We won.

Air rushed back into my lungs.
Miles blinked, then grinned, then blinked again like his brain was trying
to reboot.

God had done what He promised.
Whisper to verdict.

And the poetry of it?
That football game had looked lost too.
Miles had called it over. Said we were toast.
But in the final moments, Michigan State pulled off the impossible.

Now, we'd just lived the replay—in a courtroom.

> *"Many are the plans in a person's heart, but it is the Lord's purpose*
> *that prevails."*
> — **Proverbs 19:21**
>
> ❧ **Courtrooms write verdicts. God writes the story.**

Back in Texas, I crashed into Bible study like I was holding a golden ticket.
Told the whole story, every God-woven detail.

255

Jenni tilted her head. "So because Michigan State won, you knew you'd win?"
I grinned. "Not because they won.
Because God said they would.
And He tied it to our victory.
And then He did it—exactly like He said."

That whisper?
That wild, middle-of-a-football-game whisper?
It was real.

It changed everything.

I didn't just believe in God's existence anymore.
I believed in His voice.
I'd heard it.
I'd trusted it.
And I'd seen it play out—verdict and all.

And once you've seen God show up like that, you start noticing Him everywhere—
in the big moments, the small nudges...
and soon, in a whisper from my closet that would shake me to my core.

END OF CHAPTER REFLECTION

1. Ever had that sinking feeling you lost—only to realize later God was setting you up for a win you didn't see coming?

2. Waiting can stretch your faith thinner than diner coffee. Can you think of a time you almost gave up, but somehow kept holding on? Who (or what) helped you?

3. We all have our own "however" moments— the plot twists where God rewrites the ending. What's yours?

CHAPTER 49

When God Fixes Zippers and Blows Your Mind

The Small, Ordinary Moments Where Heaven Steps In—Just to Remind You He's Here

After the courtroom miracle, I started seeing God everywhere.
Big miracles. Small nudges.
And apparently... in the fashion accessories section.

Yes. Zippers.

I own this one blue pencil skirt. It's perfect.
Perfect color. Perfect fit.
Perfect—until the zipper decides to audition for a horror movie. Think *Jaws*, but the shark is hiding in your hip.

If I'm calm and on time? Works fine.
If I'm late, sweating like a sinner in a sauna, praying for a parking spot at church? That zipper turns into a steel-trap escape room with no survivors.

One Sunday, I'm late. Again.

I yank. I twist. I attempt an Olympic-level backbend, yanking up, down, sideways—pretty sure the judges gave me a 2.3.

Then came the full cardio workout: hopping, shimmying, and one move that suspiciously resembled the electric slide.

The zipper? Stuck in its own teeth.
Unmoved. Cold. Heartless.
Mocking me from the waistline—like it knew I was late for church.

Finally, I mutter, *"Lord... this is ridiculous. But please. I need help."*

Pause. I tried again, fully believing it would zip up.

ZIP.

Like butter on a hot skillet.

I just stood there blinking, half-expecting a choir of angels to hold up scorecards: *10/10—divine intervention.*

The next week? Same skirt. Same fight.
"Okay, Lord. Let's do this again."

ZIP.

Perfect glide. I was speechless. That could not have been a coincidence.

At this point, I'm convinced heaven has a "Wardrobe Malfunctions" department.

Eventually, I took the skirt to a tailor for a new zipper—I couldn't keep bugging heaven's wardrobe desk every time I wanted to wear it. But deep down I know: if I ever needed Him in a crunch, that zipper would zip.

Then came the blow dryer incident.

Ordinary morning. Shower done. Hair dripping. Time ticking.
I press the button.

Nothing.

Switch outlets. Juggle cords. Bang it like a bad arcade game.
Nada. Somewhere in the distance, Pac-Man wept.

I try the old "slap-it-until-it-fears-you" method.
Nothing. Just silence—like the dryer was filing for early retirement.

Finally, I plop down on the hallway floor. Wet hair, robe half-tied, looking like a raccoon who just lost a bar fight.
Big sigh.
"God, I know it's just a blow dryer. But I need this thing to work. Please. Just once more."

I press the button.

WHIRRRRRRRR.

It roared to life like angelic tech support had just rebooted it from heaven's IT department. Honestly, it sounded like a jet engine. If I'd had a cape, I could've taken flight.

And I cried.

Not because my hair survived humidity (though that's a miracle on its own).
I cried because it felt like God was saying, *Yes, I see you. Even here. Even now. Even when you look like a soggy Pomeranian on your hallway floor.*

That night, I bought a new blow dryer.
Because as much as I loved that holy hair miracle, I wasn't about to turn God into my personal appliance repair hotline.

Maybe it was coincidence. Maybe it was timing. But in that moment, I knew what it meant to me.

But out of curiosity, I tried the old one again.
Dead. Totally dead.
Like a middle school science project that had served its purpose and then gone straight to the grave.

It only worked that one time.

The one time I asked.
And believed.
And God said, *"Okay. Watch this."*

> *"Now faith is the assurance of things hoped for, the conviction of things not seen."*
>
> **— Hebrews 11:1**
>
> ✦ **Faith isn't about seeing—it's about trusting.**
> It's holding tight to what God promised—even before it shows up.

Because that's who He is.
He's not only the God of burning bushes and parted seas—He's the God of zippers, blow dryers, parking spots, and desperate hallway prayers.

The God who sees you in the chaos.
Who leans down and whispers, *Yes, child. I've been here all along.*

That hallway morning reminded me: faith isn't just for mountains and seas—it's for zippers and blow dryers too.

And once you start spotting Him in the little things, you can't help but recognize Him in the big ones—

even if they show up somewhere between a Buc-ee's billboard and a dead armadillo on I-35.

END OF CHAPTER REFLECTION

1. Have you ever had one of those tiny moments that felt tailor-made by God—so personal, so specific, there's no way to explain it except He *was there?*

2. Is there something in your life right now that feels too small—or too ordinary—to pray about? What might shift if you invited God into it anyway?

3. How would your faith look different if you actually started expecting Him to show up in the ordinary stuff—the errands, the messes, the Tuesday mornings?

CHAPTER 50

The Whisper on I-35

When God Drops a Promise in the Middle of Traffic—
and Asks You to Trust Him for the Miles Ahead

I didn't expect God to speak to me right between a Buc-ee's billboard and a dead armadillo on I-35. But there He was.

Miles was driving. I was staring out the window, watching Texas trees blur into brown-green smudges, when I heard it.
Not audibly.
But clear as day:

You will live in San Antonio. You won't need this long drive anymore. Do not worry. I've cleared the path.

I blinked. Looked at Miles. My heart skipped—not from fear, but from that deep, *this-is-God* kind of knowing.
"Miles," I said softly. "God just told me we're moving to San Antonio."

He didn't even flinch.
Just nodded like I'd asked if he wanted tacos for dinner.
"Okay, Dear."

This man. If I told him I saw a burning bush on the exit ramp, he'd probably grab marshmallows, a camp chair, and ask if we should bring a guitar too.

Here's why it mattered so much:

The court battle was over.
Maddie was safe in San Antonio—friends, school, band, even faith starting to bloom.

But one problem loomed.

Miles' ex-wife still hadn't found a job there.
And if she moved for work?
The judge's orders were clear: Maddie couldn't stay unless one of us lived there too.

So it wasn't just about being tired of the long drive.
We had to move to San Antonio if we wanted Maddie to stay in Texas.
Without one of us there to anchor her to her school, she'd be allowed to move wherever her mom's job took her.

And if she wasn't in her San Antonio school anymore, that could put the judge's order at risk—maybe even open the door for her domicile to be switched back to Michigan.

We'd wanted to live in San Antonio all along. But my job was in Austin. Miles worked from home, so he could set up shop anywhere with Wi-Fi and coffee. Me? I had to physically show up where my job was planted.

No openings with my company in San Antonio. Not even a "maybe someday."

So we stayed put.
Grateful—but stretched thin.

Until that drive.
Until God said, *I've got this.*

You'd think I'd rest in that promise.
Ha. Nope.
I started "helping."

Refreshed job boards like an Olympic sprinter.
Typed "San Antonio" so many times my laptop started sending me ads for the River Walk.

Every posting felt wrong.

And still nothing. Just a gnawing sense that pressing "apply" wasn't the assignment.

Weeks passed. Then months.
Still no job. Still no house. Still that 90-minute weekend drive.

One Friday night, somewhere near New Braunfels, I sighed hard enough to fog the windshield.
Miles kept his eyes on the road while I spiraled out loud.

"Maybe I didn't hear Him right. Maybe I just wanted it so badly, I made it up—like the time I swore God told me to buy those clearance shoes."

I shot him a look.
"I know. He didn't."

Miles glanced over.
"But... you said God told you," he said, voice cracking just enough to split me wide open.

He had believed me—fully, quietly. And here I was, unraveling, stitch by stitch—like bargain yarn that never should've been a sweater in the first place.

"I did hear Him," I said quickly. "I just don't get why nothing's happening yet."

But under all my doubt, a whisper stayed steady:
God hadn't changed.
I was just impatient.

We want miracles like Amazon Prime—fast, trackable, and preferably with free returns.

But God?
He's not late.
He's just busy arranging puzzle pieces we can't see yet.

The promise hadn't failed.
It wasn't expired.
It was just unfolding.

> *"But if we hope for what we do not yet have, we wait for it patiently."*
> — **Romans 8:25**
>
> ❧ **Real hope means trusting God's timing.**
> Even when the waiting feels endless... and the road ahead looks the same mile after mile.

And when it was ready?
We'd know.

Because the God who whispered on I-35 wasn't done speaking.

I just didn't realize His next move would come disguised as... two job offers.

END OF CHAPTER REFLECTION

1. Have you ever felt rock-solid sure God was leading you—only to second-guess yourself when nothing happened on your timeline? What did that waiting stretch actually teach you?

2. How do you handle it when someone else leans on your faith? Does it feel like a holy honor... or like you're one shaky prayer away from letting them down?

3. Why is the waiting part always harder than the believing part— even after God's already come through? (Seriously, you'd think we'd learn by now.)

CHAPTER 51

The Door I Almost Missed

When the "Less Impressive" Option is Exactly Where God Hides Your Biggest Miracle

I thought I was climbing the ladder. Turns out, God handed me a shovel— not to bury my career, but to plant something I didn't see coming.

When God gives you a promise, you'd think the only job is to believe Him. And it is—except for the hardest part: waiting.

Not hustling.
Not panic-refreshing job boards at 2 a.m.
Not tweaking my résumé seventeen times with fonts that shouted, *Hire me! I'm dazzling and emotionally stable!* (The emotionally stable part was debatable.)
Just... wait.

Waiting is not my spiritual gift.
I'm a fixer. A doer.
The "Oh, we're moving to San Antonio? Great—I'll find a job, a house, a dentist, and organic bananas by Friday" kind of girl.

So yes, I believed God.

But I also refreshed job boards like I was tracking a NASA launch countdown.

Then one day, my manager pulled me aside.
His face said, Brace yourself.

"Christine, the department you manage—it's being dissolved."

Cue Coldplay. In my head, I was boxing office supplies in slow motion, whispering goodbye to the stapler. Tragic, really.

But then—plot twist.
"You're not losing your job. We still want you. We just... don't know what you'll do yet."

So... not fired.
Just professionally "rebranded."

And that's when the lightbulb flickered.
Didn't we talk about San Antonio once?

"Hey," I said casually, "what if I worked remotely?"

One innocent question turned into a full-on pitch.
I built a binder. Tabs. Charts. Color-coded dividers. Basically, a business plan for *Christine, Inc.*

Then I strutted into the top executive's office like Elle Woods in *Legally Blonde*—if caffeine counted as confidence—and pitched that thing like it was *Shark Tank.*

My idea? A brand-new nationwide training role I'd create from scratch. Travel. Big ideas. Sprinkling sales magic like Mary Poppins with a travel rewards card.

And the wild part? They approved it.

But there were catches.
Intense travel.
Only guaranteed for a year, and then they'd "reevaluate."
Corporate-speak for: Don't get too comfortable.

And honestly? I was tired of shaky foundations.
We'd lived in "uncertain" long enough.
I wanted solid.

Still—it was a door.
Not a grand, wide-open barn door.
More like a doggy door you crawl through, praying you don't get stuck
halfway with your dignity in the air.

And something in me hesitated.
That gut-twist you get in the fitting room when a cute dress makes you
want to cry. (Ladies, you know.)

The very next day, my phone rang.
A manager from another department.

We hadn't talked in months, but he remembered my San Antonio dream.
"Well," he said, "something just opened."
No travel. No overtime. Steady.
Not flashy... but solid.

Cue dramatic music.
Slow zoom on my face.

This job? It was a step back.
It was the same role I had in Michigan.
Not the glamorous "new chapter" I'd envisioned.
More like the professional version of: *Surprise! You're back where you started.*

I hung up thinking, *Oh no, I've worked too hard to go backward.*

And then I noticed—
the gut-twist was gone.
In its place? Peace.

I decided to drive down to San Antonio, just to check it out.
To see if the office felt like somewhere I could belong.

I walked in... and it felt like home.
Not lightning bolts.
Just soul-deep ease.
Like your grandma's kitchen when biscuits are rising and you don't have to do dishes.

But still, I wrestled.

Option one: sparkle, promotions, hotel shampoos, corporate dreams—but uncertain.
Option two: quiet, humble, familiar—and steady.
Basically: promotions versus peace.

I laid it all out for Miles. Charts and everything.
He just nodded and said, "Take the one that feels right."

So I prayed.
"God, I don't need fireworks. I just need You."

And I knew.
The twist in my gut with the first job? That was God waving a giant red flag: *Don't do it, girl.*

The second job didn't come with perks.
It came with space.

The space I needed to breathe.
The space I needed...
to receive the biggest miracle of my life.

So I said no to the job I built from scratch.
And yes to the one that felt like home.

When I told my Austin manager, he blinked like I'd just said I was joining
the circus.
"You created your own job. You pitched it. And now... you're walking
away?"

I just smiled.
Didn't explain. Didn't try to make him understand.
Because in my head I already knew the truth: this wasn't just a job—it
was God's promise.

And that was okay. He didn't need to get it.

Because I'd finally learned—
you don't need everyone to understand the whisper.
You just need to follow it.

And the moment I stepped through that humble little doorway, I had no
idea I was walking straight toward the biggest miracle of my life.

END OF CHAPTER REFLECTION

1. Have you ever stared down two doors—the shiny, Instagram-worthy door and the plain, creaky one—and felt your spirit tug toward the creaky one? Which did you choose?

2. How does God usually get your attention—through peace, people, prayer, Scripture, or that gut feeling you can't shake (like heartburn, only holier)?

3. Can you think of a time when what looked like a "step backward" ended up being the setup for something way better than you could've planned?

CHAPTER 52

Goodbye Austin, Hello Home

How God Used Closed Doors, Bad Carpet, and Wild Paint Colors to Walk Us Straight into a Promise

Ever look back and think, *Wow... God just saved me from myself?*
Like, *"Thank You, Lord, for slamming that door before I bought a house with floral carpet and permanent emotional damage."*

That's what Austin was.

At the time, it felt like chaos.
Closed doors. Missed houses. Ghosted prayers.
Now? I see it.
Not chaos. *Choreography.*

God was directing every step.
And me?
I was the backup dancer who missed every rehearsal—and probably tripped over the fog machine.

Those dead ends in Austin?
Not roadblocks.
Holy detours.

If we'd bought a house there, we would've been stuck—financially, emotionally, geographically.
And worst of all, probably trapped with a mauve living room.
There's no recovering from a mauve living room.

But God saw what we couldn't.
The plan wasn't Austin.
It was San Antonio.

Once I landed the new job—the one with zero sparkle but all the peace—
we jumped in.
House hunting, baby.

We were revved up, hopeful, and just naïve enough to think it would be easy.
It wasn't.

Buying a house in a hot market is not cute.
It's *The Hunger Games*—but with fewer snacks, more paperwork, and instead of Katniss Everdeen, you're up against Chad and Madison with their $10,000-over-asking-price offers.

You find the one.
You're already picturing stockings on the mantle, Bentley playing in the yard.
Then—POOF. Gone.
Snatched away faster than your dignity in a spin class.

We lost so many imaginary Christmas trees that way.

I started wondering if we'd made it all up.
Was this a promise... or just Zillow fever?

I refreshed listings like it was a part-time job with zero benefits.
"God, did You forget my address? Or worse... did I hear You wrong?"

And then we found it.

A two-story, three-bedroom home with... let's say "personality."
The walls looked like a toddler on a sugar high had gone full Picasso—
random swirls, colors that should never meet in nature.
The carpet had salsa stains—and stories I didn't want to hear.
The kitchen appliances? I'm pretty sure Nixon baked cookies in that oven
during Watergate.
Even the light fixtures looked tired, like they were one flicker away from
retirement.

But the backyard...
A gorgeous wooden covered porch. Palm trees. Quiet breeze.
I could already picture it—sunny mornings with coffee in hand, the ceiling
fan spinning lazily above, the kind of peace you can almost taste.

And then—
that nudge in my spirit.
A whisper that stopped me in my tracks: *You've arrived.*

It was like the air shifted—warm, steady, certain.
My shoulders dropped.
The noise in my head went still.
For the first time in months, I felt... home.

I glanced at Miles, ready to explain the whole God-just-whispered-to-me
thing.
But I didn't need to. He trusts me when I say God spoke—even if it sounds
crazy.
He just nodded, like, *Okay then, this is it.*

Then he looked at the walls. Back at me.
"Another renovation?" he deadpanned.
I grinned. "We've done it before."

He sighed the sigh of a man already mentally loading a Home Depot cart while praying for a Lowe's gift card.

"Fine. But you're not picking the paint this time. That last gray was purple."

We made an offer.
It was accepted.
Just like that—it was ours.

Because the house wasn't "turn-key" enough for the HGTV crowd—what with the salsa-stained carpet, toddler-Picasso walls, and appliances straight out of a Nixon administration garage sale—nobody else wanted it.

Which meant we got it at a price that didn't make our bank account hyperventilate.

We took the profit from selling our Michigan house, rolled up our sleeves, and dove headfirst into transformation mode.

Every wall and floor practically cried out for mercy.

What once resembled a thrift store clearance aisle after a toddler's finger-painting spree began to take on new life—
one sledgehammer swing, one paintbrush stroke, and approximately 47 "we forgot this" trips to Home Depot—where the cashiers were two visits away from putting us on payroll.

Warm, sun-kissed tan on the walls. Rich wood floors flowing through the downstairs.
Upstairs, carpet so soft it felt like walking on a cloud.
Brand-new stainless steel appliances gleaming under cool granite countertops.
Light fixtures that actually worked—without flickering like a horror movie set.

By the end, it didn't just look like a house we'd fixed up.
It felt like home.
Like holy ground.

As if God Himself had stitched something sacred into the very walls.

And we had no idea.
No clue this would be the house.
The place where a miracle would show up.
The one I'd prayed for my whole life.

This wasn't just a new address.
It was a promise fulfilled.
A mission in disguise.
A setup only God could orchestrate.

So we gave thanks—for every closed door, every delay, every weird paint color.
Because each one rerouted us here.
To this exact place.
To the story He was just getting started.

Gratitude trains your heart to spot His fingerprints—even before the masterpiece is finished.

> "Give thanks in all circumstances; for this is God's will for you in Christ Jesus."
>
> — **1 Thessalonians 5:18**
>
> ❧ **Gratitude isn't just polite—it's powerful.**
> It shifts your perspective, even when nothing else has shifted yet.

And just when I thought the miracles were about drywall and backsplash, God decided to show me what He could really do with a paint can.

END OF CHAPTER REFLECTION

1. Have you ever looked back at a slammed door and realized it wasn't rejection at all—it was God saving you from yourself?

2. When has one of your messy, "this is a disaster" seasons ended up turning into something surprisingly beautiful?

3. What's one thing you can thank God for right now—even before you see the miracle show up at your doorstep?

CHAPTER 53

Barely Enough, More Than Enough

The Day God Multiplied My Paint Can

I didn't expect a holy moment in a half-painted bathroom.
But there I was—elbow-deep in lavender paint, talking to God like He was my personal Home Depot hotline.

Some women pray for a husband.
Some pray for a beach vacation.
I was out here praying for paint.

By now, Miles and I were a legit home-reno duo—DIY dream team, powered by takeout pizza, prayer, and Lowe's receipts long enough to wallpaper the house (and possibly deduct from our taxes).

We had our system: he rolled, I trimmed.
Miles attacked walls like he'd been secretly training for the Paint Olympics—smooth, steady, every stripe flawless. Gold medal in "perfect coverage."
Meanwhile, I crouched like a baseboard ninja, edging like my salvation depended on it—and trying not to baptize my leggings in Sherwin-Williams.

That weekend's project? The upstairs bathroom.
Goal: spa vibes.
Reality: pastel dinosaur nursery.

Six paint swatches later, we landed on soft lavender.
It glowed—peaceful, pretty, a little royal. Like someone had melted a candle into the walls.

Miles finished his part and came down holding the paint can like it had barely survived a war.
"There's not much left," he warned. "You'll probably need more. Don't expect miracles."

I raised an eyebrow.
"Don't expect miracles? Have you met my prayer life?"

Upstairs, I checked the can.
Tragic.
Enough to cover a toddler's tricycle. Maybe.

And there it was again—that barely enough feeling.
It had been the theme of my life lately: giving all I had, still coming up short.

I almost grabbed my keys to head for Home Depot.
But instead, I looked up and whispered, *"Okay, God. I know this is small— ridiculously small—but You fed thousands with a kid's lunch. Could You... maybe... stretch this paint too?"*

Brush in. Swipe.
Edges. Doorframe. Vanity. Mirror.
Still paint.

Behind the toilet. (Nothing tests your salvation like that corner. I nearly spoke in tongues.)

Still paint.

Light fixture. Weird nook. Second coat.
Still paint.

I slowed down, almost afraid to breathe.
Stroke. Still paint.

Until the whole bathroom gleamed lavender perfection.

I set the brush down. Stared.
The can wasn't empty.
Not even close.

A holy hush filled that little bathroom.
And I knew—it wasn't about paint. It was about being seen. About God reminding me that He notices even the smallest corners of my life—the places I forget anyone cares about.

Then I did what any rational person does after witnessing a miracle.
I bolted downstairs like I'd just won the lottery.

"MILES!"

He looked up mid-sip, steady and calm, like the rock he always is when I come in hot with drama.

I held up the can.
"You said I'd need more, right?"
"Yeah..."
"Well, I didn't go to the store. Two coats. Bathroom done. Paint left over."

He blinked. Looked at me. Looked at the can.
Like maybe it was about to start floating, blasting the *Hallelujah chorus*, and leading a parade straight to the Promised Land.

And here's the thing—he didn't mock me.
Didn't roll his eyes.
Didn't brush it off.

He just smiled, steady as ever.
Like a man who'd seen enough of God's fingerprints to stop being surprised.
That's Miles—my calm in the chaos, quietly nodding while I narrate the crazy.

That whisper in my spirit—the one saying *I see you, even here*—wasn't luck.
It was love.
The God kind.

Maybe the paint molecules formed a union.
Or maybe... God.

The God who multiplies what little we bring.
Who shows up when we're running on fumes.
Who makes a half-empty can overflow with enough.

That bathroom glowed lavender.
But more than color, it glowed with proof.

Proof that He's in the Red Sea-splitting miracles...
and the tiny, baseboard blessings too.

> *"They all ate and were satisfied. And the disciples picked up twelve basketfuls of broken pieces that were left over."*
> **—Matthew 14:20**
>
> ❧ **God doesn't just give us barely enough—**
> He multiplies, satisfies, and leaves more than we imagined left over.

I didn't know it yet...
but this was just the setup.

Because what came next?
Would blow the lid off every plan I thought I had.

END OF CHAPTER REFLECTION

1. Have you ever had God show up in such a specific, oddly personal way that you couldn't help but think, Okay... *that was just for me?*

2. Where in your life right now do you feel like you're running on "barely enough"? What would it look like to hand that can—whatever it is—over to God and let Him decide how far it goes?

3. When something happens you can't explain on paper, do you lean into wonder... or do you grab a calculator and try to make the math work? Why do you think that is?

CHAPTER 54

The Day God Said My Name

And Rewrote the Story I Thought Was Over

Mother's Day.
Also known as the holiday for crying in church bathrooms and blaming it on "allergies" like it's a seasonal sport.

I thought I'd made peace with it that year.
Polite smile packed.
Emotional duct tape ready.
The plan was simple: survive the cinnamon-scented service, clap for the amazing moms, then go home and eat cake in sweatpants.

But this time? Something felt... off.
Life in San Antonio had finally settled.
House done. Job steady. Evenings free from drywall dust and paint fumes.
For once, I could breathe.

And that's when the ache found me.
The one I thought I'd buried.
The one labeled, *Do Not Open*.

We walked into church.

Flowers everywhere.
Soft music floating.
Cinnamon-roll candles making me want to sob... and carb-load.

I smiled at the women glowing—
Some from motherhood joy.
Some from toddler snot.
Either way... they belonged.

Then the pastor said it:
"For those of you who are grieving today...
For the women who long to be mothers but haven't been able to...
We see you.
God sees you."

Boom.
Game over.
Face crumpled. Mascara tapped out.

This wasn't polite crying.
This was ugly crying—the kind where your husband freezes beside you
like, *Do I pass a tissue or call 911?*

Miles just wrapped his arm around me.
Solid. Steady.
Like he knew there was nothing to fix—just something sacred to hold.

When we got home, I went straight to the porch.
Sat in the sun, hoping it could melt the ache.
But it stuck like glue.

Why would God let me long for this... and never change the story?

Later, I pulled out a box of old photos.
Birthday parties.

Toothless grins.
Christmas mornings.
The step kids I'd loved deeply—even if only for a season.
Kids who slipped through my fingers like smoke.
Nothing stayed.

And I broke.
"I don't get it, God," I whispered.
"Why give me a mother's heart... and never let me live it out?"

Silence.
Then—
A whisper. Gentle. Clear.
"You will be a mom."

I froze.
That wasn't wishful thinking.
That wasn't grief talking.
That was Him.
I knew that voice.

I laughed through tears.
"I'm too old," I said—sassier than you should probably be when talking to the Creator of the Universe.
"Wow, God, where was this announcement ten years ago when I could binge Netflix till 2 a.m., and maybe still had a metabolism?"

Immediately, Sarah came to mind.
Ninety years old. Biology said impossible. But God said otherwise.
She had laughed at the very idea—how could she carry a child at that age?
And yet—God gave her Isaac.
Not because she was young.
Not because her faith was flawless.
(Remember, she laughed too.)
But because God is faithful.

"Christine," He whispered again.
"You will be a mom."

He said my name.

And I broke again.
But this time, peace washed over me.
Not the fake kind that ignores the pain.
The kind that sits beside you and whispers, *Hold on. There's more to the story.*

I didn't post about it.
Didn't slap it on a vision board.
Didn't even tell Miles.
But I knew—if I had, he would've believed me.
He always does.
If I say God spoke, he doesn't need proof. My word is enough.

So I tucked it away.
Not as grief anymore.
As a promise.

God hadn't said *baby.*
He said *mom.*

And I'd learned enough by now to know—
When God speaks, He means it.
Maybe it would be adoption.
Maybe fostering.
Maybe something I couldn't even imagine yet.

I didn't know how or when.
But I believed Him.
Wobbly. Wide-eyed.
But I believed.

> *"For no word from God will ever fail."*
>
> —Luke 1:37
>
> 𝄞 **His promises don't come with expiration dates.**
> If He said it, He'll do it—even if the timing looks impossible.

And what I didn't know then?

God was already putting the miracle in motion.

Not months later. Not years later.

It would start with something small.

Something I thought was just "volunteering."

Something as simple as holding a baby.

END OF CHAPTER REFLECTION

1. Have you ever had God speak right in the middle of your pain? What did He say—and how did you know it was Him and not just your own brain doing a pep talk?

2. What dreams have you quietly buried because they felt too impossible? If you cracked that drawer back open, what forgotten hopes — and maybe a few cringey diary entries with hearts over the i's — would tumble out?

3. Can you think of a time God comforted you even when nothing around you changed? How did His presence shift the weight you were carrying?

CHAPTER 55

Discovering Foster Care

(Or, That Time I Dragged My Husband
into Baby-Holding Ministry)

I thought I was signing up to hold babies.
Turns out, I was signing up for a whole new life.

A few weeks after that Mother's Day promise, I saw it. A post online:
"Volunteers needed to hold newborns born to drug-addicted mothers.
These babies need love, warmth, someone to hold them."

My heart didn't just flutter. It launched into orbit.
This had to be it. My big beginning.

I marched into the living room where Miles was deeply focused on
something spiritual—like ESPN or Harry Potter.
"We are going to hold babies," I announced.

He didn't even blink. Calm. Solid.
"No. We are not going to hold babies," he said flatly.

I narrowed my eyes. "Yes, we are," I shot back. "You're coming with me.
It's a calling."

He studied me for a long second—the way a man studies storm clouds rolling in—then sighed.
"Fine. If you believe it's from God, then okay."

That's Miles. If I say God spoke, he doesn't argue—he just prays I'm not about to volunteer us for something that requires power tools.

At the center, a sweet woman gave us a tour. Tiny newborns. Fragile little souls. Born into pain they didn't choose.
Then she said it:
"Have you ever thought about becoming foster parents? There's such a need right now."

I froze. Looked at Miles.
He looked like he'd just swallowed a bug.

We smiled politely and said the thing every couple says when they want to leave fast without arguing:
"We'll think about it."

And oh, we thought about it.

Miles went first.
"We don't need to foster," he said carefully. "We've got Maddie. Life's good. Why complicate it?"

That's when all the years of trying, praying, aching boiled over.
"You have Maddie," I said quietly.

And then came the crying.
Forget the single cinematic tear down the cheek.
This was a full-blown, blotchy, snotty, hiccupping disaster.

Miles didn't panic. Didn't try to fix it.
He just sat there and let me be a mess.

Something shifted.

"Maybe," I sniffled, "we could foster an older girl. Close to Maddie's age. No diapers. No bottles. Just love."

He didn't leap up with joy. But he nodded. Slowly. Hesitantly.
The nod of a man who counts the cost—and still says yes.

So we started.
Classes. CPR. Mountains of paperwork.

Questions like, "What would you do if a child smeared peanut butter on the ceiling fan?"
Who are these kids?!

Texas wanted every detail—income, marriage, pantry inventory.
I was just waiting for, "And your blood type, ma'am? Also, what's your stance on cargo shorts and kale chips?"

But as we learned, Miles changed in the best way.
The more he heard the stories, the more he saw it. Not red tape. Redemption.
He became the steady one in the storm, the man with the calm voice and the signed forms.

While we waited for our license, I browsed profiles of kids needing homes. Some smiled. Some didn't. All of them beautiful.

At a matching event—just caseworkers and files—we found her: a 15-year-old girl whose shy smile hooked my heart.
But we weren't licensed for her level of care.

"How do we change that?" I asked.
More training.

So we signed up. The kind that dives deeper—how to work with kids carrying heavier stories, deeper wounds.

Part of that training meant volunteering at a residential treatment center. Hard. Holy. Heartbreaking.

And that's where we met him.
A boy who stood out—quick-witted, kind, wise beyond his years.
One afternoon, he looked right at us and asked, "Have you ever thought about adopting a kid?"

He had no idea why we were there.

That night, I whispered to Miles, "Have you ever thought about adopting a boy?"
He smirked—calm, steady. "You want that boy, don't you?"

I did. But the agency said no. Too much for first-timers.
I was crushed.

That night I prayed hard.
"God, You promised I'd be a mom. But all I see are locked doors."

Later, 11:30 p.m. The phone rang.

"Would you take a 13-year-old girl tonight?" the caseworker asked, urgent. "She's a runaway. If we can't place her, she'll disappear again."

I froze. "Could she come Sunday?" I stammered. "We have a gala tomorrow..."

The caseworker's voice was sharp. "We've called every city. No one will take her."

I ran to Miles. "They have nowhere else," I blurted.

Without hesitation, he said, "Send her."

"You're sure?"
He grinned, steady as ever. "Are you sure you can miss your gala?"

Done deal.

"Religion that God our Father accepts as pure and faultless is this: to look after orphans and widows in their distress..."
— **James 1:27**

❧ **True faith shows up in how we care for the vulnerable.** Especially the ones the world overlooks, the ones who have no one else.

And then the real panic hit.
"MILES!" I shrieked. "She's a girl—and the room is blue!"

I tore through that room like Joanna Gaines on espresso. Ripping sheets. Swapping pillows and bedspreads.

The iron hissed as I smoothed the fabric for her bed. The faint scent of fresh cotton filled the air.

"Miles! I need pink curtains!"

"It's midnight," he groaned. "She's not going to care."

"Oh, I care," I said, already out the door.

I found the only 24-hour store open. Bought the pinkest curtains in Texas —possibly illegal in three states.
Back home, I ironed them and hung them like I was prepping for royalty.

Then I stopped. Looked around the room.

The hum of the iron faded.
The quiet was thick.

This was it.
She was coming.
The promise was arriving.

The same God who spoke on Mother's Day was keeping His word—just not in the way I expected.

And somewhere out there, a scared 13-year-old girl was about to walk into my life and change it forever.

END OF CHAPTER REFLECTION

1. Have you ever felt like you were standing right on the edge of a promise—heart racing, knees knocking—unsure how it would actually unfold, but you stepped anyway?

2. Is there something God keeps nudging you toward that feels way too big, too risky, or way too emotional? Be honest—what's the thing that still makes you hesitate?

3. Looking back, can you see the ways God was preparing you—even in those "nothing's happening" seasons that felt more like waiting rooms than training grounds (complete with bad magazines and stale coffee)?

CHAPTER 56

My Promised Child

The Day Rainy Walked In and Everything Changed

Miles yelled from downstairs, "Christine! She's here!"

My heart didn't just skip—it sprinted a marathon.
She's here.

I'd been pacing like an understudy about to step on stage with no script.
What if she hated us?
What if she didn't talk?
What if my lasagna ruined everything? (The fact that pasta had this much power over my anxiety deserved its own therapy session.)

Miles glanced at me, calm as ever.
"Christine," he said, steady, "if God brought her here, it's not the lasagna that's going to matter."
And of course—he was right.
(But I still made garlic bread. I knew carbs couldn't heal trauma, but I wasn't about to risk it.)

I flew down the stairs like my socks were on fire.

And there she was.
A tiny 13-year-old girl. Arms crossed tight. Eyes cautious and older than they should've been.
Jet-black box-dye hair—a teenage shield for a life already too rough for her age.

The caseworker gestured. "This is Shirley."

Without looking up, she muttered, "I'm Rainy."
Short for Shirley Lorraine, but with an edge all her own.

Rainy. Of course she was. Beautiful. A little stormy.
Exactly who God had whispered about on Mother's Day when He said, *"You will be a mom."*

Paperwork flew across the table. Pens clicked. The caseworker patted Rainy's shoulder, muttered something about catching a flight, and— poof— she vanished like a magician's assistant.

And just like that, three strangers stood in a living room, trying not to stare at each other.
One holy, awkward beginning.

Her duffel bag was heartbreaking.
A toothbrush. Travel toothpaste. A wrinkled t-shirt.
That was it.
No socks. No softness. No place to land.

So I went full "Supermarket Sweep: Foster Mom Edition."
Jeans. Shirts. Socks.
Cart flying down aisles like I was gunning for gold in Olympic cart racing.

Rainy watched me with that *is this lady okay?* face, but I caught the faintest hint of a smirk.

I kept tossing things in the cart.
"Do you need this? Of course you need this. What else? Oh—a brush. A curling iron. A blow dryer. Help me out here, Rainy."

Miles trailed behind us, steady as ever, letting me whirl like a caffeinated tornado. Every once in a while, he'd toss in something simple—solid.
"Get the hoodie. She'll wear it."
"Yeah, grab the shoes. She needs two pairs." Then, with that dad-tone that brooks no argument: "And not the off-brand ones. She needs the real thing. No daughter of mine is walking around in knockoffs."

Not flashy. Not frantic. Just steady—like the man could walk straight through a hurricane armed with nothing but dad-tone authority and a debit card.

And then I saw it—her smile.
Amused at this mom she'd just met, racing around to make sure she had everything she needed.
Someone she didn't even know, caring about her this much.

With every new hoodie, her shoulders loosened just a little.

Then the phone store.
I upgraded mine and handed her my old one.
She looked at it like I'd just gifted her a unicorn holding a winning lottery ticket.

Next stop, eye doctor.
She only had one contact lens—just one lone soldier holding down the fort.
How she wasn't walking into walls, I'll never know.
We got new contacts. Picked out glasses so cute I almost stole them.

For the first time that day, she grinned.
She was finally seeing clearly—in every way.

At home, she stayed quiet. Ate dinner. Watched us pray.

It felt strange to her at first—she told us she'd never actually eaten dinner at a dining room table as a family.

Before, she'd just grab whatever was in the fridge and eat alone. No table. No prayer. No together.

She slowly let us in.

She told us about her siblings—scattered everywhere.
Her parents—gone in different ways.
Her place in the world—lost.

Then one night, her voice barely above a whisper, she said, "I used to cut."
My stomach dropped.
"Do you still?"
She shook her head. "Not since I got here."
"Why not?" I asked.
She looked at me, calm and certain.
"Because I don't need to anymore."

No sermon. No miracle moment.
Just love. Safety. Home.

And then, one day, she called us Mom and Dad.
I ducked into the laundry room, buried my face in a towel, and cried until my knees nearly gave out.
It wasn't neat or polite—it was the kind of sobbing that leaves you breathless, because your heart can't decide whether to shatter or burst.

In that messy, holy moment, I thought of Mother's Day.
The ache. The whisper. The drawer where I'd tucked my hope away.
This was it.
The promise—alive, breathing, standing in my living room.

And even though we were technically "just fostering" her, something in me knew.

Deep in my spirit, I felt it—this wasn't temporary.

This was forever.

> "If our hearts condemn us, we know that God is greater than our hearts, and He knows everything."
>
> — 1 John 3:20
>
> ❧ **Even when you doubt yourself, God doesn't.**
> He sees the whole story—and still chooses you.

We didn't plan this. But God did.

He knew Rainy.

He knew us.

And He stitched us together with invisible threads.

She wasn't just a placement.

She was my promised child.

END OF CHAPTER REFLECTION

1. Have you ever stepped into something you felt wildly unprepared for—only to realize it was exactly where you were meant to be all along?

2. Have you ever watched someone start to heal—not because of a sermon or a "10-step plan"—but simply because they were finally safe... finally loved?

3. Is there a promise you've quietly started to give up on—but maybe, just maybe, God is still weaving it together behind the scenes — threads you can't see yet, but He's been stitching all along?

CHAPTER 57

A Sister, a Shelter, and a Soft-Hearted Husband

What to Do When God Asks You to Say Yes Before You Feel Ready

We were just starting to get the hang of foster parenting.
Barely.

We'd mastered exactly two things:
1. Surviving Target with a teenager.
2. Faking like we knew what we were doing.

Then Rainy plopped on the couch and casually detonated a bomb.
"My sister's in foster care too."
Pause.
"But she's stuck in a facility."

Facility.
In foster care speak, that's not just a location.
It's usually code for: *no one would take her.*
It usually means trauma, red tape, and fluorescent lights that hum like despair.

She kept talking.
One sister with a grandma.
Little brother with a family friend.
The other sister, Savannah? Alone.

Then came the ask.
The big one.
The one that made my heart do cartwheels while my brain screamed,
Wait, WHAT NOW?!

"Do you think she could come live here? So we could be together?"

Her voice was careful. Testing the air.
Her hands twisted in her lap, but her eyes stayed on me—hopeful, a little
scared, braced for no.
Her chin wobbled just slightly, the kind of flicker you'd miss if you weren't
looking for it.

I looked at Miles.
He had his classic "processing face."
Could've meant anything from pondering the meaning of life to wondering
if tacos were still in the fridge.

But I knew.
He was already halfway to yes.

We were brand new at this.
Like, still-thought-parenting-a-teen-meant-binge-watching *Gilmore Girls*
and buying acne wash level new.

Sure, Maddie was with us every other weekend—since she lived with her
mom most of the time—but weekend parenting is basically the training
wheels version.
No late-night homework meltdowns.
No curfews.

No daily teenage moods to decode.

And now... her sister?

"We do have an extra bed," I said slowly.

Miles smirked. "And apparently I have a soft spot for all your wild ideas."

So we shrugged.
"Why not?"

That night, I whispered a desperate prayer.
Short. Shaky. Straight to the point.
"God, if this is Your will... You're gonna have to help. Big time."

And in the quiet after, a thought flickered.
"Is this part of what You meant, Lord, when You promised I'd be a mom?"

We arranged a visit.
Three hours away.

We packed snacks, grabbed takeout, told ourselves it would be sweet.
Some sister hugs. Maybe a few laughs. A happy ride home.

We weren't ready for... the smell.
The second we stepped inside, it hit like a punch in the gut.
Sadness. Stale pizza. And maybe... something dead in the vents.

I leaned toward Miles. Whispered, "We're eating outside."
He nodded, eyes wide, slightly green.

We sat at a wobbly picnic table under a gray sky.
The wind carried faint laughter from the girls as they caught up—giggles
and fragments of stories that didn't belong in a place like this.

I tried to focus on their joy.

And on the way Rainy's whole face lit up when Savannah teased her.

But the knot in my chest wouldn't budge.
Miles looked at me.
Our married-people telepathy fired up.
His eyes said: *This is no place for a kid.*
Mine answered: *She can't stay here.*

That was it.
We had no plan.
No clue what we were doing.
But we knew one thing:

Savannah had to come home.

We weren't ready.
But we were willing.

And sometimes?
That's exactly where God starts.

> "*Learn to do right; seek justice. Defend the oppressed. Take up the cause of the fatherless...*"
>
> —**Isaiah 1:17**
>
> ❧ **A willing yes often starts with a broken heart.**

We thought we were saying yes to one more bed.
What we actually said yes to?
A firecracker. With Wi-Fi.

END OF CHAPTER REFLECTION

1. Has anyone ever surprised you with a request that flipped your life upside down—in the best (and scariest) way?

2. What does being "willing" look like for you right now—even if you're standing there in your Target sneakers, trying not to shake while you say yes?

3. Have you ever walked into a situation that broke your heart wide open... but also lit up your purpose like a neon sign?

CHAPTER 58

The Second Yes

What to Do When God Hands You More Than You Think You Can Handle

Savannah moved in like a firecracker with a suitcase.
Rainy nearly cartwheeled when we told her.
"You're kidding!" she squealed, hugged me... then yanked back like hugging me might revoke her street cred.
Sweet moment. Short-lived.

This was no Hallmark reunion with soft music and matching friendship bracelets.
Nope.
Savannah was jalapeño-on-your-pancakes spicy.
Walls up. Eyes sharp. Attitude for days.
She had zero interest in playing house or pretending we were anything but strangers under one roof.

She was smart. Observant. Hurt in ways words couldn't touch.
Rainy was thrilled... until she wasn't.
One minute they were giggling over TikToks.
The next, it was WWE SmackDown in my living room.
I could've sold tickets. Maybe popcorn.

Savannah tested every boundary like it was a competitive sport.
She pushed buttons I didn't know existed.
There were nights I cried into my pillow wondering if we'd made a mistake.
Asking God if He was sure about this.
"Lord, You brought her here. Please show me what to do... before I lose my mind."

Then came the moment that changed me.
We were having one of those emotional pep-talk-meets-prayer-meeting conversations you only see in movies.
I told her she had two paths: the hard one or the easier one.
She shrugged.
"Well, I like the hard path. That's what I'm used to."

I froze.
Not in the parenting manual.
But it hit me—peace feels weird to kids who've only known chaos.
Safety feels like a trap.
The hard path? It's the only one that makes sense.

So we walked with her. Rocky step by rocky step.

Tiny wins:

- A real laugh at dinner.
- Coming to church.
- Actually finishing a school project.
- Passing a class we thought was doomed.
- Hugging Rainy without an eye-roll (once—but it counts).

And the not-so-glamorous moments:

- Doors slammed like a demolition derby.
- Silent treatments cold enough to freeze soup.

- A bathroom that smelled suspiciously like a smoking lounge. (Pretty sure Glade doesn't make a "Teen Vaping" candle.)
- "I'm fine," said in a tone that meant the opposite.

And then... the phones.
Four of them. FOUR.
We'd confiscate one, and by midnight, she'd be texting from another like a raccoon with Wi-Fi and a burner account.

One night I caught her scrolling some random app at 3 a.m.
Collecting "likes" like they were Pokémon cards.

That's when I became Detective Mom.
Tracking apps. GPS pings.
One-woman FBI unit.

Ping.
She's supposed to be in Algebra.
She's at Subway.
Apparently, math class is no match for a $5 footlong.

We weren't perfect.
But we kept showing up.
And sometimes? That's all you can do.

No lightning bolt from Heaven.
Just a whisper:
"Keep going. I'm still here."

> "I wait for the Lord, my whole being waits, and in his word I put my hope."
>
> — **Psalm 130:5**
>
> ♪ **Waiting isn't passive**— it's choosing to trust God when everything feels stuck.

Then one night, Savannah walked past me in the hall.
No eye contact. No music swelling in the background.
Just a quiet:
"Thanks for not giving up on me."

That was it.
But it cracked something open.
And I held onto it like a lifeline.

We weren't perfect.
But we were willing.
And sometimes?
That's all God needs.

END OF CHAPTER REFLECTION

1. Have you ever said "yes" to something (or someone) before you had the faintest clue what it would actually cost—and then realized God was in it anyway?

2. Have you ever tried to love someone who seemed determined to push every button and boundary you had—and still felt God nudging you to keep showing up?

3. Who in your life right now needs you to just stay steady—even when you don't have the plan, the patience, or the perfect words?

CHAPTER 59

Divine Detours and Dents

How We Prayed For A Minivan And Got Hit By A Truck

We prayed for a minivan.
God sent a truck.

A few months into foster parenting, life was pure chaos.
Two teenagers. Enough emotional baggage to sink a cruise ship.

My car? Way too small.
And Miles? He had a two-passenger pickup truck. No room for three kids—
let alone groceries, backpacks, or anything that didn't fit in a glove box.
Back before kids, Bluetooth and good gas mileage were all I needed.
Now? I was hauling bulk Ramen, apocalypse-level Hot Cheetos, pickle jars
that disappeared overnight, and enough Takis dust on the couch to start
a crime scene investigation.

I prayed.
"God, I'd love a minivan. No idea how or when. Please... make a way."

Note to self: be specific. Like, without a truck involved.

A few weeks later, Savannah begged me to pick up some boy she'd just met.

Trying to be "cool mom," I agreed.

We stopped at Lowe's for paint.
Then a gas station for coffee and a red slushy the size of Savannah's head.

Fully caffeinated, we drove into a sketchy part of town where even Siri
wanted to turn back.
Picked up the boy.
Headed out.

I pulled up to a stop sign. Looked left. Looked right.

And then—BOOM.
A monster truck slammed into us like it had a personal grudge.

Airbags exploded. My ears rang.
For one surreal second, the world slowed down—just me in a haze of
white airbag dust, the smell of burnt propellant, and the sound of my
own pulse.

Then reality crashed back in.
The car was still moving—rolling slowly down the road like a confused
turtle.

Rainy leaned over, whispering like we were in a hostage situation,
"Mom... put it in park. Put it in park!"

Thunk. Done.

The girls jumped out like seasoned stunt drivers, yanked my door open,
and swarmed me.
"Are you okay? Mom, are you hurt?"

They grabbed my arm to pull me out.

That's when I saw the trunk.
The paint can had exploded—looked like a Sherwin-Williams crime scene.

Savannah's red slushy? A murder scene on the dash.
For five solid seconds, I thought someone had been impaled.
Nope. Just cherry flavoring.

Meanwhile, Rainy's coffee had baptized her phone.
It flickered once. Died a sticky death.
She stared at me, dead serious:
"I think God wants me to have a new phone."

I blinked.
"Miracle, huh? Not the one I prayed for—but sure."

We all stood there. Covered in paint, sugar, caffeine.
And somehow... my heart swelled.

These girls.
The way they rushed to me first.
The backwards beauty of it.
Holy.

Also, note to self: this boy is never coming over again.

Miraculously, no one was hurt.
The car? Gone.
RIP tiny trunk space.

But insurance paid it off. Clean slate.

And you better believe the first thing we did was march into a dealership
and drive home a sliding-door miracle.

Sitting there, hands on the wheel, I laughed out loud.

"God, You are something else."

He answered my prayer.
Just not the way I wanted.
Not the way I pictured.
But somehow... better.

> "*For my thoughts are not your thoughts, neither are your ways my ways,*" *declares the Lord.*
>
> — **Isaiah 55:8**
>
> ❧ **God's plan might feel like a detour—** but it's always headed somewhere good.

Because it wasn't just about the minivan.
It was about seeing my girls—new to our home, still testing if I was safe—jump out of that car and run to me, not from me.

It was about realizing that maybe... they were starting to see me as theirs.

Sometimes God's reroutes don't come with gentle whispers.
Sometimes they come with airbags, hazard lights, and a rental car that smells like old fries.
And even that can be grace.

But dents heal easier than hearts.
Because just when we thought we were finding our stride, Savannah disappeared.

END OF CHAPTER REFLECTION

1. Have you ever prayed for something good and gotten total chaos first—and then realized God was teaching you something right in the middle of the mess?

2. Can you think of a detour in your life that felt like the worst timing ever... but later turned out to be one of the best gifts?

3. What would it look like to trust God's better way right now—even if it feels nothing like the way you had it mapped out in your head?

CHAPTER 60

Loving for One Chapter

For The Times God Asks You To Be Part
Of A Story You Won't Get To Finish

June 1st started like any other last day of school.
Until it didn't.

The clock ticked.
No Savannah.
No text.
No backpack slam against the wall announcing her arrival.

That sound was usually my cue that she was home, alive, and ready to raid the pantry like a locust plague.
Hot Cheetos vanished faster than my willpower in a Target clearance aisle.

But today—silence.

I stood in the kitchen, glancing at the clock again. The hum of the fridge suddenly felt loud. Outside, a lawnmower droned in the distance. Inside, my chest tightened.

Maybe she was signing yearbooks. Or grabbing a snack. Or walking home with friends.
But the quiet pressed in heavier with every tick of the clock.

Then the phone rang.

Savannah had run away.

She'd been with us three months.
Three messy, exhausting, cactus-hugging months.
We loved her hard.
We believed it might be enough.
It wasn't.

She ran back to what she knew.
Back to chaos.
Back to the "hard path" she once told me she preferred.

That's the heartbreak of foster care—loving a child who might not stay and loving them anyway.

I saw what she couldn't.
Pep rallies. Graduation caps. Prom dresses and college apps.
I saw a future.
She couldn't—not yet. Chaos still felt safer than peace.

But oh, there were moments.

Like the night Rainy went full Whitney Houston in the minivan—you know, the diva who basically made *I Will Always Love You* a national anthem for heartbreak.
"AND IIIIIII WILL ALWAYS LOVE YOUUUUU!"
Dramatic arm waves. Deep, unblinking eye contact in the rearview mirror.

She was totally off-key—like, dogs-in-the-next-county-howling off-key. If Mariah Carey and a howling coyote had a love child—that was the sound coming from my backseat.

Savannah and I laughed so hard I begged Miles to pull over before our laughter made him swerve off the road.
Miles thought it was hilarious. It became their thing.
Whenever life got stressful, Rainy went full diva mode.
Miles grinned every time.

Sometimes I think that night alone was worth the whole placement.

And then there was the Gen Z rap playlist.
They swore it was the greatest music ever made.
To me, it sounded like someone arguing over a microwave beat while shaking a box of Tic Tacs.
But apparently that's culture now.

And Savannah's smirk—I miss it most of all.
She had a special one reserved for my cheesiest mom speeches.

You know the look teenagers give when they're pretending not to care but secretly storing every word? Yeah. That one.
Equal parts "you're embarrassing" and "don't stop."

Before she left, she finished ninth grade.
Sixteen years old, after bouncing from place to place, she managed to stick it out and complete the year—even though she'd only been with us for the last three months.

For her, that was a miracle.

Months later, Rainy got a message.
Savannah was safe.
Living with extended family.

For now, that had to be enough.

But then something unexpected bloomed.
Rainy.

Without the swirl of drama Savannah brought, Rainy could breathe.
She joined the pep squad.
Made friends.
Started loving school.

For the first time, she felt chosen.
We hadn't planned it this way.
We thought we were rescuing Savannah.
Maybe God just asked us to walk with her for a season.
Plant seeds.
Give her something to remember when the hard path gets old.

And maybe He knew Rainy needed that season, too.
To know she wasn't second choice.
To know someone stayed.

> *"O LORD, you have searched me and known me!*
> *You know when I sit down and when I rise up;*
> *you discern my thoughts from afar...*
> *Even before a word is on my tongue,*
> *behold, O LORD, you know it altogether."*
>
> **— Psalm 139:1–4**
>
> ❧ **God knows you better than you know yourself.**
> Every thought, every ache, every unspoken prayer.

God always knows.
Who will stay. Who will run.
He knows the ache of love that doesn't seem enough.

And He knows how to turn ashes into beauty—even when we can't see it yet.

Because in the end, His love is always enough—strong enough to hold those who stay, and gentle enough to follow those who run.

We didn't know what came next.
But we knew Who did.

Lord, maybe You just asked me to love her for one chapter.
I'll trust You with the rest.

And somewhere deep down, I like to think that if Savannah ever remembers our home, she'll hear Rainy's voice, loud and off-key, belting out, "And I will always love youuuu..." —and know it was true.

Even if Whitney Houston herself wouldn't have approved.

END OF CHAPTER REFLECTION

1. Have you ever loved someone knowing full well you might not get to stay in their story—and had to trust God with the ending?

2. When someone keeps running back to what hurts them, how do you keep loving without losing hope?

3. Have you ever found a hidden blessing tucked inside heartbreak— the kind only God could redeem?

CHAPTER 61

God, Guts, and Gallbladders

Finding the Divine in Your DNA

I didn't expect our kid's science class to turn into a theological showdown.
But here we were.
Amoebas.
Monkeys.
Me clutching my caffeine like it was holy water.

Maddie dropped her backpack and announced, dead serious,
"My science teacher says we evolved from amoebas... and then monkeys."

She paused. Testing the waters.

Now, Maddie loves science.
Microscopes. Brain dissections.
Asking questions I have to Google at midnight.

So naturally, I panicked.
Not visibly—I kept my mom-cool.
But inside? I was screaming, *Lord, please don't let her think You and science can't sit at the same lunch table.*

I took a breath. A long, dramatic sip.

"Some people think God used a process," I said. "Others believe He created things directly.
And if that sounds confusing? Yeah, I get it. Faith and science can feel like they're in different corners of the boxing ring.

But either way—sweetheart—you didn't come from a monkey.
You were handcrafted by a God who doesn't make junk."

Maddie tilted her head.
"So... I don't have to eat bananas?"

"Nope."

She smirked. Then leaned in with that glint kids get when they know they're onto something.
"Okay, but if people came from monkeys... why are there still monkeys? Shouldn't they all have turned into people by now?"

I blinked.
Kid logic: 1. Evolution chart: 0.

Honestly, she wasn't wrong. The monkeys at the zoo weren't exactly packing their bags for college. They looked perfectly happy swinging from trees, eating bananas, and doing—well, monkey business.

Something in her relaxed then. Relief? Maybe curiosity. Either way, it landed.

And then it hit me—proof of God wasn't just in the stars.
It was right here.
Skin. Bones. Belly buttons.

Let's start with your face.

Yes, yours.

There has never been another like it. Ever.

Even twins aren't identical—different freckles, different ways their nose scrunches when they laugh at memes they shouldn't be looking at.

Eight billion people.

One you.

That's not random. That's a designer's signature.

Fingerprints? Same story.

Custom-made.

Swirly little masterpieces. Not a knockoff.

"Indeed, even the very hairs of your head are all numbered. Don't be afraid; you are worth more than many sparrows."

— **Luke 12:7**

❧ **God sees every detail of your life—down to the hairs on your head.**

You are not forgotten. You are deeply known, unshakably loved, infinitely valuable.

Your body?

A blinking, breathing miracle.

Sixty thousand miles of blood vessels.

A heart that pumps without Wi-Fi or chargers.

An immune system that ninja-kicks germs like Chuck Norris in microscopic form.

And when you get cut?

Your blood knows how to clot, knit the skin back together, and heal.

Catch the flu?

Your body rallies the troops. Microscopic army on duty.

That's not chance.
That's built-in repair mode.
That's design.

And thank heavens for the "exit strategy."
Imagine eating pizza and... keeping it forever.
Horrifying.

And speaking of pizza—ever think about how food actually tastes good?
That's not just some happy accident.

God designed taste buds on your tongue so you'd crave what your body needs—sweet, salty, savory.
All those little fireworks that make dinner worth showing up for.

And when you've run low on fuel?
Your stomach literally growls at you.
Like a grumpy roommate yelling, *"Feed me before I start chewing the furniture!"*

Your body knows how to pull the good stuff—vitamins, minerals, energy—right out of what you eat and put it to work keeping you alive.
And it knows how to separate the junk from the good and send it on its way.
On purpose. By design.

Just like He designed your body to crave food, He also built in rhythms of rest.
He made night and day.
Light for work.
Darkness for sleep.

It's easier to rest in the dark than in the glare of daylight—and that's by design.
Not an accident. Not random.

It's a reset button.
Your body shuts down. Heals. Prepares for tomorrow.

God knew we'd push too hard.
So He stitched rest right into the spin of the planet.

(Unless you have teenagers. Then all bets are off.)

Kidneys? Bean-shaped superheroes.
Filter junk. Balance fluids. Make red blood cells. Keep bones strong.

Every time I see a "3-day cleanse" ad, I picture kidneys rolling their eyes like, "Ma'am, that's literally our job."

And because they're so important, God gave you two—so if one taps out, the other can keep things running.
Buy-one-get-one-free, courtesy of the Creator.

Pause and marvel with me for a second.
Right now—billions of cells are exchanging oxygen.
Repairing damage.
Sending electrical signals faster than a group text at midnight.

And you don't have to think about any of it.
That's not an accident.
That's artistry.

Childbirth.
One tiny sperm meets one tiny egg.
And then—like magic but better—an entire human starts forming.
Eyelashes. Elbows. Gallbladders. Sass.

Gallbladder—the mysterious organ no one notices until it suddenly decides to assassinate you.
Honestly, I picture mine sitting in the corner, arms crossed, muttering,
"You'll miss me when I'm gone."

And yes—God designed the *baby-making process* itself to be enjoyable.
On purpose.
Otherwise? None of us would be here.

And He designed men and women in a way that fits together perfectly—
body, soul, spirit. Not by accident, but by intention.

The body just knows to make milk after the baby arrives?
That's divine programming.

And the brain?
One hundred billion neurons firing thoughts, prayers, and grocery lists.
More connections than stars in the Milky Way.

No wonder I walk into rooms and forget why I'm there—traffic jam.
Meanwhile, my neurons are probably whispering to each other, *"Let's just watch her wander around for a while. This'll be funny."*

Science doesn't disprove God.
I know not everyone sees it that way.
But for me? The more I learn about the human body, the louder it screams His name.

Saying this all just "happened" is like seeing a tiered wedding cake with gold leaf and fondant flowers and saying,
"Wow, that bag of flour really nailed it."

Nope. That cake had a baker.
Your body has a Maker.

You might not see Him with your eyes.
But look in the mirror.
Wiggle your toes.
Feel your heartbeat.

There He is.
In you. Through you. Around you.

You're living, blinking, breathing proof that God is real.
And you were made on purpose.

Fast-forward. Maddie really did chase science.
She crossed that graduation stage with a biology degree in hand.

Now she's stepping straight into the medical field.
I don't know her exact title yet—doctor, researcher, healer of another kind.

But I do know this: it'll be something that helps people.
Because that's who she is.

So now, when she's studying cells or scrubbing in, I can't help but grin.
The same kid who once asked why monkeys haven't "graduated" into humans...
is now knee-deep in biology.

Still face-to-face with the proof that God was in on the design from day one.

END OF CHAPTER REFLECTION

1. Have you ever looked at your own body and thought, How *is this even possible?* What detail or design blows your mind most (besides the fact your stomach growls louder than your car engine)?

2. Have you ever had a moment where science and faith clicked together—and instead of pulling apart, they actually confirmed each other?

3. How does it change things to know you were crafted on purpose— with a unique fingerprint, heartbeat, and place in this world?

CHAPTER 62

Why My Dog Thinks I'm a Time-Traveling Wizard

(And Why Trusting God Is Kind of the Same Thing)

Our dogs think we're either gods, wizards, or vending machines with anxiety.

Every time we walk through the door, they lose their minds.
Tails spin like helicopter blades.
Eyes bug out.
Bodies shake like a phone on vibrate.

"YOU CAME BACK! I THOUGHT YOU JOINED WITNESS PROTECTION, BUT YOU'RE HERE!"

Maddie once said our dogs probably think we're wizards.
She's not wrong.

To them, disappearing and reappearing with groceries or Amazon boxes must feel like pure sorcery.

Here's the thing—
They have no clue where we've been.

We could've gone to war.
Or space.

To them, it's all magic.

One time, I walked in and caught our dog Bentley face-first in a pecan pie—like it was his birthday, Thanksgiving, and Mardi Gras all rolled into one.

He looked at me like, *"Lady, if God didn't want me to eat this, He wouldn't have given me teeth."*

Another time?
He ate a four-pound block of Buc-ee's fudge.
Didn't even chew—just inhaled it like he was competing in the Candy Olympics.

I Googled "dog fudge overdose" and braced for a vet bill the size of our mortgage.
But there he was, tail wagging like nothing had happened—basically hosting his own MasterClass: *"How to Pick Desserts When Your Humans Ditch You."*

They don't understand Target runs.
Or school pickup lines.
Or why I sometimes walk in muttering, *"I just need five minutes of silence."*

They're loyal.
Confused.
Soft.
And blissfully clueless.

And here's where I have to pause and admit—
Sometimes I wish I could trust God the way my dogs trust me.

Because the truth?
I'm basically them.

I pace the hallway of life.
Barking at the unknown.
Pressing my face against the window, convinced God has forgotten me.
Forgetting He *always* comes back.

We don't know what He's doing.
We pray, *"God, where are You?"*
But He hasn't left.

He's just been busy—
Moving things we can't see.
Answering prayers we don't even know how to ask.

Just not on our schedule.

Their timeline is *now.*
Mine is *later.*
Sounds familiar.

Like my dogs don't understand Amazon Prime,
I don't understand how God hears billions of prayers at once.
Or how galaxies come out of His breath.
Or how He weaves my mess into something meaningful.

But you know what?
The dogs don't need the details to feel safe.
They just need to know I'll come back.

And if my dogs can trust I'll return from CVS with more than toothpaste,
surely I can trust God to come back for me with more than I even know
to ask for.

Sometimes I picture Him the way my dogs picture me—
Standing just beyond the door, arms full of things I know they'll love,
waiting for the right moment to come in.

They're pressed up against the window.
Ears twitching at every sound.
Certain I'm on the way.

That's the kind of faith I want.

Genesis says we're made in God's image.
Not little gods, but mirrors.

We love. Forgive. Dream.
Dance barefoot in kitchens.

We burn pancakes and laugh anyway.
We're chosen. Known. Wanted.

God made oceans. Stars. Planets.
And mosquitoes.
(Still waiting for an explanation. Pretty sure sin is involved —
or maybe mosquitoes are just Satan's interns).

Then He looked at all of it and said,
"You. I want you in My story."

So no—we won't understand everything God does.
We're not supposed to.

Just like my dogs don't know where I've been,
We don't know why God delays, detours, or seems silent.

But one day, maybe we'll see the full picture and go,
"Ohhhhhhh. That's what You were doing."

Until then?
We wag our tails.
We stay close.

We trust.
And we live in the wild joy of knowing—

The One we thought left? Never did.

END OF CHAPTER REFLECTION

1. Have you ever felt like God was distant — only to realize later He was right there the whole time?

2. What can you learn from your pet's tail-wagging trust that would help your faith today?

3. Can you think of a moment you looked back and said, "Ohhhh — that's what You were doing, God"?

CHAPTER 63

Faith, Floorplans, and the Home We Didn't Plan For

Trusting God's Blueprint When Yours Falls Apart

Our house was bursting at the seams. One more person and we'd be stacking bunk beds in the pantry, praying nobody came in craving Doritos at midnight.

For over a year, we'd been hinting—okay, borderline begging—Miles' mom, Judy, to move to Texas.
He's her only son.
Maddie's her only grandchild.
And Michigan winters? The kind that freeze your eyelashes on contact.

It felt like a no-brainer.

But Judy truly loved the change of seasons in Michigan—
crisp falls, snowy winters, tulips in spring.

She knew we weren't moving back there, though.
And in the end, being with family—the ones who loved her and wanted her close—meant more than any postcard-perfect autumn.

It wasn't just sunshine and grandkid snuggles drawing her here.
Judy had been through a few surgeries, and being 1,300 miles away during health scares gnawed at Miles.

He wanted to bring her soup when she was sick.
Change lightbulbs without booking a flight.
Have her laugh echoing through our house instead of across the phone line.

We wanted her here—her no-nonsense wisdom, her grounding presence.

And I was excited too—it felt like the final puzzle piece of the prophecy God whispered to me back at that women's conference. Marriage. Maddie. Miles' mom. It was as if this had been God's blueprint all along, and now the pieces were finally locking into place.

One small problem.
Okay, three.

Rainy had moved in.
Maddie needed space.
And our house was out of bedrooms, patience, and electrical outlets.

In my dream world, the new house would also have a private pool—because in my head, that was just as essential as running water.

So we prayed.
Dreamed.
Scrolled listings like it was a full-time job.

We toured open houses like contestants on *Fixer Upper: Chaos Edition.*

We pictured Judy's future room—
where she'd stack her favorite coffee mugs beside towers of hardcover books—

and build her small-town murder mystery library—the one with creaky floors and a possibly homicidal librarian.

And somewhere in all that scrolling, I remembered the whisper I'd written down years earlier:
"Bring Miles, Maddie, and his mom closer to Me."

Back then, I didn't know how.
But now? The pieces were moving.

Miles' faith was growing.
Maddie's was blooming.
Judy believed in God, sure, but church wasn't her thing yet.

If she lived with us, she'd see faith up close—no pressure, just presence.

So I prayed bold, terrified prayers.
"Lord, if this is really You... help our house sell fast. Help us find the right one. And please... don't let us live out of our car while trusting You."

We listed our house with no backup plan.
Leapt first. Looked second.

Boom. First showing, first offer.

And I? Promptly panicked.

"What if this ends with us in a tent behind Walmart?"
I mean, I like camping—but not the long-term, shampoo-in-a-bottle, explain-to-your-neighbors kind.

The next morning, I adjusted one little filter.
I had been treating private pools like salvation requirements.

This house didn't have one—

but it did have a community pool right across the street.

I clicked anyway.
And gasped.

Five bedrooms.
(Later six—once we put up a wall and claimed some bonus space.)

Master downstairs.
Four upstairs—including one screaming "Judy's Room" in big neon letters.

Bathrooms for everyone.
Movie-night loft for Monopoly games that might require repentance afterward.

"I think this is it," I said.
And miracle of miracles? Miles didn't argue.

We FaceTimed Judy to show her the room.
She smiled and said, "Wow, this is really nice. But that hot pink and black has to go. Can we paint it light blue, please?"

Honestly, it looked like Barbie had a midlife crisis and moved into Hot Topic.
Judy was not amused.

The house even had room for Bonny's bed. Back in Michigan, Bonny and our Bentley were best buds. Now they'd be reunited—two happy dogs under one roof.

Everything clicked—fast. The sale. The purchase. Early access before closing.

For a moment, I just stood in the empty doorway and let it sink in.

A month earlier, I'd been holding tight to my own blueprint—
my must-haves, my pool, my "perfect plan."

Now I was standing in something better.

When God steers, you don't need the whole map.
Just a whisper and a moving truck.

This wasn't just more space.
This was surrender.

Faith with drywall.
Trust with a floorplan.

I thought I wanted a blueprint.
God gave me a home with room for miracles—
and Judy's book hoard.

"Trust in the Lord with all your heart and lean not on your own understanding; in all your ways submit to Him, and He will make your paths straight."

— **Proverbs 3:5–6**

❧ **Trust isn't about knowing every detail.**
It's about knowing Who's holding the blueprint.

END OF CHAPTER REFLECTION

1. Have you ever leapt without a backup plan—just went for it—and trusted God to catch you? What pushed you to say yes?

2. Is there someone in your life you feel nudged to point toward God—not with pressure, just with presence? What might that look like?

3. When's the last time God swung a door so wide open you knew—no way this was coincidence?

CHAPTER 64

Twinkle Lights, Panic Prayers, and a Maybe-Forever Kid

Loving With Open Hands When Your Heart Wants To Hold On Tight

Buying a house with faith is like putting on mascara before skydiving.
You hope it ends well.
But you know there's a good chance you'll smear mascara halfway to your ears on the way down.

The house came together like divine choreography.
Every door opened.
Every box checked.
It felt like God Himself was directing traffic—possibly while humming show tunes.

We moved fast.
More space. More light. More breathing room.

It felt like a house where healing could actually move in, kick off its shoes, hang soft lights, and stay awhile.

So I strung up twinkle lights like a caffeinated Joanna Gaines.
Target runs. Snacks. Pillows. The works.
If HGTV had a category called "Cozy for Wounded Teenagers," I was going
for gold.

But Rainy's heart wasn't settled yet.

She still texted people from her past—
biological family, old friends, people who kept pulling her backward.

Her parents? Missing in action.
No court check-ins.
No programs.
No proof they even remembered she existed.

One night, she looked up at me with glassy eyes.
"Why don't they care about me?"

I wanted to scream.
Shake someone.
Throw furniture.
Possibly all three.

Instead, I wrapped her in a hug and said,
"Rainy, you are smart, brave, beautiful. I don't know why they're not
doing what they should. But I know this—God loves you. He brought you
here for a reason. You are not forgotten."

God whispered,
"Just listen. She'll tell you what she needs."

So I did.
No sermons. No fixing.
Just presence.

She opened up slowly.
Told me her mom still called her sisters—but not her.
She was the invisible one.
The forgotten one.

Then came the gut punch.

She'd been talking to a family friend up north.
Someone who wanted to adopt her.
A maybe-forever home.

Back to her tiny hometown, where the biggest event of the year was probably a pancake breakfast in the church basement with a raffle prize of a jar of pickles and a scented candle.

For her, it was comfort. For me, it was fear.

Because deep down, I felt like the backup plan—
safe to lean on until something better came along.

And still, my heart kept leaning toward hers.

Part of me wanted to hang more twinkle lights in her room, stock it with her favorite snacks, and make it so cozy she'd never want to leave.

The other part wanted to bolt my heart shut.
Swallow the key.

Miles felt it too.
He took her to every appointment.
Showed up for every football game she cheered.
Joked with her. Encouraged her.

Loved her quietly—with late-night snack runs and perfectly timed dad jokes.

If Rainy said, "Dad, I need more pickles. There's none left," he was already grabbing his keys like her wish was his command.

It was his way of saying, *You matter. Just as much as Maddie.*

Every time she mentioned leaving, it felt like another thread in my chest unraveled.

But that's foster care, isn't it?
You sign up knowing your heart might shatter.
You're the safe harbor—not always the forever home.

So I prayed.
"God, put her where she'll be loved. Even if it's not here. Just make sure it's safe. Whole."

"The Lord is close to the brokenhearted
and saves those who are crushed in spirit."

— Psalm 34:18

🕊 **When hearts ache, His presence doesn't leave.**
He stays closer than breath.

And I felt it—
Peace.
Small. Flickering. But real.

I didn't know if she'd stay.
But I knew this:
She'd already unpacked in my heart.

And God's love—woven into every hug, every snack, every twinkle light—would go with her, wherever she went.

We thought buying a house was the big leap of faith.

Turns out, the bigger leap was answering to a name I wasn't sure I'd ever hear.

Next stop: Target.

The mascara aisle.

And one word—spoken out loud, in public—that changed everything.

END OF CHAPTER REFLECTION

1. Have you ever loved someone knowing they might not stay—but you went all in anyway? What pushed you to risk it?

2. How do you sit with someone's pain when you know you can't fix it?

3. Who in your world feels invisible right now—and how could you remind them they're seen?

CHAPTER 65

When "Mom" Feels Like a Crown

The Beauty And Heartbreak Of Holding
A Title You Might Not Get To Keep

Some kids tiptoe into your heart.
Others blast through the front door like they've been launched out of a cannon—leaving Hot Cheeto fingerprints on your soul.

After Rainy had been with us for a while and our home finally found a rhythm, we said yes to a few more foster kids here and there.
Not many.
Just enough to remind us that every child carries a different story.

Some stayed a weekend.
Some long enough to carve their names on our hearts.

The little girls?
Mostly sweet.
(Well, except that one who could've had a side hustle in horror movies. My eardrums are still in recovery.)

When they cried for their parents, I was right there—
holding them, praying over them, whispering,

It's going to be okay.

My nurturing spirit went full mom mode.
I felt like God always gave me the right words to say.

The boys?
Whole different rodeo.
Tiny hurricanes with backpacks.
Trauma, chaos, zero chill.

Meltdowns over cereal.
Tantrums over air.

One kid had so much energy, I half expected Red Bull to sponsor him.
The school would call and say, "He's...uh...doing that thing again."
What thing?
Oh, just ricocheting off walls like he'd swallowed a trampoline.
(If I'd bottled his energy, I could've powered half of Texas.)

We hung on for dear life.
Then—slowly—the chaos softened.
They laughed louder. Flinched less.
The colts became kids again.

But Rainy—she was different.
Being with her didn't feel like foster parenting.
I didn't feel like her foster mom.
I felt like her mom.

We bonded over shopping sprees, hair appointments, and movie nights
with enough snacks to feed a marching band.

We bleached out the harsh black dye from her runaway days.
Golden highlights lit up her whole face.
Once her hair was back to blonde, people started saying she was my mini-me.

And honestly? My heart puddled.

Then came the nails.
Good grief, the nails.
Long, glittery, velociraptor claws.

I'd watch her tap her phone screen and think:
How do you text that fast?
How do you zip your jeans?

Honestly, if she scratched her head too fast, she could've picked up a radio signal.

She was fabulous.
And I was just the mom footing the bill.

And then it happened.
Target. Mascara aisle.
She yelled across two rows of lip gloss:

"MOM!"

At home, she had been calling me mom.
But this was different. Not just at home. Not whispered.
Out in public—loud, certain, like she meant it.
Target's mascara aisle as our witness.

I turned without thinking.
Not "Christine."
Not "Miss."

Just... Mom.

For half a beat I froze. *You mean me?*
Then I answered like I'd been doing it forever.

That word fit like a crown I never asked for—but would never take off.

And in the middle of Target, between mascara and lip gloss, God whispered:
See? I keep My promises—even in aisles you didn't expect.

Miles noticed—how she said it, how I lit up when she did.
Not with flowery words—he never needed those.

But with consistency.
He was there.
On the bleachers. In the waiting rooms.
In the little sarcastic back-and-forths that made her smirk and secretly relax.

If Rainy complained, "Dad, my phone charger's broken," he'd show up five minutes later with three backups—like the Charger Fairy had made a late-night run.

He was just... an awesome dad.

But still—Rainy talked about leaving.
That family friend up north kept coming up.

I wanted her to find happiness—truly, I did.
But deep down? It felt like we were the backup plan.
And that stung.

Because I wasn't just loving her like a foster mom—I was loving her like a forever mom.
But I wasn't sure she saw me that way.

For me, it was like standing on the edge of a cliff.
Because in my heart, she was already mine.
And there's no boxing that up.

Through every twist and tear, I clung to this:

> *"And we know that for those who love God all things work together for good, for those who are called according to His purpose."*
>
> — Romans 8:28
>
> ✿ **Even the messiest chapters aren't wasted.**
> God weaves every detour, every heartbreak, every victory into a bigger story.

But one question kept looping in my head like a bad Top 40 song:
What if she chooses someone else?

And worse—
What if I lose her right after she finally called me Mom in front of the whole world?

Okay... Target isn't technically the whole world.
But in that moment?
It sure felt like it.

I thought "Mom" was the crown.
Turns out, Rainy had one more question—spelled out in teal letters—that would change everything.

END OF CHAPTER REFLECTION

1. Have you ever loved someone like family—even before you had the "official" title? What did that stir up in you?

2. Do you remember the first time someone called you a name soaked in love—Mom, Dad, sister, friend? Did it undo you a little?

3. How do you keep pouring out love when you're not sure if the person you love is going to stay?

CHAPTER 66

Will You Adopt Me? (Yes! Yes! A Thousand Times Yes!)

The Moment She Chose Us, And Heaven Agreed

I didn't see it coming.
Not like this.
Not spelled out in teal letters that would stop my heart mid-beat.

I'd wanted to be a mom my whole life.
Not just a lunch-packing, field-trip-chaperoning mom.
The forever kind.
Soul tied. Can't untangle us.

God had whispered the promise.
I didn't know when.
I didn't know how.
I just held on like a kid clinging to a balloon in a hurricane.

Jamie—Rainy's CASA worker—called.
"I'm driving down to visit Rainy."

Casual, I thought. Snacks. Small talk. Nothing dramatic.

Wrong.

She showed up with a bag of teal letters, like Hobby Lobby exploded in her car.

Rainy grinned. "Everyone sit down."
We obeyed like kindergartners, each taking a seat at the dining room table.

Miles and I sat down next to each other, trading a look that said: *Something was definitely up.*

Rainy spilled the letters.
"Unscramble these."

Miles dove in like he was training for the crossword Olympics.

"Would," he announced proudly.

Rainy rolled her eyes. "No!"
Jamie's husband laughed. "Nice try. Not the word."

The suspense was thicker than Texas humidity.

Miles pieced it together.
"Will you..."
Then "A D O..."
Then the "P" and "T."

My heart finished before my brain:
WILL YOU ADOPT ME?

The air stilled.
Like even heaven held its breath.

Her smile changed.

Brave. Hopeful.
Like she was betting her whole heart on our answer.

She handed Miles a folded letter. "Read it."

He glanced at me, eyes glassy. "You want to—"

"You read it," I whispered.

He began, voice shaking:

"I know I'm not the best kid, and I'm not so easy to handle, but thank you for loving me and treating me like your own. I'm so thankful that God placed me here when He did. God knew this is what I needed. January 28th will always be a special day for me."

I was gone already—undone before he even finished the first paragraph.

January 28th.
The day she first showed up on our doorstep with nothing but a duffel bag and a guarded heart.
Now here she was, calling it special. Holy. Home.

Miles looked up. Eyes locked on me as if saying: *Christine, this is your dream. Coming true.*

He kept reading:

"Thank you for not giving up on me when I was a bad kid and started so much trouble. You may not be my real parents, but in my heart you always will be. Both of you treat me better than my parents ever did, and it's only been a year since I've been here. I told Jessica I was going to ask this question, and she said okay. February 16th I will be getting moved to adoption court, so then you both can adopt me officially right after that. I love you both so very much!"

Then, because she's Rainy—extra and wonderful—she ended with a poem:

"I didn't give you the gift of life, but in my heart I know,
The love I feel is deep and real, as if it had been so.
For us to have each other is like a dream come true.
No, I didn't give you the gift of life.
Life gave me the gift of you."

We were puddles.
Laughing. Crying. Laughing while crying.

I finally choked out,
"And the answer is YES!"

In my head, I was screaming it Nicholas-Sparks style on a beach somewhere:
"Yes! Yes! A thousand times yes!"

She'd called me "Mom" before.
But this was different.
This was her choosing us.

Her grandparents—who loved her fiercely—gave their blessing.
Her CASA worker, Jamie, and her caseworker, Jessica, had seen how much
she was thriving.
Everyone had quietly hoped for this day.

But God?
He'd known since day one.

He'd been weaving this messy, heartbreaking, beautiful, miraculous story
long before I prayed my first *please-make-me-a-mom.*

She asked.
We answered.
And heaven whispered back—YES.

> "Many are the plans in a person's heart, but it is Lord's purpose that prevails."
>
> — **Proverbs 19:21**
>
> ♫ **We can dream, strategize, make lists—**
> but God's plan is the one that sticks.

Because when His promises show up on your doorstep—sometimes written in teal letters—
you'll know it was worth every tear, every prayer, every second.

We thought the question was the big moment.
Turns out, adoption day makes mascara cry for mercy.
Maybelline didn't stand a chance.

> "The LORD of hosts has sworn:
> 'As I have planned, so shall it be,
> and as I have purposed, so shall it stand.'"
>
> — **Isaiah 14:24**
>
> ♫ **God doesn't make backup plans.**
> When He speaks it, it's done.

END OF CHAPTER REFLECTION

1. Have you ever waited so long for something that when it finally came, you almost couldn't believe it was real?

2. What promise from God are you still clinging to with white knuckles, trusting He'll deliver?

3. Who has chosen you—looked you in the eye, picked you—and changed your story forever?

CHAPTER 67

Forever, Signed In Ink and Tears

The Day the Judge Made It Official—
and My Mascara Called It Quits

I thought adoption day would be quick.
Sign a paper.
High five.
Done.

Nope.
Emotional Olympics.
Mascara running for its life.

Rainy's question had been the spark.
This was the finale.
Big. Loud. Holy.
A tear-soaked touchdown dance.

There was a 90-day waiting period.
Legal stuff.
But her bio-parents hadn't shown up in years, so no one expected last-minute drama.

(Though I still half-waited for someone to jump out yelling, "OBJECTION!" Perry Mason-style.)

We gathered her people—Maddie, Jamie (her CASA angel), friends who'd stood in both mess and miracle.
June 8th was circled on the calendar like it was Christmas and a Beyoncé tour combined.

"Hey," I told Rainy, "you can change your name in court if you want."
She lit up. "Yes!"

"Rainy" fit.
"Shirley" never had.

Middle name? Shrugs—until I said, "Rainy Rose?"
She hesitated. "But Maddie's middle name is Rose..."

Maddie grinned. "Then we're rose sisters."

Boom. Sold.

Miles pointed to his arm tattoo—a dragon holding a rose.
"Maddie was born in the Year of the Dragon," he said.
"Now this ink's for both my girls. My two Roses."

Cue the lump in my throat.

We got crafty—poster boards and glitter. Signs:
• *My Forever Family*
• *The Awesome Dad Between His Two Roses* (Miles insisted).

Underneath, the word *Thorn* was scribbled out like it had been banished from the kingdom.

The night before court, I couldn't sleep.

What if something went wrong?
What if she changed her mind?

Morning came anyway.

I whispered, *"God, You promised I'd be a mom. I pictured a swaddled newborn— not a teenager with perfect eyeliner and a phone charger collection. But You were right on time. Thank You."*

We even hired a videographer named Fabio.
Yes, Fabio.
And yes, he was as fabulous as you're imagining.

Courtroom time.
Rainy stood before the judge.
Brave. Sparkling.
And underneath: *Am I safe now? Am I finally chosen?*

She handed me a box.
Inside—a necklace with one word: Mom.

I clutched it like it was proof the promise was real—because it was.

Miles opened his box—a bracelet stamped Dad.

No speeches.
Just her eyes saying, *Thank you for choosing me.*

We gave her a ring—three small diamonds.
"You in the middle," I said, voice wobbling. "Mom and Dad forever beside you."

Her smile cracked wide open.
Big. Real. Unguarded.

I thought my heart couldn't take more—but there was still one more gift.

A silver heart box engraved—
Rainy Rose Pilgrim - Forever Our Daughter - June 8, 2018.

The judge smiled.
Miles wrapped his arm around Rainy, kissed her head just like he does with Maddie.
Because now, he had two daughters.
Same dad.
Same love.

Then came the words we'd prayed to hear:
"It is with great, great pleasure that I grant this adoption and forever make Rainy yours—and you forever Rainy's."

Applause erupted.
I'm convinced heaven joined in.

And just like that, the whisper God spoke on Mother's Day wasn't a whisper anymore. It was a legal decree, signed in ink and sealed in tears.

Mascara? Gone.
Dignity? Questionable.
Gratitude? Beyond words.

I walked out of that courthouse a weepy mess in slightly-too-tight heels.
But don't mistake me for weak—
I was a mother.
Officially. Legally. Forever.

And may God help anyone who tries to mess with my kid.

Thank You, Lord, for writing a story I never could've imagined—
but will spend forever thanking You for.

Some prayers are so big, they echo across the years.
And when God answers?
You feel the holy weight of every second you waited.

And every second was worth it —because forever had finally come.

> *"Oh give thanks to the LORD, for He is good,*
> *for His steadfast love endures forever!"*
>
> **— Psalm 107:1**
>
> ❧ **God's love doesn't have an expiration date.**
> Forever means forever.

END OF CHAPTER REFLECTION

1. Has God's timing ever caught you completely off guard—in the best way—like He was waiting to surprise you?

2. When has God taken your careful little blueprint and rewritten it into something bigger than you imagined?

3. What's your "forever moment"—the kind that split your story into before and after (and maybe made your mascara file for early retirement)?

CHAPTER 68

When Pain Makes Room for Purpose

How God Can Use Your Deepest Hurt to Write Your Best Chapter Yet

Pain doesn't knock first.
It barges in—muddy shoes, bad attitude, steals your last brownie—and wrecks your heart.

Then it has the nerve to say, "This is for your growth."

Oh really, Pain? Cool. Where's the refund desk?

But here's the wild thing—God uses it.
Like a Master Chef walking into your emotional kitchen, spotting burnt toast and shattered eggs, and saying:
"Perfect. Watch this."

I used to think my dream of being a mom was simple:
Pray. Wait. Get pregnant. Done.

Except... it didn't happen.

CHRISTINE PILGRIM

IVF became an emotional rollercoaster—needle pokes, hormones, tears—
and not even free snacks. (The least they could've done was hand out
Oreos.)

The hormones were so intense I cried at dishwasher commercials.

And when it failed? I was gutted.

I remember lying face-down on the carpet one night, crying so hard my
face left a watermark in the rug.
"Please, God," I whispered. *"Just this once. Let me be Hannah. You opened her
womb. You split a sea. Surely You can do this for me."*

Silence.
The silence was louder than my prayers.

It felt like the end.
But it wasn't.
It was the middle of a miracle I couldn't see yet.

Because if I had gotten what I wanted when I wanted it…
I might've never seen her.

A sad teenage girl out there, praying for someone like me.

God wasn't saying "no."
He was saying, *"Not yet. I've got someone else."*

He wasn't punishing me.
He was preparing me.

I don't believe God caused my infertility. That's not Him.
But I know this—He refused to waste it.

He filled my empty nursery with loud music, TikToks I don't understand, and makeup explosions on every surface.

He filled it with love.
Messy, loud, holy love.

Every tear.
Every negative test.
Every night I whispered, *"Did You forget me?"*

God was already breadcrumbing me *straight to her.*

And maybe that ache in your chest right now?
It's not the end.
It's the setup for a divine plot twist.

God doesn't sit on a throne with a clipboard watching you suffer.
He rolls up His sleeves.
He turns ashes into beauty.

And sometimes the day that feels like your worst...
Becomes the doorway to your best.

I handed Him burnt toast.
He gave me a daughter.

I wasn't Hannah in the way I prayed for. But He still gave me a child I can call mine.

And the taste of that miracle?
Sweeter than anything I'd ever imagined.
And zero needles involved.

> *"You intended to harm me, but God intended it for good to accomplish what is now being done, the saving of many lives."*
>
> **— Genesis 50:20**
>
> 🎶 **What was meant to break you? God's already flipping it for good.**

> *"He heals the brokenhearted and binds up their wounds."*
>
> **— Psalm 147:3**
>
> 🎶 **God doesn't ignore our pain.**
> He steps in and heals what feels beyond repair.

END OF CHAPTER REFLECTION

1. Have you ever watched something that broke you end up becoming strangely beautiful —like God had been writing a bigger story underneath the pain?

2. Is there an ache in your chest right now that feels like silence— but might actually be God setting you up for a Hannah-style plot twist?

3. Could it be that your "not yet" isn't God forgetting you—but Him whispering, *"Hold on, I'm still writing"*?

CHAPTER 69

Whispers, Goosebumps, and Holy Text Messages

How God Used My Phone Plan for Eternal Purposes

I never planned to become God's messenger.
Especially not via text.

One Thursday, my phone buzzed, and suddenly I was sweating like I'd
been asked to defuse a bomb.
If this wasn't from God?
I'd officially be the weirdo who thought she had divine Wi-Fi.
Unlimited plan, apparently.

Hearing from God isn't what you think.
No booming voice from the clouds.
No scrolls floating down with neat bullet points.
(Although, Lord, if You're taking suggestions...)

It's quieter.
A whisper that makes your soul sit up straighter.
Goosebumps you can't explain.
A knowing you didn't create.

Once you've heard it, you can't un-hear it.

A friend once asked me what it sounds like when God speaks.
Fair question. I used to ask it too—over and over—before I finally recognized His voice.

Here's the tricky part: it's not a voice you hear with your ears.
It's in your thoughts.

But it's clear.
Sometimes it feels like a conversation—gentle, steady, almost like someone is speaking right to you.
Other times it's just knowing.
Like—there's no way I came up with that on my own.

Not loud.
Not harsh.
Quiet, but undeniable.

And if you're rolling your eyes right now? I get it. I've been that skeptic too. But this is what happened.

That day when my phone buzzed, a text message popped up from a friend in Michigan:
"Diana just lost Tom."

I froze.

Tom and Diana weren't just married.
They were married-married.
Holding-hands-in-the-peanut-butter-aisle married.
The kind where even Tuesday night errands felt romantic.
She didn't just lose a husband.
She lost her best friend, her co-pilot.

My heart sank.

I prayed:

"God, I don't know what to say. Please help me not make this worse."

And then I felt it—
a warmth, a stillness.
Like the sun on your face with a cool breeze wrapped around you.

The Holy Spirit.
Words landed in my heart:
"Tom is right here with Me, right by My side. Do not worry."

I froze again.
Do I actually text her that?
Is that even allowed?
Should I slap a disclaimer on it? "Holy Spirit may or may not be involved"?

The whisper came again:
"Tell her. She needs to hear it."

I knew I could be wrong. But I also knew the weight of those words wasn't from me.

Heart pounding, I hit send.

Seconds later, her reply came.
Not confused.
Not doubting.
Peaceful.

She told me she'd already seen her mom—who had passed away—in a vision, welcoming Tom into Heaven.

Diana saw a vision. I heard a whisper. Same God, same message—just delivered in two different ways.

Two women, a thousand miles apart, hearing the same holy message from God Himself.

Then came one more whisper:

"Diana's vision is true. She will see them both again someday.
I want her to take care of herself and her children. I will never leave her side.
You cannot imagine what Heaven will be like.
But I have big plans to use Diana here.
She just needs to trust Me."

More goosebumps.
I could hardly breathe.
But I typed and sent it anyway.
Because I knew Who gave me the words.

Diana said it was the greatest gift she'd received.
Not flowers.
Not casseroles.
Not sympathy cards.

This—
a message from a God who still speaks.

And me?
I wasn't some holy guru.
I was just the mail carrier.
Delivering hope I didn't write but couldn't keep to myself.

That Thursday, God reached through grief and used a phone to bridge the pain.
We didn't get all the answers.
But we got just enough to breathe.
Just enough to believe that Heaven is real.
That love still speaks.

That God never stops whispering.

And one last nudge, straight to my soul:
"You're hearing Me. Keep listening."

The girl who once doubted God now gets holy goosebumps on a random Thursday.

Friends, God doesn't just talk—
He changes the listener.

And sometimes...
He might even ask you to hit send.

"Each of you should use whatever gift you have received to serve others, as faithful stewards of God's grace in its various forms."
— **1 Peter 4:10**

❧ **Your gifts aren't random.**
They're tools God hands you to deliver hope.

"My sheep listen to my voice; I know them, and they follow me."
— **John 10:27**

❧ **God's voice is personal.**
And once you've heard it, you'll recognize it forever.

END OF CHAPTER REFLECTION

1. Have you ever felt that little holy nudge to reach out—when it made zero sense on paper—but you couldn't shake it?

2. How do you usually recognize God's whispers—through goosebumps, peace, a Scripture, or just that deep-down knowing you didn't come up with yourself?

3. Who might God be asking you to "hit send" for today—a text, a call, a word of hope—that could land exactly when they need it most?

CHAPTER 70

Judy, Jesus, and the Kidney That Never Needed Saving

Proof That God Speaks — and Sometimes He's Way Ahead of the Chart

I wasn't planning to write a medical miracle into my life story.
But then my mother-in-law moved in.

When Miles' mom, Judy, arrived, I pictured cozy dinners, family bonding, maybe a few cute grandma moments.
Not a guest role on *Grey's Anatomy: Senior Edition.*

Judy was in her late seventies—sharp, tough, the kind of woman who'd duct tape a severed arm and finish folding laundry before admitting she needed help.

Then the bomb dropped.
Breast cancer. Already in her lymph nodes.

Chemo. Surgery. The whole terrifying drill.

And just when we thought it couldn't get worse—doctors found tumors on both kidneys.
The urologist didn't sugarcoat it.
"We might be talking removal. Of both."

Miles looked at me one night and said, "I might have to give her a kidney.
She could never survive dialysis."
And he meant it. No hesitation.

Meanwhile, I was unraveling.
So I prayed the desperate kind of prayers—hands gripping the sink, tears soaking the counter.

And then... stillness.
Like God walked into my kitchen and whispered:
"The tumors are not malignant."

I froze. I knew that voice.
I grabbed a scrap of paper, scribbled it down, sealed it in an envelope, and hid it in my dresser.
Not because I doubted Him—because I knew one day I'd need proof.

Chemo began. It wrecked her.
It stole her hair, her energy, her privacy—
but never touched her sass.
Judy marched through it like a warrior queen demanding the remote control.

Then—one random Tuesday—the doctor said,
"Only one in ten respond this well." He paused. "Looks like you're the one."
Cancer: gone.

I nearly high-fived Jesus through the ceiling.
Miles and Judy walked in calm as cucumbers.
I was doing mental cartwheels.

"I knew it!" I shouted. "God cured you!"
Judy arched an eyebrow. "Still have those kidney tumors."
I grinned. "They're not malignant."

Here's the thing—the doctors had already said they couldn't know for sure without surgery to cut them out to check. Normally cancer grows fast, and if those tumors didn't? Maybe they weren't a problem.

But I knew. I knew what God told me.

She gave me that classic Judy look—suspicious, like I'd tried to forge God's signature.

Weeks later, scans came back.
Tumors stable. Just monitoring.

Yes, the doctors had their charts. But I had my envelope.

That's when I pulled the envelope from my dresser.
"Read this," I said.

She opened it.
The words stared up at her:
God told me Judy's kidney tumors are not malignant.

Everything went still.
No beeping timers. No dishwasher hum.
Just a flicker of peace in her eyes—like maybe, just maybe, she believed it too.

Years later, those tumors? Still harmless. Still monitoring.
No surgery. No dialysis.
Just Judy in her recliner, hair grown back, sass fully restored, binge-watching *NCIS* like she's waiting for a call from Agent Gibbs.

Life isn't perfect. But it's peaceful.

And that scrap of paper is still in my drawer—

proof that God speaks, proof that He heals, proof that sometimes He hands you an umbrella before the storm even shows up.

She moved in, and I thought we'd argue about proper dishwasher loading.

Instead, we ended up on holy ground—

with a side of *NCIS* reruns.

And I wouldn't trade a single second of it.

> *"The Lord sustains them on their sickbed and restores them from their bed of illness."*
>
> — **Psalm 41:3**
>
> ❧ **God is healer, even in the hardest nights.**

> *"The prayer of a righteous person is powerful and effective."*
>
> — **James 5:16**
>
> ❧ **Your prayers move mountains, even when you can't see it yet.**

END OF CHAPTER REFLECTION

1. Have you ever looked back and realized God had you ready before you even knew what was coming—like He slipped the umbrella into your hand before the storm ever showed up?

2. Is there a whisper or promise you tucked away—maybe even scribbled down on paper—that you need to pull out and remember today?

3. Who in your world needs you to hit your knees for them right now—to be their prayer warrior in the scary stuff—and how can you show up this week?

CHAPTER 71

Confessions of a Former Skeptic

For Anyone Who's Ever Wanted Proof
but Got a Whisper Instead

If you'd told me years ago that God would one day speak directly to me, I would've laughed.
Out loud.
While Googling the nearest exit.

Me? Hearing from God?
That was for prophets, nuns, and people who fold fitted sheets without swearing.

I wasn't just doubtful.
I was president of the Doubters Club—laminated card, sarcasm punch card included. Our annual convention? Just me and a mirror.

"God spoke to you? Sure. Or maybe it was just the echo in your own head."
"You felt peace in chaos? More likely adrenaline finally wearing off."

I could poke holes in other people's spiritual stories faster than a toddler with bubble wrap. Relentless. Messy. And smug about it.

Then something shifted.
Not fireworks. Not an angel with a clipboard.
Just quiet. Goosebumps.
Thoughts too kind, too steady, too patient to be mine.

The crack opened.

One night, heavy-hearted, I whispered into the dark:
"God... are You there?"

The silence didn't feel empty.
It felt full.
Like someone was holding the other end of the line.

No flashing lights.
No Morgan Freeman voice booming from the sky.
But it split my doubt wide open.

So I tried again:
"Okay, God. If You're real—prove it.
No angels. No confetti cannons. Just something I'll know is You."

And He did.
At first it was just comfort. Peace I couldn't manufacture. A steady
knowing that I wasn't alone.

But then I wanted more. Not just feelings—words. A voice.
And after years of asking (and half-believing my own prayers), I finally
heard Him.
I think He'd been speaking all along—I just didn't know how to listen.

And the more I leaned in, the more I heard.
The more I heard, the more I trusted.

It wasn't overnight.

Not wandering one day, walking on water the next.
It was clumsy. Slow. Beautifully messy.

Years of crawling toward Him with skinned knees and prayers that started,
"God, I don't know if You're listening... but..."

And then one day, I realized—
I wasn't just hoping God was real.
I knew it.

Because once you've heard His voice—really heard it—you can't un-hear it.
It's like tasting fresh cream after years of powdered stuff. You'll never go back.

Of course, the enemy still whispered garbage:
"You're not good enough."
"That wasn't God. Just wishful thinking."

Classic devil. Same tired script, zero creativity. Honestly, he should hire new writers—or at least fire his PR team.

But now I know better.
I know who God is.
I know who I am because of Him.

One truth.
One hope.
One name: Jesus.

> "And this is the testimony: God has given us eternal life,
> and this life is in His Son."
>
> — 1 John 5:11
>
> ♣ Hope isn't wishful thinking—it's already a gift, wrapped in Jesus.

Not just a wise guy in cool sandals.
Not just a dusty Sunday school trivia answer.

He's it.
The Way. The Truth. The Life.
The only one who actually sticks.

> "I am the way and the truth and the life.
> No one comes to the Father except through me."
>
> — John 14:6
>
> ♣ Jesus isn't just pointing the way. He is the way.

No striving.
No scoreboards.
No religious Fitbit tracking your spiritual steps.
Just grace.
Just Him.

And if you're standing where I stood—one foot in faith, the other knee-deep in doubt—hear me:
You're not broken.
You're searching.
And searching? That's sacred.

Ask. Knock.

Bring your coffee-stained journal and shaky prayers.

> *"Ask and it will be given to you; seek and you will find;*
> *knock and the door will be opened to you."*
>
> — **Matthew 7:7**
>
> ❧ **God isn't dodging you. Keep knocking. He's right there.**

God isn't offended by your questions.
He's not hiding.
He's waiting.

Because that's what good Fathers do.

And if He can break through to a sarcastic, skeptical, grace-needing mess like me?
Trust me.
He can reach you too.

Pull up a chair, friend. Coffee's on.
He's still listening.
He's still speaking.
And yes—He still calls former skeptics.
(Take it from me: retired president of the Doubters Club.)

END OF CHAPTER REFLECTION

1. Have you ever been in that spot where you questioned everything—but still couldn't shake the sense that maybe, just maybe, God was real?

2. What would it look like if you stopped rushing, leaned in, and actually gave Him space to whisper?

3. If you could ask God one raw, honest question today—and know He'd answer—what would you ask?

CHAPTER 72

Jesus, Pancakes, and the Thing I Couldn't Deny

How I Went from Doubting Everything to Believing for Real

If belief were a class, I'd be the kid in the back with crossed arms, muttering, "Prove it."

And then came the word that wrecked me:
Believe.

Seven letters that sound like a bumper sticker until your life's on fire and suddenly you need it like oxygen.

It's the flashlight when you're stumbling through the dark.
The gut instinct that whispers, *Don't quit.*
The stubborn pulse of hope when everything in you screams, *Why bother?*

But I didn't grow up nailing this belief thing.
When people said, "You just gotta believe!" I rolled my eyes so hard they nearly sprained.

It sounded like a bad holiday movie.
Cue fake snow. Cue cocoa mugs. Cue eye-roll.

But real belief?
The kind that rewires you from the inside?
That's not a bumper sticker.
That's survival.

Getting there wasn't easy.
I doubted.
I Googled things like, *Is God real or am I losing it?*

One night, with cold pizza in my lap and mascara streaks on my cheeks,
I whispered:
*"God, if You're real, show me. Not goosebumps. Not a butterfly landing on my
Bible. Just something I can't shrug off as coincidence."*

And He answered.
Not with fireworks.
Not with clouds spelling "HELLO."
Just steady words pressed into my heart.
Patient. Gentle. Clear.

That's when I realized:
God isn't scared of questions.
He isn't turned off by doubt.
He just sits with you and waits.

Like He pulls up a chair and says, *Take your time. I'm not going anywhere.*

I wasn't trying to start a fight.
I just wanted to know if faith was real—
or if I was one bad day away from believing in Bigfoot too.

And when I finally believed?

Not in some vague "higher power."
In Jesus.

Something shifted.
Not fireworks. Not instant perfection.
But deep down, my heart whispered:
Yes. This. This is what I've been missing.

Belief didn't make my life neat.
But it made it possible.
Peace in the chaos.
Hope in the waiting.

And yeah—sometimes it looked like pancakes at The Flapjack Shack.
Because God shows up anywhere. Even at breakfast.

I get why people doubt.
I doubted everything too.

But think about this—
We already believe plenty we've never seen.
History books. Ancient kings. Columbus crossing the ocean.
But when it comes to Jesus? Suddenly it's "Too far-fetched."

Really?

This story has outlived empires.
It's survived fires.
It's still here. Still changing people.
And it's the only story where the hero dies for the villains—
and then comes back to invite them to dinner.

Without Jesus, we're fumbling in the dark.
Like flipping a broken light switch.

Only Jesus turns on the power.

> "Salvation is found in no one else, for there is no other name under heaven given to mankind by which we must be saved."
>
> — **Acts 4:12**
>
> ❧ **Only Jesus saves.**
> Jesus isn't just one option on the menu—He's the only One who can actually save.

And the first people who followed Him?
They didn't risk their lives for a rumor.
People die for lies all the time. But not lies they made up and knew were fake.
Nobody gets tortured for their own bad prank.

They believed because it was real.
Because they knew for sure.
They saw Jesus with their own eyes—alive after He died.

> "Now in what I am writing to you, before God, I do not lie."
>
> — **Galatians 1:20**
>
> ❧ **Paul staked his whole reputation on the gospel being true.**
> Nobody signs up for beatings and prison over a bedtime story.

So no—you can't argue someone into belief.
But you can live it.
Love big.
And yes—invite them to pancakes.

Because sometimes the best sermon isn't in a church at all.

It's at a diner booth. With coffee. And syrup.

And a God who shows up anywhere He's invited.

(Worked on Miles. Shoutout to The Flapjack Shack. Michigan's unofficial IHOP for confused skeptics everywhere.)

"Accept the one whose faith is weak, without quarreling over disputable matters."

— **Romans 14:1**

Less arguing, more grace.

People aren't debated into the Kingdom—they're loved in.

"Nothing can separate us from the love of God that is in Christ Jesus our Lord."

— **Romans 8:38–39**

God's love doesn't come with an unsubscribe button.

Nothing—no mistake, no failure—can break it.

"Whoever has the Son has life; whoever does not have the Son of God does not have life."

— **1 John 5:12**

This is the bottom line. Life is Jesus. No Jesus, no life. Simple.

END OF CHAPTER REFLECTION

1. Where does your belief feel like it is right now—steady, fragile, or just barely holding on?

2. Was there a moment when choosing to believe in Jesus shifted something deep in you?

3. Who in your life might be quietly watching your faith story, waiting to see if it's real?

CHAPTER 73

When Trust Feels Like a Tightrope In Crocs

Why Faith Feels Wobbly Until You Realize
God's Been Spotting You All Along

Faith is like Wi-Fi—sometimes strong, sometimes barely one bar.

Some days I strut like a faith champion.
Other days I'm side-eyeing heaven like, "Yo, God—did You hit mute?"
while clutching a chipped mug of reheated coffee.

We toss "faith" around like confetti.
Put it on throw pillows.
Use it as a hashtag.
But let's be honest: half the time we're whispering, "Okay... but what does
that even mean? And is there a YouTube tutorial?"

The dictionary calls faith "complete trust." Cute.
But if you've ever been stood up, scammed, or Venmo-swindled, "complete
trust" feels less like theology and more like a pyramid scheme.

Then there's "belief without proof."

Excuse me?

I read 200 Amazon reviews before I buy ChapStick.

I want evidence. Charts. Maybe a Consumer Reports article, minimum.

So yeah—faith felt risky.

Like bungee jumping with a cord I bought off Facebook Marketplace—where half the reviews say "arrived broken" and the other half say "RIP Uncle Steve."

But here's what I've learned:

Faith isn't blind. It just sees differently.

It notices patterns. Perfect timing.

Those moments that are way too precise to be luck—no matter how badly you want to chalk it up to coincidence.

I used to roll my eyes when people said, "God told me."

Sounded like an overcaffeinated brain with a Jesus filter.

But now? I lean in like I'm about to hear Taylor Swift drop an unreleased track.

"Now faith is confidence in what we hope for and assurance about what we do not see."

— **Hebrews 11:1**

❧ **Faith isn't a blind guess.**
It's a white-knuckle grip on the God who won't let go.

Because I've heard Him too.

And no, it doesn't sound like me giving myself a pep talk in the bathroom mirror.

It's peace that makes no sense.

Wisdom I couldn't Google.

Truth I didn't want to hear—but desperately needed.

Here's what trusting God really feels like:
A tightrope walk.
In Crocs.
On a windy day.
While carrying six bags of groceries.

You wobble.
You panic.
You rehearse your obituary.

But every single time?
He steadies you.
He catches you.
And somehow—you make it across.
Laughing, mascara smeared, shoes squeaking, dignity questionable... but alive. And you know you didn't make it through on your own.

> *"So we fix our eyes not on what is seen, but on what is unseen.*
> *For what is seen is temporary, but what is unseen is eternal."*
> — **2 Corinthians 4:18**
>
> ❧ **Faith isn't about ignoring reality—it's about grabbing onto forever.**

Because faith isn't about ignoring the wobble—it's about keeping your eyes locked on the One holding the rope.

END OF CHAPTER REFLECTION

1. Have you ever hit a season where your faith felt foggy, fragile—or just plain terrifying? What did you do with that ache?

2. Can you remember a time you heard a whisper that was so undeniably God, you couldn't explain it away?

3. What's one wobbly step of faith you could take this week—even if it feels like crossing a tightrope in Crocs on a windy day, wondering if your dignity will make it across too?

CHAPTER 74

The Moment I Knew For Sure

How a Free TSA Upgrade Became My Burning Bush

Faith isn't pretending everything's fine.
It's trusting God is still God—even when you're wobbling.
He's not asking for perfect faith.
Just real faith.
Mustard-seed small.
Even if it sounds like: *"Lord, I believe... but wow, am I struggling over here."*

"I do believe; help me overcome my unbelief!"

— **Mark 9:24**

🍃 **God isn't offended by doubts.**
He shows up right in the middle of them.

That was me.
I didn't start with mustard-seed faith.
I started with "God, I need neon lights, arrows, and maybe a skywriter over Times Square" kind of faith.

And one day—I got one.

Not the kind I expected.
But the kind only He could pull off.

Everyone has that moment.
The one where the fog lifts.
The one that finally makes doubt pack its bags and leave.

Mine happened at an airport.

I was flying home from that Austin job interview—nervous, second-guessing everything.
Then I saw it: the longest TSA line I'd ever laid eyes on.
I knew I was going to miss my flight.

Then came the whisper: *"Look at your ticket. You have TSA PreCheck."*

> *"Whether you turn to the right or to the left, your ears will hear a voice behind you, saying, 'This is the way; walk in it.'"*
>
> — **Isaiah 30:21**
>
> ❧ **God's whispers may be quiet—but when they come, you know.**

I pulled out my ticket, the one I'd stuffed in my purse, and there it was—big, bold letters: **TSA PreCheck.**

Which made no sense.
I didn't have it.
I'd never applied for it.

That flight was in 2014. I knew TSA PreCheck existed, but I had never applied for it and definitely didn't have it on my ticket when I flew in.

Years later, I'd learn about a short-lived TSA program—running in 2014 and ending in 2015—that sometimes slipped random travelers into PreCheck.

So yes, that explained how it might have shown up on my ticket.

But here's what it didn't explain: how I heard a whisper telling me to look, when I had no idea random selection was even possible.

That part? That was God.

It felt like God leaned over and said:
"Told you I'm real."

That was it. The moment that slammed the door on years of doubt.
Not a burning bush.
Not an angel with a clipboard.
Just a boarding pass I couldn't explain.
And a whisper I knew absolutely did not come from me.

And I knew.
Deep down, unshakable.
God is real. Alive. Personal.

I don't know what your moment will look like.
But if you keep asking, you'll get one.
Not as a party trick.
Not as proof for the whole world.
But as a love note with your name on it.

That day, He didn't give me a five-year plan.
He gave me a whisper.
And a free TSA upgrade.

Honestly, the holiest thing that's ever happened in an airport—unless you count Chick-fil-A waffle fries.

That was the day I stopped Googling *"Is God real?"*
And started living like He was.

TSA PreCheck: 1. Doubt: 0.

END OF CHAPTER REFLECTION

1. Have you ever had a whisper moment—when God broke through the noise and made it personal, just for you?

2. Have you ever asked Him for confirmation—and the answer came so perfectly timed it couldn't have been coincidence?

3. What's your version of TSA PreCheck—a small, unexpected gift that grew your shaky faith into something steadier?

CHAPTER 75

Jesus Doesn't Carry a Clipboard

And He's Not Mad At You Either

Let's clear up one of the biggest spiritual mix-ups:
Jesus is not Heaven's hall monitor.

He's not stomping around with a clipboard muttering, "Tsk, tsk, late to church again."
He's not circling your name in red ink when you hit snooze on Sunday or blowing a holy whistle because you skipped Bible study after your toddler glued herself to the dog.

That Jesus?
Yeah... I don't follow Him either.

The real Jesus isn't keeping score.
No tally marks for good deeds.
No cosmic spreadsheet of "oopsies" versus "quiet times."

If He had a clipboard at all, it would have just one word on it, in giant bubble letters: **BELOVED**.
Probably with doodles of sheep and fish.

Jesus didn't come for the polished and perfect.

He came for the messy ones.

The limping, guilt-dragging, *"I'm back again with my baggage, Lord"* kind of people.

(So... basically all of us.)

> *"For the Son of Man came to seek and to save the lost."*
>
> — **Luke 19:10**
>
> ❧ Jesus came looking for the broken— not the polished pretenders acting like they had it all together.

Here's the kicker: He didn't just rescue people.

He told us to copy Him.

Be kind to everyone.

To feed the hungry. Heal the hurting.

Open our doors and welcome outsiders.

Fun fact: Jesus Himself was an immigrant once, carried into Egypt as a baby.

So when we care for strangers, when we set a table for someone who doesn't belong, that's not just being "nice."

That's being like Him.

> *"Do not forget to show hospitality to strangers, for by doing so some people have entertained angels without knowing it."*
>
> — **Hebrews 13:2**
>
> ❧ Every guest matters. You never know when heaven might be standing at your door.

And then there's my favorite Jesus mic-drop moment.

A woman was caught in adultery.
Dragged through the streets.
Thrown in the dirt.
Surrounded by a mob of men gripping rocks.

Jesus walks in.
Kneels beside her.
And starts writing something mysterious in the dirt.

(I like to imagine He was listing out their sins one by one—"Hey Joe, tax fraud, Tuesday." Or maybe He just doodled, *"Drop the rocks, guys."*)

Then He says: *"Let the one who's never sinned throw the first stone."*

Silence.
Rocks hitting the ground one by one.
Men backing away slowly—like Homer Simpson melting into a hedge.

> *"Let any one of you who is without sin be the first to throw a stone at her."*
>
> — **John 8:7**
>
> ❧ **Jesus didn't just defend her—He blew up their pride parade and replaced it with grace.**

Then He looked at her and said,
"I don't condemn you. Now go and leave your life of sin."

Notice the order?
Not, *"Go get your act together, then I'll love you."*
But, *"I love you already. Let's change your life together."*

Love first.
Grace first.

Relationship first.

But don't miss this—He didn't give her a free pass to keep wrecking her life.
Grace isn't a hall pass to sin more; it's the power to live differently.
Forgiveness comes first, but real love also says, *"Now let's walk a new way."*

That's Jesus.
No clipboard.
No whistle.
No naughty list.

And if you've been avoiding Him because you think He's tracking every failure, hear me:

He's not crossing your name off. He's calling your name out.

Not to shame you.
To save you.

END OF CHAPTER REFLECTION

1. When you picture that moment in the dirt—rocks dropping, grace standing tall—what part hits your heart the hardest?

2. "Grace first, change second." How does that flip what you were taught about faith—and what does it stir up in you now?

3. Jesus forgave the woman, but He also called her to leave her old life behind. How does that challenge the way you think about forgiveness and change in your own life?

CHAPTER 76

Jesus Flips Tables—Not People

He's After Your Heart, Not Your Report Card

Jesus never said,
"Clean up and then come close."

He said,
"Follow Me."

Even when you're shady.
Even when you're a hot mess.

Zacchaeus? A tax scammer.
The woman at the well? Worn out and used up.
Peter? Basically a walking outburst in sandals.

Jesus still called them.

Somewhere along the way, people changed the script.
"If you sin, you're going to hell."
Wait, what? Hold up.

Here's the truth:
If sin alone sent people to hell, we'd all be toast.

Literally. Burnt Pop-Tarts.

It's not sin by itself that sends someone away from God—
it's rejecting the only One who came to rescue us from it.

> *"For it is by grace you have been saved, through faith—and this is not from yourselves, it is the gift of God."*
>
> — **Ephesians 2:8**
>
> ❧ You don't earn grace. You just unwrap it.

Jesus doesn't care about your religious résumé.
He's not grading you on attendance.
Or on how many casseroles you've carried to the potluck.
He's not scrolling through your "good deeds spreadsheet."

He wants your real heart.
Not your checklist.
Not your "I only messed up three times this week" report card.
Just... you.

I used to think God kept score.
Miss church? Minus ten.
Cried during a Hallmark movie instead of reading my Bible? Flag on the play—fifteen-yard penalty.

But no.

> *"There is now no condemnation for those who are in Christ Jesus."*
>
> — **Romans 8:1**
>
> ❧ No shame. No clipboard. No guilt buffet.

Grace doesn't expire.
Jesus doesn't roll His eyes.
He doesn't mutter, "Seriously, again?"

He's not the lunch lady of Heaven slopping guilt onto your tray.
He's the one who cooked the meal—
And saved you a seat.
Mess and all.

> *"We love because He first loved us."*
>
> — 1 John 4:19
>
> ❧ Love came first. Before the cleanup. Before the "yes."

What does Jesus actually want?
Not your perfection.
Not your performance.
Just your heart.

He'll handle the rest.

And if you're wondering if He "flips out" on people?
Nope.
Only tables.

And if He flips anything in your life, it won't be you—
it'll be the lies, the shame, and the chains trying to keep you from Him.

> *"Come to Me, all who are weary and burdened, and I will give you rest."*
>
> — **Matthew 11:28**
>
> ❧ **Rest isn't a prize for good behavior.**
> It's a gift for the exhausted.

END OF CHAPTER REFLECTION

1. Ever catch yourself trying to "earn" God's love—like He's keeping score—only to realize He already handed it to you, no strings attached?

2. Can you remember a time you braced yourself for judgment... but what actually showed up was pure grace?

3. What would it look like if you finally dropped the act and just rested in Jesus—mess, exhaustion, and all?

CHAPTER 77

The Day the Lost Sheep Stopped Climbing Fences

The True Story of a Runaway Sheep and a Very Patient Shepherd

The grass was fine.
Plenty of space. Sunshine. Safety.

And yet there I was—eyeing the fence like it had personally insulted me.

The other sheep grazed politely, tails flicking like they were in a sheep shampoo commercial.
Me? I was plotting my great escape like a teenager sneaking out past curfew.

One glance over my shoulder.
No Shepherd in sight.
Then—*boop!*—one leg over.

And just like that, I was gone.
Headed toward some glittery distraction that promised more but delivered less.

(Like buying cheap shoes online—looked amazing in the ad, fell apart the minute I wore them).

Ever felt like the odd one out in God's flock?
Yeah. That was me.

If there were a "Most Likely to Wander Off" award, I'd win every year. My yearbook photo would show me grinning, holding grass I stole from the neighbor's yard, proud like I'd pulled off the heist of the century.

I swear He looked at the angels more than once, sighed lovingly, and said, "Welp... Christine's off-roading again. Somebody grab My sandals."

And every single time I wandered?
Jesus came after me.

> *"Suppose one of you has a hundred sheep and loses one of them. Doesn't he leave the ninety-nine... and go after the lost sheep until he finds it?"*
> — **Luke 15:4**
>
> ❧ **That's love. Relentless, pursuing, undeserved love.**

Not with a lecture.
Not muttering, "Seriously, again?"
He came Himself.

The Good Shepherd.
With compassion in His eyes.
Grace in His hands.
And sandals that have definitely seen some miles.

> *"I am the good shepherd... I know my sheep and my sheep know me."*
> —**John 10:11,14**
>
> ❧ **Jesus isn't distant. He knows your name, your fears, your scars—**
> and He still calls you His. Even when you wander, He never forgets where you belong.

When He found me, I was usually a mess—
Wool matted.
Pride tangled in emotional barbed wire.
Insisting, *"I'm fine! Totally fine!"*

Spoiler: I was about as "fine" as week-old gas station sushi.

But He didn't scold me.
He picked me up.
Dusted me off.
And carried me home.

Here's the twist—
I *knew* I was the lost sheep.
I just didn't know you could be found... and still fully loved.

I thought I had to be "spiritually Instagram-ready" first.
At least buy one of those leather Bibles with the tabs so I'd look like I knew what I was doing.

But Jesus didn't wait for my polish.
He came for my pain.

I didn't find Him because I was clever.
He found me because He's committed.

I remember one of my lowest moments.
Sitting in my car in a Target parking lot, crying into a McDonald's bag,
convinced God must be so disappointed in me.

I wasn't praying.
Wasn't reading my Bible.
Just drowning in guilt.

But even there—in my self-dug ditch—He showed up.

Eventually, I stopped running.
Stopped chasing "better pastures" that were really just AstroTurf.
(Like trading steak for a soggy fair corn dog: looks fun, leaves you broke
and sticky.)

Because I realized—
The best pasture isn't out there.
It's wherever the Shepherd is.

Let's be real—sheep aren't geniuses.
They panic.
They walk into things.
They follow each other off cliffs.

If I were a literal sheep, I'd have leaves stuck in my wool, a limp from
falling in a hole, and probably a Chick-fil-A sauce packet stuck to my hoof.

But that's the point.
It's not about the sheep's IQ.
It's about the Shepherd's heart.

> *"My sheep listen to My voice; I know them, and they follow Me."*
> —**John 10:27**
>
> ❧ **His voice is steady and unmistakable.**
> When we hear it, our only job is to follow.

And His heart?
It's wild about you.
Even when you doubt.
Even when you're messy.
Even when you're convinced He's done chasing you.

He's not.

The lost sheep story isn't for "other people."
It's for all of us.

Because we all wander.
We all need a love that doesn't quit when we do.

So if you've been wandering—breaking promises, missing chances, thinking you've gone too far—hear me:
You're not too late.
You're not too lost.
You're not too much.

The Good Shepherd knows exactly where you are.
And He's not coming to shame you.
He's coming to save you.

> "The thief comes only to steal and kill and destroy; I have come that they may have life, and have it to the full."
>
> — John 10:10
>
> ✤ The enemy drains joy. Jesus restores it.

Now that I've stopped climbing fences...
Now that I've let Him carry me home...

Well, friend—this runaway sheep?
She's not lost anymore.

Because once you've been carried by grace—once you've felt the arms of the Good Shepherd—you stop looking for greener grass.
You already found it.

I'm home.

And okay, yes—sometimes I glance at the fence.
But nothing out there beats the peace in here.

Somewhere nearby, I picture the Shepherd chuckling—
Sandals by the door.
Just in case.

END OF CHAPTER REFLECTION

1. Ever had a "lost sheep season" — wandering, doubting, trying to DIY life — and ended up face-planting in the AstroTurf anyway?

2. How does it hit you to know Jesus would leave the 99 just to come find you — messy wool, Chick-fil-A sauce packet on your hoof and all?

3. What "fence" are you still tempted to climb — and what would it look like to stay close to the Shepherd instead?

CHAPTER 78

Sugar, Snow, and Second Chances

The Weekend We Stopped Being Strangers

I thought the hard part was over.

Turns out, God wasn't done with plot twists.

He handed me two kids, a mountain of paperwork, and a stuffed animal named Wilber.

This wasn't "The End." Not even close.

But it was the end of me begging for proof that God was real.

I know He is now.

I've seen too much. Felt too much. Heard too much to pretend otherwise.

These days?

It's not about proof.

It's about trust.

And trust usually comes wrapped in instructions that make zero sense—but turn out way better than my plans.

Enter: Autumn and Jaxson.

Two siblings.

One teenage girl with enough sass to power a small city.

One little boy who could dismantle your ceiling fan in three minutes flat—for fun.

Autumn was 14. Gorgeous. Guarded.
Way too smart to fall for fake kindness.

Jaxson was 9. Sweet as pie.
But also? He had the curiosity of a mad scientist and the attention span of a squirrel on espresso.
If something could be taken apart, he'd find a way.
Then he'd look at you like *you* were the crazy one for expecting it to still work.

They came as a package deal.
They also came with laughter, noise, healing, trauma, and chaos—with a capital C.

Let's be honest. Teenagers are hard.
Parenting one you just met? One with layers of hurt you didn't help write?
That's next-level hard.

You're jumping into a book halfway through, guessing the plot, hoping you don't ruin the ending.

And it hurt.
Every time I pulled close, Autumn pulled away.
Some days hugging her felt like hugging a hedgehog.
With lip gloss and combat boots.

One night, after another blowup, I crawled into my closet.
Sobbed into a hoodie sleeve. Whispered, *"God... maybe I can't do this. Maybe I was wrong."*
And I heard it. Calm. Steady.
"She is yours. Forever. Don't give up."

Autumn came in like a wildfire wrapped in glitter.
Beautiful. Bold. Absolutely convinced I knew nothing.

She was fluent in sarcasm and skepticism.
The eyeliner was thick. The necklaces were chokers.
And the eye rolls? Olympic level.

She was nothing like Rainy.
She needed different love.

And I was trying—really trying—to let her be her without commenting on every dramatic outfit or vampire-level makeup choice.

But I'm a mom. I have opinions.
And holding them in felt like trying not to sneeze in a silent church sanctuary.

When things got rough, I'd drive to H-E-B (a Texas grocery store chain) and cry in my car in the parking lot.

Cue the emergency call to Lindsay—our foster care director and personal lifeline.
Part counselor. Part cheerleader. Part emotional SWAT team.

"I don't think I'm cut out for this," I'd cry. "Like... is there a return policy on foster parenting?"

And Lindsay—God bless her—would talk me off the ledge with her wisdom, humor, and grace.
"She's scared. She feels safe with you now, so she's letting the fear show. You're doing great. Keep going."

So I'd wipe my face.
March into H-E-B for some emergency chocolate therapy.
And drive home like a mom on a mission.

Then I'd head upstairs to Autumn's room.
We'd sit and talk.
Sometimes for five minutes. Sometimes for hours.

I'd listen—really listen.
Not just to her words, but to the fear underneath.

And in the middle of those messy, beautiful conversations, I'd feel God
nudging me.
Whispering just the right words.
Soothing her heart.
Soothing mine.
Helping us find our way back to each other.

And slowly... things shifted.

Her makeup got softer. Her clothes more gentle.
Her walls? Not gone—but lower.

She started showing up as herself.
Not the version she thought she had to be to survive.

Then came the trip to Chicago.

My sister called to plan a birthday party for our mom.
Mom's health was fading. This might be the last one.

I started booking a flight.
And God whispered: *"Take Autumn."*

Uh... come again?
A solo trip? Just the two of us?

But the whisper didn't stop.
So I said yes.

Got the paperwork. Packed snacks.
And braced for impact.

Cue: The Airport Coffee Incident.

We're in line. I order my black coffee.
Then drown it in sugar like it's a science experiment.

Autumn, who was basically a walking Instagram model and could've
walked a runway, looks at me and says,
"You probably don't need that much sugar."

Y'ALL.
I could feel my soul leave my body.
It wasn't cruel—just careless. But wow, it hit hard.

I called Miles. Whispered, "Come get her."
He chuckled. "Really?"

God whispered: *"Your feelings are hurt. That's all. Talk to her."*

So I did. We sat down together right there on the airport carpet.
I told her about my weight struggles. My insecurities.
How I knew she didn't mean it—but it still hurt.
Something shifted—we started over.

We got on the plane, and I prayed: *"Lord, please make this the best trip ever.*
Help us bond. Give me the right words to say to her."
I meant it—with every fiber in me.

"You will seek me and find me when you seek me with all your heart."
— **Jeremiah 29:13**

❧ **God isn't hiding. He's waiting.**

413

At the hotel, I asked for a better room.
We got Room 2304—pretty sure it was the top floor. Gorgeous skyline view. It felt like God whispering, *I got you.*

We walked the city streets laughing together through snow flurries.
Chased taxis like amateur tourists.

We took goofy photos with her emotional support stuffed animal, Wilber—who, by the way, got more camera time than either of us.

Wilber posed with sculptures, fountains, hotel pillows.
He got his own chair at breakfast. A prime spot on the windowsill "to enjoy the view."
Honestly? Wilber was living his best life.

Then came Navy Pier.
The Ferris wheel spun over the Chicago skyline lights.
Lake Michigan stretched dark and endless behind us.
And somewhere between the spinning and the laughter, Autumn softened.
A wall came down.
So did mine.

That weekend, Mom and Autumn talked.
At Mom's birthday party, Autumn slid into the seat beside her.
Mom caught my eye across the table and smiled.
"You have another beautiful daughter," she said. "She's a wonderful granddaughter. You should be proud."

My heart swelled.
She knew.
She remembered the little girl who played with dolls in that red playhouse, dreaming of being a mom.
Now I had Rainy.
And somehow, she knew Autumn was mine too.
Special. Chosen.

Maybe that's why God nudged me to bring her.

So Mom could see.

So she would know my dream had been fulfilled.

Not once, but twice.

> *"Trust in the Lord with all your heart and lean not on your own understanding."*
>
> **— Proverbs 3:5**
>
> ♪ **Faith isn't about figuring it out.**
> It's about following Him—even when it makes zero sense.

She met my mom there—for the first and last time.

And I held onto that moment, thanking God right there in Chicago for whispers that make no sense...

Until they do.

It wasn't just about sugar or coffee. It was about trust. Healing. Grace that shows up—even on airport floors and Ferris wheels.

Back at the hotel, Autumn curled up by the window with Wilber, watching the snow fall outside. And I knew—she wasn't just visiting my world anymore. She was letting herself belong in it. Letting herself be loved.

And that?

Was the real miracle.

END OF CHAPTER REFLECTION

1. Have you ever had a moment that looked ordinary on the outside—but shifted everything on the inside?

2. Has God ever whispered something that felt confusing at first... but later you realized it was exactly what you needed?

3. Where is God asking you to trust Him right now—not because it makes sense, but because you know His heart does?

CHAPTER 79

Operation Wilber

The Day God Proved He's in the Details—Even at Disney

When Autumn and Jaxson first came to us, church was... let's just say "reluctant."
Think dragging a cat into a bathtub.
While the cat is holding a grudge and a side-eye sharp enough to cut glass.

But little by little, something changed.
We prayed together.
We sang—loud, off-key, possibly offensive to angels.
We argued on the way and repented during the second worship song.
God was quietly knitting a family together.

Then came Winter Storm Uri.
Texas tried to be a snow globe. It failed miserably.

Power? Gone.
Heat? Nope.
Toilets? Non-flushable frontier nightmares.

It was offensively cold.
The kids scooped snow into buckets like survivalist penguins.

We melted it on the stove—on the rare occasions the power graced us with its presence during the rolling blackouts.
And what was it for? Drinking water? Cooking?

Nope. Flushing toilets. Foster care glamour at its finest/worst.

Meanwhile, the kids were cooking snow like it was ramen.
We laughed to keep from crying.
And when a pipe burst and flooded part of the house, we decided tears were valid too.

But here's the thing—God was there.
In the snow soup.
In the blackout board games.
Even in the eventual insurance payout that got us new floors.

Sacred moments don't always come with candles and worship music.
Sometimes they come with frozen plumbing and prayers for working toilets.

And that storm taught me something:
God cares about the big disasters—and the tiny inconveniences.
And I was about to learn just how much... from a pink stuffed animal named Wilber.

Fast-forward to Disney World.
My personal happy place.

Autumn loved it too—but mostly because her emotional support stuffed animal, Wilber, came along for the ride.
Wilber wasn't just pink fluff and thread.
He was a gift from Jonathan—the first boyfriend who didn't make me want to call in the FBI.
He was kind, respectful. Actually took her to church. Major upgrade.

Wilber went everywhere with her.
He was her comfort.
Safety.
Proof that love might not always hurt.

After Autumn and I bonded on our trip to Chicago,
she told me she believed Wilber was the glue that healed our relationship.
To her, Wilber meant things could get better.
That she could be okay.

Then one tragic afternoon in Epcot... Wilber vanished.

One minute tucked under her arm.
The next—gone.

Autumn froze. Then panicked.
Tears came fast.
This wasn't about a toy. This was about every loss she'd ever had.

Miles and I saw the panic on her face and knew this was go-time.
"There will be no more rides," I announced,
"until we find that stuffed animal!"

All the kids were officially activated.
"Operation Wilber" was underway.

We retraced every step.
Aquarium. Bathrooms. Benches.
We prayed like Pentecostals and bribed like mob bosses.

"If you ever want to see that Guardians of the Galaxy ride again," I warned
the siblings,
"you better come up with that stuffed animal!"

And then—miracle.

Wilber turned up in lost and found.

The look on Autumn's face nearly cracked my heart in two.
She clutched Wilber like he was her heartbeat.
Like having him back meant maybe everything broken could be found again.

And right there in the middle of Epcot, God whispered to me:
"See? I care about what matters to her too."

> *"Are not two sparrows sold for a penny? Yet not one of them will fall to the ground outside your Father's care... So don't be afraid; you are worth more than many sparrows."*
>
> — **Matthew 10:29-31**
>
> ❧ If God notices sparrows and stuffed animals, imagine how much He notices you.

Because He does.
He sees the trauma.
The heartbreak.
The grief.

And the little things too.
Like a stuffed animal in a crowd of tourists.
Like a girl learning she's safe, loved, and worth finding.

> *"So do not fear, for I am with you... I will strengthen you and help you."*
>
> — **Isaiah 41:10**
>
> ❧ Fear doesn't vanish. But neither does His presence.

We had no idea, in that moment at Disney with a stuffed animal named
Wilber,
that we were inching closer to something even bigger.
Something permanent.
Something sacred.

That night Wilber sat in the hotel window, quiet—
like he knew what was coming next.

> *"And we know that in all things God works for the good of those who
> love Him..."*
>
> **— Romans 8:28**
>
> ❧ Nothing's wasted. Not pain. Not detours. Not even a lost
> **stuffed animal.**

END OF CHAPTER REFLECTION

1. What's your "Wilber"—that little thing that makes you feel safe,
   even if nobody else gets it?

2. Do you really believe God cares about the tiny stuff—the lost-and-
   found moments, the random heartbreaks, the details nobody else
   notices?

3. When has God used a messy, inconvenient season (you know, the
   kind that makes you want to cry in the bathroom) to actually pull
   you closer to the people you love?

CHAPTER 80

Fist Bumps and Broken Hearts

When Joy and Sorrow Shared the Same Room

Two years after they arrived, we adopted Autumn and Jaxson. Together.

If you're picturing mahogany benches and tissues passed down the row—stop.
This was Zoom court.

Forever families, brought to you by Wi-Fi, leggings, and mute buttons no one could find.

We crammed into one little rectangle.
Miles and me up front.
Autumn and Jaxson behind us.

Then he appeared—the same judge who finalized Rainy's adoption.
Smiling like this was the best part of his job.

"Kids," he said softly, "no more CPS. No more foster care. You are now officially Pilgrims."

I turned just in time to see it.

Autumn and Jaxson glanced at each other—small, knowing smiles tugging at their faces.
No words. Just two kids who'd been through too much.
Then quietly, deliberately, their knuckles met.

A fist bump.

It wasn't loud.
It wasn't staged.
It was survival and relief in one tiny gesture.

Like they were saying: *We made it. We're safe now. Together.*

Small. Silent.
Everything.

We celebrated Zoom-style.
I dressed up—even though the fanciest courtroom I saw that day was my dining room table.
Lipstick for the laptop camera. Heels no one could see.

Miles wore Michigan State pajama pants.
The judge's Wi-Fi froze mid-sentence.
But it didn't matter.
We were family. Officially.

Joy was thick in the air.
But heartbreak wasn't far behind.

From day one, we prayed the siblings could stay together.
Two more sisters were out there.
We kept the door open. We hoped. We waited.

Then the call came.
Mia—just a year younger than Autumn.

From a Residential Treatment Center.

She wanted to live with us.
We said yes without hesitation.
Because siblings belong together.

Mia was clever. Artistic. Beautiful.
But untethered.
Carrying wounds you couldn't see, but could feel.

She came. She left. She ran.
Over and over.

Not just from us—but from many houses.
Chasing something she couldn't name.

She wasn't with us anymore.
She had run again.

Then the phone rang.
Mia was sixteen.
A car. A crash.
And she was gone.

Air vanished from the room.

When the kids heard, their screams gutted me.
They clung to each other like drowning souls grabbing the same raft.

Ava was with us by then—the youngest sister.
She had dreamed of all four kids living under one roof again.
But that dream was gone.

I stood in our living room.
Watching hearts break in real time.

No words.
Just sobs.

"God... help," I whispered.
"Show me what to do."

And He came.
Not with answers.
Just presence.

> *"The Lord is close to the brokenhearted and saves those who are crushed in spirit."*
>
> — **Psalm 34:18**
>
> ❧ **Your pain pulls Him closer, not farther away.**

"Just stay," He whispered.
"Just hold them."

So I did.

No speeches.
No solutions.
Just arms around shaking bodies.
Just love that refuses to leave.

That year, joy and sorrow didn't just dance.
They took turns leading.

One day—
a silent fist bump in a Zoom courtroom.
The next—
holding my kids as they screamed for a sister who wouldn't come home.

But through it all, the same God stayed.

Through the laughter.

Through the sobs.

Through the courtroom screen.

Through the hospital call.

> *"He heals the brokenhearted and binds up their wounds."*
>
> **— Psalm 147:3**
>
> ♪ He's the healer who stays and makes new what was **shattered.**

And we learned—

joy and grief can share the same room when love refuses to walk out.

END OF CHAPTER REFLECTION

1. Have you ever been in that tug-of-war between grief and faith—wondering which one was going to win? What kept you standing when you thought you might fall?

2. Can you remember a moment when God didn't show up with answers or quick fixes—but just... Himself? How did you know He was there?

3. When have joy and sorrow pulled up chairs at the same table in your life—and what did that moment teach you about His love?

CHAPTER 81

The Voice That Led Me Home

(And Kept Me From the Shiny Trainwreck)

If I'd ignored God's voice—that "yucky gut feeling" I couldn't shake—I wouldn't be here.
Not even close.

I'd probably be stuck in traffic somewhere in a rented Nissan Altima—burned out, over-caffeinated, smiling on the outside but dying on the inside.

But I'm not there.
I'm here.

Here with an incredible husband who loves God—and me—even when I'm hangry.
He's a rockstar dad to our kids. We live in sunny San Antonio.
Our home is full of laughter, lipstick and loud love.
It's chaotic—but the good kind. The sacred kind.

Here with a career I love. The kind that fits like a custom blazer with pockets.

But to get here?
I had to turn down the shinier job.
The one that screamed *You've made it!*
And listen instead to the whisper: *Don't do it, girl.*

If I'd said yes to shiny, I would've missed sacred.
Rainy beaming when people say she looks like me.
Autumn bringing me flowers "because my mom deserves it."
Jaxson knocking every night just to say "I love you."
Ava presenting me with glitter-covered Tinkerbells—because she knows
my favorite fairy.

Shiny would've cost all of that.

Later, when life finally felt steady, I thought, *Maybe it's time to climb again.*
I even started eyeing other companies—tempted by "more" and "bigger."

But in the middle of my restless scrolling, God made it clear: *Stay. Right
here. Your next promotion will come where you already are.*

> "Trust in the Lord with all your heart and lean not on your own
> understanding; in all your ways submit to him, and he will make
> your paths straight."
>
> **— Proverbs 3:5–6**
>
> ❧ **You don't need the whole map—just the Guide.**

I had followed His voice this far, so I chose to trust Him again.
And it paid off.

Rumors started—someone was retiring.
Their role? Way out of my league.
I wasn't certified. I'd need to pass tough exams.
The kind that make grown men cry into briefcases.

But then I heard it. God's voice, steady and sure:
"This is it. This is for you. Go for it. I've already cleared the way."

> *"Whether you turn to the right or to the left, your ears will hear a voice behind you, saying, 'This is the way; walk in it.'"*
> — **Isaiah 30:21**
>
> ❧ **God's whisper is steady—even when your steps feel shaky.**

And I knew that voice.
When He says yes, you go.

There was just one problem—I couldn't take the exams without permission.
So I called the man who would become my future boss.
I told him I knew I could do it. I spoke with confidence.
He listened. And then he gave me the chance.

There was something in his voice that told me he believed in me.
Sometimes, one voice of belief is all it takes to unlock courage you didn't even know you had.

I studied. Passed the first exam.
Failed the second.
I was crushed.

But God hadn't said "almost."
He'd said, *"This is for you."*

So I wiped my face, drove to Houston for a prep class, studied like my life depended on it, prayed like it really did—and passed.

I called my future boss.
"Great," he said. "Now pass the next one. I know you can do it."

His belief lit a fire in me before my own had even sparked.
I wasn't about to let him—or God—down.

I passed the next exam. First try.
And this time, I didn't just trust God.
I trusted me.

A few months later, the phone rang.
"We'd like to offer you the position."

I squealed, happy-danced, and shot a grin toward Heaven.
On paper, it made zero sense. In His plan, it made perfect sense.

Two years later, God widened the path even more—another promotion,
with a new title and provision. Another *only God* moment.

None of it was ladder-climbing hustle.
It was the whisper that led me here.
The one that led me home.
And kept me from the shiny trainwreck that would've cost me everything
that mattered.

> *"For I know the plans I have for you,' declares the Lord, 'plans to prosper you and not to harm you, plans to give you hope and a future."*
> **— Jeremiah 29:11**
>
> **He's not winging it with your life.**

> *"In all things God works for the good of those who love Him..."*
> **— Romans 8:28**
>
> **Not one detour is wasted.**

END OF CHAPTER REFLECTION

1. Have you ever brushed off that gut feeling—only to realize later it was God trying to protect you?

2. Can you think of a time God whispered "stay" when everything in you wanted to bolt?

3. Where might He be asking for your yes right now—even if it makes absolutely no sense on paper?

CHAPTER 82

The Career Cha-Cha

How Two Steps Back Still Led Me Forward

God knows how to orchestrate a rescue mission.

When I started this new role, I was clueless.
Deer-in-headlights clutching a laptop clueless.
And to make it even more fun?
It was right after... well, you know. That global chaos chapter we'd all like to skip in history books.

So there I was—working from home.
Staring at my screen like it held the cure for awkward silence.
I could type like lightning, sure. But none of that helped when I had no idea what I was doing.

In my old position? I was excellent.
I knew it inside and out.

My time in Austin? That had been management. A promotion.
But when we moved to San Antonio, I chose the safe position.
Right back where I started.

It felt like a step back.
But really, it was just the Cha-Cha—two steps back, waiting for the beat, before the next big step forward.

Then came the exams. Two down. Another passed. Promotion.
Two steps forward.
And now? Promoted again.
Proof the Cha-Cha works if you don't quit the dance.

But when I was first offered this new position, everything was new.
New systems. New rules. New everything.
And I had to learn it fast enough to teach other people—without passing out.

Enter Lisa.
The MVP. The legend. My mentor.
My fairy godmother—appearing daily on a laptop screen.

She had a laugh that could light up a room and chase away nerves in an instant.
And she showed up—every single day.
Patient. Steady. Answering a million questions without once making me feel dumb.

She always ended with the magic words:
"You're doing great. You're a quick learner."
Cue the invisible parade I threw in my head.

Lisa didn't just train me—she sprinkled confidence over every step.
We lived in different states, but the screen between us became our bridge.
We were a dream team.

And when it was time for me to fly solo, she gave me a virtual hug and let me go.
Her magic wand wasn't sparkles or spells—it was patience and kindness.

I was ready—because she made me ready.

Then came my "special ops squad": The Brain Trust.
(I'm looking at you, endless work group chats).
The geniuses who translated corporate Greek into English.
The ones who helped me turn "Wait, what?" into "Yep, I've got this."

There was also one wise woman—my unofficial crisis coach.
She taught me how to handle tough situations without hiding under my
desk or setting the building on fire. (Both tempting options.)
She let my inner comedian out.
Every conversation ended the same way: both of us laughing, and her
sighing, "Oh, I needed that laugh today."

And now? I've got a new boss—just as amazing as the one who first
believed in me.
Different season, same gift.
God keeps placing the right people in my life, right when I need them.

All those years I envied my sister Denise with her amazing career—and
now, God finally handed me mine.

I love my new position—it feels like a gift straight from God.
The kind of work that challenges me but also fits like it was made for me.
Yes, it's a rollercoaster—full of shifting rules and surprise turns.
But even there, I see His fingerprints.
I see how He surrounded me with the right people and steadied me for
each step.

> *"Trust in the Lord with all your heart and lean not on your own understanding."*
>
> — **Proverbs 3:5**
>
> ❧ **You don't need to figure it all out.**
> Trust the One who already knows the way.

And here's where the two worlds—the work and the personal—collided. Because while God was equipping me with the right people for my job, He was also reminding me of the whisper He'd given me years before: *"Bring Miles, Maddie, and Judy closer to Me."*

No how-to guide. No timeline.
Just a whisper.

I told Denise during that retreat, and her eyes lit up.
"Christine, I sensed the exact same thing."
Confirmation. Holy goosebumps.

I don't hear God with my ears.
Not out loud.
It's quieter than that—but stronger too.
A whisper that sinks deep and won't let go.

I hear Him in my thoughts—clear, steady, impossible to ignore.
And if that sounds a little wild to you, that's okay.
I used to wonder the same thing.
But once you've heard Him, you just know.

No thunder. No skywriting.
Just a calm, certain voice cutting through the noise:
"Hey. This way."

> *"Whether you turn to the right or to the left, your ears will hear a voice behind you, saying, 'This is the way; walk in it.'"*
> — **Isaiah 30:21**
>
> ♪ **He's not silent. His voice is always guiding—**
> sometimes whispering, but always steady.

So we followed.
We moved to Texas.

Now we laugh around the dinner table.
Pray over meals.
Cheer for each other.
Cry with each other.

We're living that whisper—one messy, beautiful, holy step at a time.
Not because I'm fearless.
Not because I've got it all figured out.
But because I listened.

> *"My sheep listen to my voice; I know them, and they follow me."*
> — **John 10:27**
>
> ♪ **You are His. You are known.**
> He's still calling you by name.

And because His voice didn't just lead me to a job...
It led me to my people.
To my purpose.
To a life I couldn't have built on my own.
To home.

Sometimes life really is a Cha-Cha.

Step forward. Step back. Spin around.
But when God leads the dance? You'll always land exactly where you're supposed to be.

Lisa, the Brain Trust, every boss who believed in me—they weren't accidents. They were choreography. God's way of proving He's in the details, guiding every step of the dance.

Turns out—I can dance after all.
(Okay... maybe not on an actual dance floor. But the Jesus Cha-Cha? That one, I've got.)

END OF CHAPTER REFLECTION

1. Who showed up for you in a season when you felt way in over your head—the kind of person who made you believe you could actually do it?

2. Have you ever taken what felt like a step backward, only to realize later it was God's setup for something bigger?

3. Can you think of a time when God's whisper was so clear, it shifted your whole direction—and you just knew it was Him?

CHAPTER 83

Wild Hearts and Rooftop Rescues

How God Turns Chaos Into Calling

By age twelve, Jaxson had already earned a full set of "parental achievement badges":

- Indoor Graffiti Badge – spray-painted his action figures. Indoors. With the windows closed. The whole upstairs reeked like a body shop.
- Rooftop Explorer Badge – cut out a second-story screen and climbed onto the roof. Out there just laying back like it was his personal Airbnb planetarium.
- Fire Safety Failure Badge – tried to roast marshmallows on his bedroom carpet, leaving a permanent circle of charred black. I'm convinced the carpet still smells like s'mores.
- Kitchen Bomb Squad Badge – hard-boiled an egg in the microwave... without water. (It exploded. The kitchen looked like an omelet had met a hand grenade. Genius.)

Parenting Jaxson felt less like raising a child and more like starring in my own Saturday morning cartoon.

Comedy. Chaos.

And a constant soundtrack of, *"What in the WORLD?!"*

Jaxson was the kid I worried about most.

I knew girls.

I'd been one.

Raised a few.

I spoke fluent estrogen.

Boys?

Different species.

No manual. No warning label. Definitely no mute button.

Jaxson came into our life like a tornado in a toy aisle.

Touching everything.

Breaking most of them.

Questioning everything.

And usually hiding the evidence.

When Rainy's retainer went missing, we knew who had it.

If the house smelled like nail polish? Mystery solved—curiosity had struck again.

He kept us on our toes in the most unforgettable—and occasionally flammable—ways.

But here's the thing: God didn't call us to raise perfect kids.

He called us to love them.

And Jaxson needed love in bulk.

Along with structure.

And about a thousand repeated instructions a day.

> *"Start children off on the way they should go, and even when they are old they will not turn from it."*
>
> **— Proverbs 22:6**
>
> ❧ **Every seed of love, truth, and faith you plant will grow—** maybe slower than you'd like, but it will grow.

Then one day, something shifted.
Beneath the chaos, a gentleman was emerging.

We taught him to hold the door.
Say please and thank you.
Put others first—especially the ladies.
(With all the girls in the house, he didn't really have a choice.)

"Ladies first," I told him.
"Even if they take forever?" he asked.
"Especially then," I said.

Bit by bit, it stuck.
Respect. Kindness. A new layer of responsibility.
Pretty soon, he was racking up Chivalry Badges—tiny medals only moms can see.

Now?
He takes out the trash.
Mops the floors.
Helps with groceries.
Complains only 30% of the time—which is basically sainthood for a teenage boy.
He definitely has a heart to serve.
That's his Household Helper Badge.

One-on-one, he's pure gold.
Funny. Smart. Affectionate.
The kind of kid who hugs you goodnight and whispers, "I love you, Mom," and melts your entire soul.
And yes, I mentally pin a Soul-Melter Badge on him every time he does it.

He dreams big.
Some days it's the military. And honestly? He looks pretty sharp in that ROTC uniform.

Other days, being an entrepreneur.

Once, it was a storm chaser.

(Not my favorite phase, but at least he never tried to build a tornado in the backyard... yet.)

And lately? Maybe some kind of mechanical repairman.

His curiosity makes him want to fix anything that's broken—including vacuum cleaners.

He tinkered with ours once, and somehow... it worked again.

Pretty sure it involved equal parts confidence and random button pushing.

So naturally, I awarded him the Household Hero Badge—for services rendered to appliances everywhere.

One week he's planning to save the world.

The next, he's inventing gadgets out of duct tape and determination.

It's equal parts inspiring and terrifying—because with this young man, you never quite know if you're getting genius... or smoke alarms.

Whatever he chooses, one thing's certain:

God's got something incredible planned for this once-wild-hearted kiddo.

We used to wonder how we'd survive him.

Now we wonder what amazing things God is preparing him for.

> *"...He who began a good work in you will carry it on to completion until the day of Christ Jesus."*
>
> **— Philippians 1:6**
>
> ❧ **Kids aren't finished products. Neither are we.**
> God's still at work.

Because this once-wild-hearted boy?

He's learning how to channel that energy into purpose.

The same grit that climbed rooftops and roasted carpet marshmallows...

might just be the grit God uses to change the world.

> *"For my thoughts are not your thoughts, neither are your ways my ways," declares the Lord. As the heavens are higher than the earth, so are my ways higher than your ways and my thoughts than your thoughts."*
>
> **— Isaiah 55:8–9**
>
> ♪ **Even in chaos, God's plan is bigger, better,**
> and way funnier than anything we could dream up.

Because this kid? He's going to be something great.

And who knows—maybe one day he'll trade in his badges for medals, patents, or uniforms.
But for now, his proudest badge is the one he doesn't even see:

Beloved son, chosen by God.

And that's the best badge of all.

END OF CHAPTER REFLECTION

1. Have you ever felt completely unequipped to parent or guide someone—and wondered how on earth you'd make it through? What did God do in that gap?

2. What quirks in a kid (or even in yourself) might actually be little breadcrumbs pointing to future greatness?

3. Could the chaos you're in right now actually be the early signs of someone becoming exactly who God made them to be?

CHAPTER 84

The Roller Coaster, The Himalaya, and the Book That Broke Me (In the Best Way)

How a Seatbelt, a Spin Ride, and a Quiet Daughter Changed Everything

Ava was our last little whirlwind.
The final puzzle piece.
Not a perfect fit at first—but somehow, she made the picture whole.

She was different from the others.
Quieter.
A watcher before a talker.
She seemed to hold everything in like a volcano—silent until she finally erupted when she was angry or upset.
But even in her silence, she changed the whole dynamic.

We've had laughs.
We've had tears.
And enough emotional baggage to fill a luggage carousel.

Family vacations?
Pure chaos on steroids—with sunscreen, churros, and someone always losing a shoe.

Especially if an amusement park is involved.
Now listen, thrill rides are not my jam.
I like roller coasters. Sure.
But I prefer the kind that don't try to rip my face off.

One summer in Ohio, Ava and I split up from the rest of the adrenaline junkies.
I made the mistake of picking a "safe" coaster with Ava.
Middle schoolers and grandmas were riding it.
Perfect.
Or so I thought.

Here's the thing.
That season?
I was seventy pounds heavier.
And *not* feeling fabulous about it.

We climbed in.
One seatbelt.
For both of us.
I pulled. I shoved. I begged physics to be my friend.
Nope. That buckle wasn't closing unless we called in the jaws of life.

I jumped out faster than a cat from a bathtub.
Told Ava she'd have to ride alone.
Smiled big, like it didn't sting. But inside? Something cracked—not just pride, something I couldn't laugh off.
I decided right then: this would never happen again.

> *"The Lord is close to the brokenhearted and saves those who are crushed in spirit."*
>
> **— Psalm 34:18**
>
> 🔊 **God doesn't run from pain.**
> He sits with you in it and starts the healing there.

Fast forward an hour.
We braved *The Himalaya.*
It spins. It squishes. It turns the outside rider into roadkill.
So I took the death seat.

We climbed in. Ava looked down at the seatbelt.
Then she looked at me with wide eyes.
"There's only one seatbelt."

I prayed like I've never prayed before.
"God, if You love me, don't let her ride this one alone too.
I got the message. I'm working on it.
Just give me this win."

We pulled, we tugged.
Then...click. Victory.
Pretty sure an angel personally buckled that belt while heaven high-fived me.
And I laughed the whole ride—not because it was fun, but because God had just proved He's got the best sense of humor.

Now? Seventy pounds lighter, I want a rematch with that first coaster.
Not to prove anything.
Just a victory lap.
Because that day didn't defeat me.
It woke me up.

But Ava?
She was fighting her own roller coasters.
The kind you don't see at amusement parks.

Therapy helped us both. I'm learning to speak "Ava"—a language of sideways glances, silence, and quiet questions that mean everything.
She's learning to trust that she's enough.
That she always was.

> *"Start children off on the way they should go, and even when they are old they will not turn from it."*
>
> — **Proverbs 22:6**
>
> ❧ **Every small act of love matters.**
> Even when you can't see the results yet.

And then came Mother's Day.
She walked up shyly, holding a gift bag with one of those fill-in-the blank little books inside called *What I Love About Mom*.

Ava doesn't aways say her feelings out loud.
So this? This was gold.

I opened it slowly, one page at a time.
Each line hit harder than the last.
Some of my favorites:

- "I love hearing stories about your life." (Well, she's going to *love* this book.)
- "I'm humbled by your intelligence." (Can we get that engraved somewhere?)
- "It makes me laugh that you think you're fat because you're not. You're so pretty." (Apparently, she forgot about *Ohio*. But I'll take it.)

- "I'd be lost without your presence."
- "I wish I had known you when I was younger."
- "Thank you for everything. I love you, Mom."

And I broke. Tears, the kind you can't stop.
Because in all the moments I thought I was failing...
When she stayed quiet.
When I wondered if love was landing.
God was weaving what I couldn't see—until that moment, book in hand.

That tiny treasure wasn't just a gift.
It was proof that love was working. Proof that God was healing. Proof that even the quietest daughters have the loudest ways of saying, I love you. I see you. You're my mom.

And now? Ava's not nearly as quiet anymore.
She tells stories. She opens up. She laughs loud.
She trusts us with her heart—because she knows this is her family, her safe place.
She's come so far from the girl who once kept everything inside.

> "(Love) It always protects, always trusts, always hopes, always perseveres."
> — **1 Corinthians 13:7**
>
> ❧ **Real love sticks around.**
> It changes lives—including yours.

That shy gift shattered me—in the best possible way.

Because of Ava, I know this: God takes messy moms, wounded daughters, roller coasters, Himalayas, and seventy-pound wake-up calls...
And He writes them into love stories worth keeping forever.

God's plot twists don't always come with trumpets.
Sometimes they come tucked in a little book full of crooked handwriting.

And that's when you know for sure—
the story isn't just yours anymore.
It's ours.

END OF CHAPTER REFLECTIONS

1. Have you ever had a moment that embarrassed you—or broke you—and you swore, "Never again"?

2. What's one word, gesture, or moment of encouragement you still cling to?

3. Where do you think God might already be working quietly—before you even notice?

CHAPTER 85

The Full Circle God

When Every Tear and Prayer Finally Makes Sense

A few weeks after Maddie's 18th birthday, God dropped a mic.

Miles and Maddie. Baptized.
Same day. Same church.
Same me, ugly-crying so hard I nearly needed a towel service.

Miles on one side. Maddie on the other.
They went under—came up glowing.

And I thought: *This. Right here.*
Every tear. Every prayer.
Every *"God, are You even listening?"*—worth it.

> *"Take delight in the Lord, and he will give you the desires of your heart."*
>
> — **Psalm 37:4**
>
> ❧ The waiting feels long, but God never forgets His promises.

Maddie's mom came and watched it all.
Under my breath, I whispered, *Lord, let Maddie's light lead her mom home to You someday.*

Because Maddie? She's a walking lighthouse.
She's seen too much of God's hand to ever go back to *maybe He's not real.*

A few weeks later, over spaghetti—because all our best theology happens over carbs—I asked,
"Hey, Maddie, you didn't believe in God at first. What changed?"

She shrugged.
"Too many miracles. God's real."

Boom.
My heart puddled right there on the dining room floor.

And the best part?
I didn't convince her.
God Himself did what only He can do—made faith undeniable.

Fast forward.
Maddie's 25 now.
A college grad.
Medical career ahead.
Still shining that same light into the world.

And here's what I know now:
Not one mile of this Michigan-to-Texas rollercoaster was wasted.
Not the miles. Not the tears. Not the waiting.
God was planting seeds the whole time—
and now there's fruit on every branch.

Five kids.
Each one a living answer to prayer.

A whole new generation chasing Him.

Evidence that the same God who carried me through doubt is now holding them steady in faith.
More than an answered prayer—a legacy being rewritten.

And just when I thought God had finished His full-circle surprises with Maddie, He had one more up His sleeve: Judy.

Miles's mom moved here thinking she was signing up for one grandkid.
Surprise! She's got five.
A grandma-of-the-year trophy.
And a Christmas shopping list that could make an elf cry.

But a few years back, doctors dropped words that froze the air.
Cancer.
Kidney tumors.
The kind of news that hangs in the room like it owns the place.

We prayed. We waited. We hoped.
And God moved.

And now—years later?
Cancer—still gone.
Kidneys—still working like champions.

The doctor's only advice?
"You could gain a little weight."

Miles heard that and basically declared a culinary state of emergency.
Butter in everything that held still long enough.

Not just a medical win.
A divine plot twist.
A reminder that God writes better endings than we dare imagine.

> *"And we know that in all things God works for the good of those who love him, who have been called according to his purpose."*
> — **Romans 8:28**
>
> ❧ He's weaving every messy, miraculous step into a masterpiece.

And Miles himself? Don't get me started.

Stubborn as a mule—
and that grit makes him the most loyal, steady husband and dad I know.

He's not flashy. He's not loud.
MSU pajama pants when he's relaxing at home.
Michigan State shirts pretty much everywhere else.
Dad jokes so dry they could spark a wildfire.
And for reasons known only to him—sharks and Minions.

But beneath the sarcasm and sports gear?
A man who shows up.
Every. Single. Time.

I've watched him carry this family through it all—
Foster care chaos. Job changes. House moves.
Deep grief. The daily circus we call home.

He fixes the mess no one sees.
Holds the line when I want to quit.
Makes sure we laugh when life feels heavy.

Miles may never stand on a stage or chase applause.
But he is, without question, the quiet hero of our story.
We need him more than he knows.

Picture him: MSU pajama pants, a grocery bag in one hand, this family in the other.

That's our guy.

God didn't throw this family together by accident.
He crafted it.
Chose it.
Signed His name on every chapter.

And He's not done.

What's next? I don't know.
But if there's one thing I've learned, it's this:
The best is never behind you.
It's always ahead.

And that's the real miracle.
Every full-circle moment points to the Author who isn't finished yet.

Not with me.
Not with Miles.
Not with Judy.
Not with the rest of us.

Not with you.

He's still holding the pen.
That's where the story really turns.

And if you're wondering where to find Him?
Check the water.
Check the hospital room.
Check the dinner table, right over a plate of spaghetti.

Because God shows up best right where life feels most ordinary—bread broken, laughter shared, and love passed around like it's never going to run out.

END OF CHAPTER REFLECTION

1. Where have you seen a full-circle moment only God could pull off?

2. Who are you still praying will find their way home to Him?

3. What miracle in your own story makes you certain God is real?

CHAPTER 86

The End... of the Beginning

This is where I pause, look back, and see God's fingerprints on every page of my story.

You know my dream. I wanted to be a mom.
For years, it felt like my prayers went straight to voicemail.
The waiting dragged like a bad Netflix series.
The heartbreak cut deep.
The silence? Louder than a toddler with a drum set.

But God hadn't forgotten me—not for a second.
He was just writing a plot twist I couldn't see coming.
Hands down, His script beat mine by a mile.

Rainy.

My first promised child.
My Sunshine.
Not born of my body, but stitched into my soul forever.
She made me a mom.

She arrived at 13; she's 22 now.
Studying to heal bodies and hearts.

Every time she sends me a heart emoji, mine does Olympic-level cartwheels.

Born with a hole in her heart, she had surgery as a baby.
Doctors warned she'd need a valve replacement "one day."
Last year, "one day" showed up.

We prayed the easy fix would work.
It didn't.
Open-heart surgery was the only option.

Ten years ago, that news would've flattened me. This time, my faith had roots.
The God who gave her to me wasn't letting go now.

And He didn't.
She came out whole—and sassier than ever.

My beautiful first daughter, my Sunshine—the one who first made me a mom.

Always my Sunshine.
Our Treasured Rainy.

And then came Autumn.

My flower-bearing, fiercely independent, compassionate Sweet Girl.
She went from eye-roll champion to hugs that melt me like butter on a biscuit.

She's got a passion for animals that borders on full-time zookeeper status.
Two dogs, two birds, hamsters, and mice she swears are "very sweet." (If she brings home a llama, I'm drawing the line.)

She arrived at 14; now she's 19.

College girl. Future psychiatrist.
Let's be honest—she's been psychoanalyzing us since day one; the diploma is just catching up.

Her gifts undo me.
A necklace with all the kids' names engraved? Sobbed.
A wall hanging that says "Greatest Parents"? Sobbed harder.
Tears might be my love language—and she's fluent.

My gorgeous second daughter, written into my life at just the right time, forever a piece of me.

Always my Sweet Girl.
Our Cherished Autumn.

And then came Jaxson.

Part boy, part spring-loaded football.
First year of high school—already diving into football, basketball, track.

I can already picture it: us in the bleachers every Friday night.
Miles—living his best life as a proud sports dad.
Me—who doesn't even like sports—shaking pom-poms and pretending I know what's going on.
But I'll be there. Loud. Proud. Faking it like a pro.

Every night he knocks on my door:
"Goodnight, Mom. I love you."
And my heart turns into a Hallmark movie.

Arrived at 9; now he's 15.
Video game obsessed. Still allergic to laundry.
He'll haul trash and rake leaves.
But clean his room? That would require a court order and possibly a hazmat team.

He's mine, though. Forever.
I wanted Alexander in his name; didn't win that one—
so I call him Jaxson Alexander anyway.
He won't admit it, but it makes him feel special. Seen. Loved.
Even the dogs have Alexander as their middle name.
They're fine with it. Zero complaints.

My bold and tender boy, who taught me that motherhood can sound like
Friday night stadium lights and end with "Goodnight, Mom. I love you."

Always my Jaxson Alexander.
Our Unstoppable Jaxson.

And finally—Ava.

Our glitter-sparkle Princess with big feelings and even bigger hair tools.
She arrived at 13. Now she's 16.
Her room? A pink explosion that met a salon and decided to stay.

She's wildly creative—painting, building, sewing, making jewelry.
Once, she handed me a handmade Tinkerbell with glowing wings.
I nearly burst into glitter myself.

She's come so far.
Brave. Funny. Bold enough to try new things.
Dreaming of a career in law enforcement or the military.
And knowing her, she'll do it.
Because once she sets her mind on something, she doesn't quit.

She's the final puzzle piece—completing our big, messy, beautiful family.

She's not just part of this family—she is our daughter. Forever.
Adoption day is planned and coming soon, but heaven already stamped
it official.

My radiant youngest daughter, who carries enough sparkle and strength
to turn ordinary days into wonder.

Always my Princess.
Our Precious Ava.

Every single one of them?
Evidence that God hears prayers—especially the desperate, tear-stained,
"why-not-me" ones.
I didn't carry them in my womb—I carried them in my prayers.
Now they live in my heart, rent-free, forever.

And me? Changed.

Sure, I've dropped 70 pounds with some left to go.
But the real transformation? Not on the outside. In my heart.
God's still working on me—and thank goodness He doesn't quit.

Because the real change?
I believe now. Fully. Loudly. Unapologetically.
I trust Him. I follow Him.
Even when it's terrifying. Even when it makes zero sense.

This whole thing started with a whisper.
Every chapter since? Proof He's real.

---

*"Therefore, if anyone is in Christ, the new creation has come: The old
has gone, the new is here!"*

— 2 Corinthians 5:17

🕊 **Your old story is over.**
The new one has already begun.

459

I was writing down the miracles as they happened—so I would never forget.

I started writing this book over a decade ago—shaking, worried people would think I was nuts for saying I hear from God.

Fear told me to bury it—like the man who buried the talent God gave him instead of using it.

Faith told me to dig it up and share it.

> *"His master replied, 'Well done, good and faithful servant! You have been faithful with a few things; I will put you in charge of many things. Come and share your master's happiness!'"*
>
> **— Matthew 25:23**
>
> ❧ **Don't bury what God's given you. Even if it feels small, it matters.**

And looking back?

It's a good thing I waited.

Because who knew how much life would happen in the past ten years?

The miracles. The heartbreak.

The full-circle moments that make you laugh and cry in the same breath.

Now, when I tell the story, it's not just theory.

It's lived.

Every bit of it—messy, miraculous, and true.

> *"And we know that in all things God works for the good of those who love him, who have been called according to his purpose."*
>
> **— Romans 8:28**
>
> ❧ **Nothing is wasted. Not pain. Not waiting. Not mistakes.**

So if you're still wondering if God is real—aching for proof—don't stop now.

Ask Him. Boldly. Ask like you expect an answer.

Seek Him. Hard. Like you've lost your lifeline.

Knock. Pound. Refuse to quit—even if your knuckles bleed.

Push past the silence.

Push past the fear.

Keep knocking until heaven answers.

I promise you—He's listening.

And when you break through, you'll know it wasn't wasted.

That's what I did.

I didn't whisper polite little prayers.

I chased Him like He was oxygen—like I was running out of air.

And when I finally caught Him?

Doubt didn't just fade.

It died.

If you run after Him with everything in you—He will meet you.

He will show you what He's shown me.

And once you've seen Him for yourself?

You'll never go back to wondering.

You'll know.

"Being confident of this, that he who began a good work in you will carry it on to completion until the day of Christ Jesus."
— Philippians 1:6

❧ **God finishes what He starts. Every time.**

Because the Author of your story?
He's not finished.
He's already holding the pen.
And His script beats yours by a mile.

So don't set down your faith—not now.
The next chapter is coming.
And it's going to blow the cover off every doubt you've ever had.

END OF CHAPTER REFLECTION

1. Which part of this story stirred something in you?

2. What promise are you still holding tight to?

3. Where might God be inviting you to chase Him with your whole heart?

EPILOGUE

Thank you for walking this journey with me.
May your own story be filled with wild grace, unexpected joy, real faith—
and the unshakable certainty that God's been with you all along, every
step of the way.

The end... of the beginning.

A Final Prayer for You

Hey God,
You see the person holding this book right now.
You know every detail of their story—every heartbreak, every hope,
every dream that still feels out of reach.

Would You remind them they're not forgotten?
That You're closer than their very breath?

Give them courage when fear tries to run the show.
Peace when life spins out of control.
Joy that sneaks up on them in the middle of ordinary Tuesdays.

Most of all, let them know—really know—they are loved.
Chosen.
Never alone.

And when Your voice feels far away, make Your whisper so clear they can't miss it.
Amen.

Now It's Your Turn

Close this book. Take a breath. Talk to Him.

It doesn't have to be fancy. It doesn't have to sound like church.

Whisper. Ramble. Cry. Laugh.
He's listening. Always.

Ask Him your questions.
Tell Him your fears.
Hand Him your dreams.

Then wait—because He *will* show up.
And when He does, you'll know.

So here's my challenge:
I dare you—yes, you—to try. Just once.

Pray like you mean it.
Ask like you expect an answer.

Because the same God who carried me through my mess, my miracles, my motherhood, my whole wild story—is ready to step into yours.

And when He does?
Your life will never be the same.

Your story isn't over.
God's still holding the pen.

"Then you will call on me and come and pray to me, and I will listen to you. You will seek me and find me when you seek me with all your heart."

— Jeremiah 29:12-13

✿ **"God isn't just in my story—He's already waiting in yours."**

ABOUT THE AUTHOR

Christine Pilgrim spent years wrestling with a see-saw faith—believing in God one moment and doubting His very existence the next. Determined to know the truth, she searched until the silence gave way to His unmistakable voice. She lives in San Antonio, Texas, with her family, learning daily to follow the God who speaks.